A Confluence of Minds

The Rabindranath Tagore and Patrick Geddes Reader
on Education and Environment

> P.S. I have just written this about Dr Patrick Geddes
>
> What so strongly attracted me in Dr Patrick Geddes when I came to know him in India was not his scientific achievements, but, on the contrary, the rare fact of the fulness of his personality rising far above his science. Whatever he has studied and mastered have become vitally one with his humanity. He has the precision of the scientist and the vision of the prophet, at the same time, having the power of an artist to make his ideas visible through the language of symbols. His love of Man has given him the insight to see the truth of Man, and his imagination to realise in the world the infinite mystery of life and not merely its mechanical aspect.
>
> Rabindranath Tagore
>
> August 4, 1920

Rabindranath Tagore on Patrick Geddes in his Foreword to Amelia Defries's book, *The Interpreter Geddes, the Man and the Gospel*

A Confluence of Minds

The Rabindranath Tagore and Patrick Geddes Reader
on Education and Environment

Edited by
BASHABI FRASER,
TAPATI MUKHERJEE and AMRIT SEN

Special Advisor
NEIL FRASER

Luath Press Limited
EDINBURGH
www.luath.co.uk

First published in India 2017 by The Director, Granthan Vibhaga, Visva–Bharati

Revised edition first published in the UK 2018 by Luath Press

ISBN: 978-1-912147-25-0

The authors' right to be identified as the authors of this book under the Copyright, Designs and Patents Act 1988 has been asserted.

The paper used in this book is recyclable. It is made from low chlorine pulps produced in a low energy, low emission manner from renewable forests.

Printed and bound by Bell & Bain Ltd, Glasgow

Typeset in 11 point Sabon by Lapiz

Photographs (except where indicated) courtesy of the Rabindra-Bhavana Archives

© the contributors

Contents

Foreword	7
Introduction	9
Rabindranath Tagore on Education	23
The Vicissitudes of Education (1892)	25
The Problem of Education (1906)	31
My School (1917)	40
The Centre of Indian Culture (1919)	55
An Eastern University (1921)	72
A Poet's School (1926)	86
The Parrot's Training (1918)	96
Sriniketan (1924)	99
The First Anniversary of Sriniketan (1924)	101
Patrick Geddes on Education	105
The World Without and the World Within (1905)	107
The Fifth Talk from my Outlook Tower: Our City of Thought	112
The Education of Two Boys	126
The Notation of Life	139
Scottish University Needs And Aims	144
Rabindranath Tagore on the Environment	153
The Religion of the Forest (1922)	155
Can Science Be Humanized? (1933)	164
The Relation of the Individual to the Universe (1913)	166
'Introduction' to Elmhirst's address, 'The Robbery of the Soil'	175
Patrick Geddes on the Environment	183
Cities, and the Soils They Grow from	185
The Valley Plan of Civilisation	195

V: Ways to the Neotechnic City	206
Life and its Science	215
The Sociology of Autumn	221

Letters 231

Plays and Poetry 253

Foreword

THE LATE 19TH and early 20th century had witnessed the flowering of a Renaissance in Bengal and India with a vibrant connection with the West. The intellectual exchanges between Rabindranath Tagore and Patrick Geddes was part of this exchange. While both Tagore and Geddes were engaged with experimentations in education and the environment, they sought to radiate these experiments into their communities and beyond. Both shared a sense of globality and sought a free movement of ideas across borders.

The present volume brings some of these major ideas for the contemporary reader to appreciate the visionary qualities of these thinkers who alerted us to the dangers posed by rote education that was insensitive to the ecology and the community. While Geddes was more of a polemical writer, Rabindranath created a body of poetry and drama that could sensitize the audience to these issues.

Visva-Bharati and Edinburgh Napier University had collaborated on a UGC-UKIERI project titled 'The Scotland India Continuum of Ideas: Tagore and his Circle'. The present volume is one of the two books that are being published on the basis of the project. This book is a collection of some of the most relevant writings of the two thinkers where there reveal the confluence of ideas; a separate volume will bring together critical evaluation of these ideas in contemporary times. Together these complementary volumes should provide a cohesive idea of the interface between these visionaries.

Since the volumes will address a global audience, most of the texts by Tagore have been cited from the *English Writings of Rabindranath Tagore* (in 4 vols.) published by Sahitya Akademi. Wherever we have used other translations, the source has been mentioned.

While we are deeply grateful to the UGC and UKIERI for funding the project, we would like to express our gratitude to Professor Swapan Dutta, Vice-Chancellor, Visva-Bharati and Professor Amit Hazra, Registrar Visva-Bharati for providing the necessary publication grant.

We sincerely hope that readers who are deeply committed to the cause of education and the environment will appreciate this volume.

Tapati Mukherjee & Amrit Sen

Santiniketan
Visva-Bharati

Rabindranath Tagore and Patrick Geddes: An Introduction to their Ideas on Education and the Environment

Neil Fraser and Bashabi Fraser

Rabindranath Tagore[1] and Patrick Geddes were towering intellectuals from their respective nations, India and Scotland, and both polymaths, who had much in common, not least in their powerful thoughts on education and ecology. They met between 1918 and 1930 (as Geddes was in India for much of this time) and kept up a lively correspondence till Geddes' death in 1932. As the letters reveal, they had a lot of respect for each other.[2] Both were critical of the education around them, as they wanted close bonds with nature, and a regeneration of the land and improvements in the lives of villagers. Both reflected on the local but were also international in their outlook, especially in their thinking on the role of universities. But there are also contrasts between them, for Geddes was a scientist and a planner, whereas Rabindranath was first and foremost a creative artist. Rabindranath admired science and wanted it as a core subject in his university, but he was cautious with Geddes' love of diagrams and 'plans'. Geddes began his career in Botany, being a pioneer ecologist, but then moved more to the Social Sciences and was a Professor of Civics and Sociology in the University of Bombay. He did analytical scientific work, but with time, he became more interested in synthesizing the sciences, exploring their inter-relations. Rabindranath describes Patrick Geddes in a letter written on 4 August 1920, which is reproduced later on in this *Reader*: 'What attracted me... was not his scientific achievements, but, on the contrary, the rare fact of the fullness of his personality rising far above his science. Whatever he has studied and mastered has become vitally one with his humanity.' One could apply 'fullness of personality' and 'one with his humanity' to Rabindranath himself.

The focus on education and on environment was chosen for this Reader because of their centrality to the thinking and work of both men. Rabindranath was very unhappy about his own experience of formal education and went on to set up a school in 1901 and later a university, Visva-Bharati, established in

---

1. Henceforth Rabindranath. There were many Tagores who were illustrious, so in order to differentiate Rabindranath from the other talented members of his family, we will use his first name. In Bengal, writers and other famous men are mentioned by their first names, e.g., Bankimchandra (Chatterjee), Jagadish Chandra (Bose).
2. See Bashabi Fraser, Ed., *The Tagore Geddes Correspondence* (Shantiniketan: Visva-Bharati, India, 2004, 2nd Rev Edn) and *A Meeting of Two Minds: the Geddes-Tagore Letters* (Edinburgh: Wordpower Books, 2005), 3rd Rev Edn.

1921 at Shantiniketan.[3] Geddes organized international summer schools for some twelve years in Edinburgh, was a consultant for planning universities, including Tagore's own university and the Hebrew University in Jerusalem, and for a time organized home schooling for his own children, as did Rabindranath till his children were able to attend his school at Shantiniketan. In fact, Rabindranath and Geddes had experience of home schooling as boys, not just in pedagogic subjects but in diverse activities like wrestling and exercise on parallel bars in the case of Rabindranath and nature study with his father in their garden in the case of Geddes, and they both practised art at home.

Both men thus sought a holistic approach to education and emphasized harmony with nature. They stressed the need to nurture sympathy in human beings for their fellow beings and for their environment as they were concerned with the inter-relation between education and the environment, advocating 'unity'. Geddes was a pioneer ecologist who taught about evolution and man's responsibilities for conserving resources. Tagore wanted schooling which was close to nature and also wanted to improve the life of local villagers, whom he saw frequently suffering malaise which education, with university leadership, could help to address. Geddes too felt strongly about this and encouraged his son Arthur to take a leading part in it. They believed in the efficacy of science for a rounded education and in interdisciplinarity which did not compartmentalize humanities and the sciences. In their desire for holistic education and creative learning, they wanted poetry, music, painting and plays to be part of the curriculum, as exemplified by Rabindranath's tireless writing of songs, poems, plays, operas and dance dramas which were performed by his students (and across Bengal) and Geddes's pageants, masques and poetic exercises – which were published in *The Evergreen*.[4]

Rabindranath Tagore on Education:
An early essay (the 'Vicissitudes of Education', published when Rabindranath was 31) reflects his own experience of Indian education. He writes about the 'joyless education our boys receive', about 'school work which is dull and cheerless, stale and unending'. He saw the major problem in the use of English as the medium of teaching and by teachers who were inadequately trained, and even given to physical punishment of their wards. He believed that education needs to be much closer to the students' own lives, reflecting their experiences. Students are unable to cultivate thought or imagination when the education is imparted in a language and literature whose references

---
3. Rabindranath refers to it as Santiniketan. We have adopted Shantiniketan to indicate the way it is pronounced with a palatal 'sh' in Bengali.
4. Patrick Geddes, ed. *The Evergreen*, parts 1-4, 1895.

are rooted in a culture they are unfamiliar with. The examples Rabindranath gives are of haymaking and of Charlie and Katie snowballing, which a Bengali child would be unable to imagine. The use of the Bengali language would help to 'unite our language with our thought and our education with our life, ensuring a rootedness of education to the region where the child belonged'. Rabindranath speaks of the significance of Bankimchandra Chatterji's *Bangadarshan* in this connection as a magazine that had characters and narratives a Bengali audience could identify with and relate to. The urgent need for schooling to be in the mother tongue remained a strong strand in the education policy formulated by Rabindranath.

As has been said earlier, Rabindranath established a school in Shantiniketan in rural Bengal, in the Birbhum district. In 1906 he wrote an essay 'The Problem of Education' where he notes that most schools function like factories, using mechanical methods that aimed at churning out products which were symmetrical, not recognizing the individuality of each child, and thus riding roughshod over each child's creativity. He anticipates Foucault when he writes of 'the prison walls of schools'. Schools need to get children interested, rather than offer an education that has no correspondence with what parents talk about at home. He advocates that teachers and pupils should live together and grow up with nature i.e. in schools which are not like closed institutions (e.g., prisons), but are close to 'earth and water, sky and air', in the spirit of the forest hermitage of ancient India, where the students lived with their Guru, their teacher, who was a family man and learning was a holistic experience involving shared daily chores as well as lessons.

In order to overhaul an unimaginative system of education, Rabindranath believes that the committed teacher is a prerequisite for good education, the teacher who encourages creativity and welcomes curiosity in his pupils. He is most critical of Bengali parents who bring up their children in an atmosphere that is divorced from their own culture and feels that the sons of the rich who are ferried to school and have their books carried for them, have their capacity for growth and freedom curbed and stunted: 'Freedom is essential to the mind in the period of growth'. Pupils should do work in school gardens rather than be prepared for a life of a pampered elite. Children must learn simplicity like sitting on the floor, as plain living can free the learning environment from the clutter of equipment. In his school, where possible, the school still holds classes out-of-doors, each class meeting under the benign shade of a tree. In cities, Rabindranath recommends schools being built away from the congested parts, in green spaces where the child will learn about trees by climbing them, rather than from descriptions in text books, letting the joy of association with the natural surroundings making learning memorable and refreshing.

The philosophy of his school in Shantiniketan is developed by Rabindranath in 'My School', an essay published in 1917. He describes the object of education as 'freedom of mind' (children encouraged to think for themselves) and stresses the atmosphere or ethos of the school. In fact, in 'A Poet's School' which he writes later, he says that what he has offered is an atmosphere where the child's mind can grow feely and creatively. Shantiniketan is almost idyllic, a place where the children grow up amidst nature, a point that is stressed by Rabindranath as the ideal environment in its unfettered setting and expanse. Once again he stresses that schools should not be like factories and should not stifle love of life. He offers his students freedom and nurtures self-help. In this essay, Rabindranath offers a paean to the ideal teacher, who acts from a love and joy of life and literature, in Satish Chandra Ray, who came like a refreshing spring shower for a year to his institution at 19 and died at 20, but left a deep impression of how learning and play could be imperceptibly intertwined in an atmosphere of voluntary participation. He is Rabindranath's 'living teacher'. There is a unity in truth which means that there is no separation of the intellect from the spiritual and physical. Personality should be born of love, goodness and beauty. Here again he goes back to the forest hermitage, the *tapovan*, which he believes that India should 'cherish', this 'memory of the forest colonies of great teachers', where master (guru) and students shared 'a life of high aspiration'. Here is the idea and practical realization of the campus university. As one pupil of Rabindranath's institution, Amartya Sen, said 'the emphasis here [in his school] was on self-motivation rather than on discipline, and on fostering intellectual curiosity rather than competitive excellence.'[5] Another pupil, Mahasweta Devi, wrote 'we were taught in our school that every animal, every cat, every bird, had a right to live. From childhood, we were taught to care for nature, not to break a single leaf or flower from a tree'.[6]

Rabindranath points out how Europe's intellect and culture have their source in Europe from which its life blood flows, which informs and structures the education it offers in her educational institutions. Similarly, India's source of light and life can only be found in India, in her past and in tracing a continuity in her evolution. Importing European education to India will prove stultifying and deny the growth of the Indian mind. He makes a difference between the conscious mind which is on the surface and the unconscious mind which is 'fathomless', the latter being the soul of man's[7] being which

---

5. Amartya Sen, The Argumentative Indian: Writings on Indian Culture, History and Identity (Harmondsworth: Penguin Books, 2005), p.114
6. Quoted by Fakrul Alam and Radha Chakravarty, Eds., The Essential Tagore (Harvard and Visva-Bharati) from Mahasweta Devi, The Land of Cards p.viii, p.21.
7. Rabindranath's use of the term 'man' encapsulates both women and men, which has subsequently been replaced by 'human beings'.

finds expression in poetry, music and art, underscoring man's creative impulse which, in his collection of essays, *The Religion of Man* (1931), he identifies as his creative principle.

When Rabindranath published his essay 'Centre of Indian Culture' (1919) he was very much involved in the preparation of his international university, Visva-Bharati, a nest where the world meets. He envisaged Visva-Bharati as a centre of Indian culture, and not just being a centre of intellectual life but also a centre of economic life, as in rural reconstruction and also as an institution to which scholars and teachers from the West and East will come and participate in an atmosphere of mutual exchange. He recognised a need for a diversity of languages (as India has) and close connections with the cultures of other societies. He believed that music and art have to be part of culture and he established music and art as academic disciplines in his university. He also emphasized that there has to be room for all religions. He looked to Ireland in the Dark Ages for an example of education which flourished by having strong local roots (including the Irish language as a medium of instruction) while the rest of Europe was beset by war. The subsequent destruction of Irish seats of learning and the imposition of English on the nation, resulted in long years of suppression for Ireland.

After his visit to England in 1912 and the winning of the Nobel Prize for Literature in 1913, Rabindranath became a world figure travelling to several countries on invitation to address gatherings, and meet key people – intellectuals, artists and political leaders. Through his travels, interactions and writing, he strove to bring the East and West closer together through 'co-ordination and co-operation', 'to unite the minds of the East and West in mutual understanding' and to effect this, he speaks of having established an 'Eastern University' (Visva-Bharati) where the meeting of minds can effect a synthesis, bringing the closer world together. Synthesis is a term that Patrick Geddes uses in his own writing on education, one of the trio of 'S's that Geddes identifies, the other two being Sympathy which is also used by Rabindranath (as has, as has been noted earlier) and Synergy, which is generated by energetic activities.

In 'An Eastern University' (1921) Rabindranath discusses what universities should be. They should be places where East and West work together in the common pursuit of truth. Students from the west can study the different system of Indian philosophy, literature, art and music at Visva-Bharati. It should be a University which 'will help India's mind to concentrate and to be fully conscious of itself, free to seek the truth and make this truth its own wherever found, to judge by its own standard, give expression to its own creative genius, and offer its wisdom to the guests who come from other parts of the world'. The article also includes a critique of existing institutions of education.

In 'A Poet's School' (1926) Rabindranath expands on the atmosphere he has sought to create in his school. He writes about learning to improvise and develop a creative life and finding freedom in nature. The school seeks to engage students in music, painting and drama in the open-air. It endeavours to counter assumptions many boys bring with them, e.g., that certain kinds of work are only to be done by a paid servant. The boys 'take great pleasure in cooking, weaving, gardening, improving their surroundings, and in rendering services to other boys, very often secretly, lest they should feel embarrassed. Their classwork has not been separated from their normal activities but forms a part of their daily current of life.' The school faced many obstacles e.g., parents' expectations, the upbringing of teachers, the traditions of the 'educated' community, and the need to attract funding, but the atmosphere created helped to overcome these problems. The boys thus developed a sense of responsibility which forms the basis for a holistic education that assists character formation. The references in these essays are to 'boys' with whom the school at Shantiniketan was started. In subsequent years, girls were admitted to the school and the university became a mixed institution. In fact, the reputation of Rabindranath's institution was such that Jawaharlal Nehru, the first Prime Minister of independent India, sent his daughter, Indira, to Rabindranath's institution where she was educated for a year.

Many of India's leading pre-independence and post-independence thinkers/scholars/artists have been educated at Shantiniketan, including such luminaries as the film director, Satyajit Ray[8] who too has written about his debt to Rabindranath's atmosphere of creative learning at his institution, which nurtured a knowledge and value of an education rooted in Indian tradition, the local, while being open to the ideas of the world.[9] Of this experience Ray says, 'I consider the three years I spent in Santiniketan as the most fruitful of my life… Santiniketan opened my eyes for the first time to the splendours of Indian and Far Eastern art. Until then I was completely under the sway of Western art, music and literature. Santiniketan made me the combined product of East and West that I am.'[10]

In the two edited sections from Rabindranath's reflections in 'Sriniketan', which is the name of the Institute for Rural Reconstruction at Surul (Shantiniketan's twin institution), he discusses why service to society should

---

8. Satyajit Ray was awarded the La Lumiere and won the Oscar for his lifetime's work.
9. Patrick Geddes coined the slogan, 'Think Global, Act Local' in what has become impetus for glocality.
10. In Sen, p. 115. The spelling 'Santiniketan' is retained when quoting from the original texts which are referred/included to here.

be part of education. He believes students and academics at universities should share a life with the tillers of the soil and that the humble workers in the villages should be part of an ideal educational institution. He advocates that human beings (both his students and the villagers) should be in infinite touch with nature in an atmosphere of service to all creatures, while practising a certain 'detachment' from the material world, gaining from a climate of uninhibited creativity which fosters a deep contact with (wo-)man's 'thought, emotion and will'.

The final piece in this section, is a delightful parable about education, called 'The Parrot's Training', published earlier, in 1918. In this story, Rabindranath shows how the paraphernalia of education in elaborate buildings and equipment, can mean losing sight of the recipient of this whole exercise – the student – whose needs and propensities should be the central consideration in an educational system, but is sidelined by unimaginative and self-serving decision makers. In his ironic story, the king's parrot is at first lively, singing and playful in its unrestricted setting, till the king's advisors point out how cheeky and fearless the parrot is. On the advice of his ministers, the king decrees that things are put right to tame and teach the parrot a lesson. Everything is done for the parrot's education from constructing a gilded cage, to providing a silver chain and finally clipping of the poor bird's wings. The voice of the bird is no longer heard and when the king comes on an inspection tour of the progress of the bird's education, he discovers the body of the tiny bird amidst this huge machinery, its mouth stuffed with pages from textbooks. Patrick Geddes was a strong admirer of this short-story as he calls for action against rote learning: 'the Parrot be Avenged!' (see his letter to Rabindranath written on 11 June 1908).

The letters between Rabindranath and Geddes, are a source for their ideas on education as well as the environment. For example, in Rabindranath's letter to Geddes dated 9 May 1922, the former says that he started his school 'with one simple idea, that education should never be dissociated from life'. He then says 'the institution grew with the growth of my own mind and life'. He contrasts this organic approach to the planner's approach adopted by Geddes, which he admires but temperamentally cannot adopt.

Patrick Geddes on Education
Like Tagore, Geddes was a critic of most existing schools. In his 'The World Without and the World Within' (1905) he argues most schools do not stimulate their students' imaginations – the in-world of memories and plans is neglected – meaning they grow up unable to plan and therefore unable to act on the basis of plans. Geddes refers to the In-World of Memories and Plans against the Out-world of Facts and Acts. In 'The Notation of Life' he speaks of the

Inner life. Rabindranath too speaks of the Inner Life and the Outer Life, 'to distinguish between the quotidian life from the life of the mind'.[11]

In his 'Our City of Thought', Geddes discusses science and education. The strength of science is in its requirement to do fieldwork (systematic observation) – something education in science should practise (as shown by the Scottish medical scientist Joseph Lister and by the Scottish geologists). The diagnostic survey was a favourite tool of Geddes' – recommended for example in town planning. But here he complains that too much of the education of the time teaches the non-empirical ways of old psychology or utilitarian economics. Science, in particular, needs direct contact with nature. Reflecting his own progress into the social sciences, Geddes argues that biology is a necessary preparation for sociology. He also argues that societies should be understood historically – even through the reading of ancient sacred texts for what they tell us of societies operating in a different environment from those of the present day.

In his 'The Education of Two Boys', he describes the home schooling for his own children, contrasting it with British public schools ('standardising schools'). He talks about the wide range of occupations he took up in his youth and those of his children. Two of Geddes' passions in his life came from his upbringing – the garden of his family home (leading to his passion for nature study and botany), and experimental methods, including data collection by survey (which he brought to his own practice as a town planner). The nature ramblings – as he had the freedom to scour his family garden in Perth and the landscape beyond along the Tay – developed his power of observation from this close association with his surroundings, making him the naturalist and humanist he was.

Geddes was a great believer in learning via recognizing the interdependence of academic subjects (see 'The Notation of Life'). He developed elaborate diagrams to illustrate this inter-relatedness, diagrams that he called 'Thinking Machines'. This simple but amazing method was adopted by Geddes when he briefly faced the threat of blindness and was unable to read or write in his usual copious manner. He then used a sheet of paper which he folded up into four and later nine sections and used each section to accommodate a thought which could be interlinked vertically, horizontally and diagonally to other thoughts, in what looked like a noughts and crosses pattern. A particular starting point he used for this 'Thinking Machine' was in showing the links between Place – Work – Folk (devised by the French sociologist, Le Play), the basis of the subjects Geography – Economics – Anthropology. Geddes

---

11. Sabyasachi Bhattacharya, *Rabindranath Tagore: An Interpretation* (New Delhi: Penguin Books, 2011), 'Introduction', p. 7.

sees Sociology as embodying all three. He came to Sociology from Biology, which he saw as a necessary preparation. An example of his recognition of the elements within Sociology is in his letter to Tagore on 15 April 1922, when he refers to 'this diagram-plan of my department'. He goes on to say these subjects embody, in academic jargon, the 'unity of life.' Rabindranath, has, in different contexts, referred to 'unity' as the ultimate goal for mankind, of educational institutions with the surrounding country, of the urban with rural, of 'man' with nature, of 'man' with his fellow human beings. In his letter dated 9 May 1922, Rabindranath in his reply to Geddes's letter, which is mentioned above, concedes that his university is not planned in this way; it is rather 'a living growth', what may be described as organic in its very development.

In his section on 'Our City of Thought', Geddes mentions the three stages in the development of people who have contributed to the progress of civilization, the '(1) Precursors, (2) Initiators (3) Continuators', not in a steady mapable movement, as there have been 'dormant periods', but through continuators who have passed the torch of progress on 'between initiative growth-waves'.

Like Rabindranath, he believes that science at city institutions cannot stay divorced from contact with nature which ensures the continuity of life, using the example of roses grown in flower vases, which is, untenable.

> If our study is not in nature, of rocks, or forces, but like Ruskin's in Venice, of the stones and human significance of cities, then shall we need to set our laboratory on their High Street; yet with scan of their plains to hills and sweep of the valley section of their civilization. So we shall come in the succeeding article more particularly to this Outlook Tower in Edinburgh. But before taking up its work of civic interpretation for city people.

In 'The Education of Two Boys' he mentions his own 'curious perversion at 15', when he was given to practical joking. It is an embarrassing memory, but he realizes that they were a result of him not finding an outlet for his creative mind, his restless curiosity which is channeled later on as he discovers his joy in creative learning. Thus in the summer he joined a 'real joiner's workshop' in the mornings, followed by art school during the day and the laboratory in the evenings. This is what the adolescent needs, immersion in activities which occupy the mind and fire the imagination through practical methods of

---

12. For an analysis of the significance of the correspondence between Geddes and Rabindranath, see Fraser, *A Meeting of Two Minds*, 'Introduction', pp. 12-51.

learning. He believes in a holistic education and is critical of a system that aims at creating 'manly men' rather than 'man-in-the-universe.' Speaking of his own children, he finds how journeys in a boat with a fisherman on the Tay, and learning to swim, led to his son joining a laboratory at Millport and his daughter becoming a student. With special reference to his son, he notes the boy's natural instincts for discovering and exploring the world creatively, which bears fruit in his multifaceted talents finding expression in diverse endeavours and achievements, till his life is cut short tragically during his service in the First World War.

Patrick, with his younger son, Arthur Geddes, who went on to become a geographer, helped in the planning of Tagore's university at Shantiniketan. Patrick's letter to Tagore on 10 November 1922 sets out questions he needs to know (e.g. for how many students should they plan and for what departments should they plan?). He also enquires about the meaning of the International University. He refers Tagore to plans in Brussels and comments that they are a development of the annual summer schools in Edinburgh[12], which he ran for a dozen years, attracting a range of well-known intellectuals (e.g., William James from Harvard).

Geddes' belief that universities can play a crucial role in the renaissance of a country is to be found in his 'Scottish University: Needs and Aims'. He argues there that Scotland then was behind the rest of Europe in reforming her universities. He gives two proposals which are notably sensitive to the needs of students: 1. The building of halls of residence (a project in which he had been actively involved in Edinburgh) and 2. Support for students studying abroad and in this connection, one can mention the later revival of the Scots College in Paris.

Rabindranath Tagore on the Environment

Much of Tagore's thinking on the environment goes back to the forests which once covered India and the forest hermitages which developed there. He writes in 'The Religion of the Forest' about the kinship of man with creation:

> The hermitage shines out, in all our ancient literature, as the place where the chasm between man and the rest of creation has been bridged. Nature stands on her own right, proving that she has her great function, to impart the peace of the eternal to human emotions.

Poets like Kalidasa are warning about the unreality of luxury in contrast to the purity of the forest. Tagore develops these thoughts in his essay 'The Relation of the Individual to the Universe'. He contrasts the inspiration India draws from the simple life of the forest hermitage with the West's idea of subduing nature. He emphasizes our harmony with nature. One poem included here is his 'Homage to the Tree'. The goal of human life is to be peaceful and at-one-with-God. These ideals, shared by the Upanishads and Buddhism, are opposed to the policy of self-aggrandisement and greed that has motivated much human enterprise.

Greed is analysed by Rabindranath in his Introduction to Elmhirst's address entitled, 'The Robbery of the Soil'. With the rise of the standard of living in India, greed is encouraged, it 'breaks loose from social control'. Cities are a prime cause, they are 'unconscious of the devastation [they are] continuously spreading within the village'. A further factor identified is the rapid decay of India's family system. The personal ambition of one member of the family is usually enough to lead to this decay. A career of plunder can outstrip 'nature's power for recuperation'. The result is exhaustion of water, cutting down of trees etc. – what is now termed desertification. Rabindranath took the evidence for these effects in the villages around Shantiniketan very seriously and believed universities should respond through community engagement and practical endeavour. He founded an Institute for Rural Reconstruction (Sriniketan) to address them, which was led by Leonard Elmhirst, an English agriculturalist with input from Arthur Geddes at one stage. Elmhirst gave an address about *The Robbery of the Soil* which Tagore introduced with the talk reproduced here. Elmhirst and Tagore both deplore a loss of community enterprise in many villages – evident in the lack of action to prevent erosion and to keep ponds clean. The result was poor crops leading to inadequate diets, which, coupled with the high prevalence of malaria and general lethargy, created a sense of despondency in the rural hinterland of Shantiniketen. Patrick Geddes' son, Arthur, worked at Sriniketan for two years, doing teaching and village surveys, which assess and seek to address the situation (some of the surveys became the fieldwork for his PhD which he submitted later on at Montpellier, entitled *Au Pays de Tagore* 'In the Land of Tagore').

Patrick Geddes on the Environment
Understanding the environment was central to Geddes' work throughout his life. He refers often to the central influence of the garden of his parents' home in Perth and the countryside around it. Geddes believed that nature study should be a subject in schools and was responsible for initiating it in schools. Botany was his scientific discipline. Reilly has called him 'one of the first modern ecologists'. He moved into social sciences (later becoming Professor of Civics and Sociology in the University of Bombay in 1920 as has been noted earlier) beginning from a belief that these sciences (sociology

and economics) are a sub-species of biology. He believed rules of conduct for men could be derived from physical and biological laws. He recognized that resources like coal are finite and that one could have a balance-sheet for the sum of energy available. Resources need to be conserved. He sought to understand the issues created by a growing population (debating this with John Ruskin). Like Rabindranath he advocated co-operatives. He critiqued the economists' use of 'utility' to measure the value of goods in favour of intrinsic value in terms of life-giving qualities.[13]

Geddes' *Talks from my Outlook Tower* includes two essays on ecological themes. 'Cities and the Soil They Grow From'(no.2), has a historical discussion of deforestation and malaria in the Mediterranean region, and the need for regional planning of afforestation. 'The Valley Plan of Civilisation'(no.3), discusses the social significance of occupations according to topography between mountains and the sea. He discusses pastoral societies, wood-workers making tools, rice-growing, corn-growing, following a trajectory that signifies mankind's progress and industries. Industrialisation changes, but does not obliterate, this analysis. In both these extracts Geddes adopts an approach based on economic stages of history, a particularly Scottish approach to analyzing history (as in Adam Smith's *Wealth of Nations*).

We have included a chapter from Patrick Geddes' seminal publication, *Cities in Evolution* (1915). This discusses how town planning changed 19th century cities, ameliorating the grimness of the early industrial age (which Geddes called the paleotechnic age, a retrogressive step after the Neolithic stage). Beautifying cities tends to be dismissed as sentimental, but Geddes argues there is a good case for the conservation of nature, for creating parks in urban spaces and for the reclamation of slums within cities. We see that his experience of his parents' garden in Perth and the green hinterland beyond which had beckoned him and aroused his naturalist's enthusiasm remains a living memory in his town planning as he proposes breathing green spaces in urban scapes.

Geddes frequently takes up an argument that Arts and Sciences should not be compartmentalized. Two examples are in two issues of a short-lived journal he founded in 1895, *The Evergreen*. In the spring issue, entitled *Life and its Science*, he discusses how science on the one hand, and poetry and painting on the other, handle Nature and Life. He sees science in a process of rewriting its manuals. In poetic prose he describes how the beginning of life among insects, birds, and flowers in spring time happens: 'As poetic

---

13. See J. P. Reilly, *The Early Social Thought of Patrick Geddes,* Ph.D. thesis (1972), ch. 2 &3, unpublished. New York: University of Columbia.

intensity and poetic interpretation may be true at many deepening levels, so it is with the work of the painter; so too with the scientific study of nature'. We are invited to consider how research can throw new light on the problem of evolution and, in turn, how ideas of evolution can help us 're-organise the human hive'. And then through renewal of the environment, the painter and poet may find 'new space for beauty and new stimulus of song'.

In the Autumn issue of *The Evergreen*, in 'The Sociology of Autumn', Geddes argues that analysis in art or science, can be rebuilt as synthesis. A favourite idea of Geddes is that understanding can be enhanced by looking into related areas/disciplines, a form of sympathy. He goes on to discuss synthesis in relation to cities, and particularly the seasons and cities. Autumn is viewed as the typical season of cities, being the season of both decadence and renewal (rebirth/renaissance), 'autumn is the urban spring' while 'spring the urban autumn'. Geddes finishes with a sentence which might sum up his philosophy, the conclusion of Voltaire's Candide, 'we must cultivate our garden'. This can be the individual garden and the collective garden built through cooperation, which needs careful planning and nurture and which will bring about what Rabindranath calls, 'creative unity'.

The sections on education and the environment are followed by selected letters which have been discussed where relevant in the above sections. The letters are followed by extracts of Rabindranath's play, *The Waterfall* (*Muktadhara*) and a poem, 'Homage to a Tree', which embody the themes of this *Reader*.

The Waterfall ((Muktadhara) is a play by Tagore which anticipates the modern environmental concern over big dams. The arrogant royal engineer has built a machine (like a dam) to stop water from the waterfall. For him it has its own justification as a technological marvel (even though many are killed in its construction). But the real target of the dam seems to be to create drought conditions for a group of subjects (the Shiu-tarai) who are to be 'punished'/displaced for having a different religion and appearance. The devotees of God Shiva are shown singing praises for victory. A schoolmaster is shown coaching his students to mouth aggressive cries against the Shiu-tarai uncomprehendingly, applauded by a government minister. The Crown Prince on the other hand sympathises with the Shiu-tarai and acts to destroy the machine, but he is swept away by the waters he releases. Through this self-sacrificing act, he restores freedom and dignity to his wronged subjects. The moral for man is not to try to subdue nature and not to treat a group of subjects as dispensable.

In the poem 'Homage to The Tree' Rabindranath meditates on trees as 'friend of man'. The tree is symbolic of a living earth: 'you urged a continuous war to liberate the earth from the fortress-prison of aridity.' As a powerful Romantic poet, he recognizes its intrinsic aesthetic appeal 'you were the first to sketch the living image of beauty'. In this poem we can see once again Rabindranath's vision of the forest and the space it provides for reflection and growth as its trees show 'how power can incarnate itself in peace', the peace that comes from a silent and nurturing presence that embodies life.

Education and Environment were considerations that remained close to Rabindranath and Geddes's life and thought, as reflected in their work, both in their writing and in their pragmatic and creative projects, the educational institutions they established, the socio-cultural issues they addressed, the continuity they saw as they evaluated tradition and embraced modernity. Both contributed to a sustainable future for humanity, through their belief in coordination and cooperation, through harmony and sympathy in a synthesis that puts mankind in touch with nature, challenges the rural-urban divide and gives educational institutions a key role in engaging with, gaining from and uplifting the surrounding environment through holistic education.

Neil Fraser
Bashabi Fraser

Rabindranath Tagore on Education

Rabindranath Tagore taking a class in Santiniketan

The Vicissitudes of Education (1892)[14]

HUMAN BEINGS CANNOT be content with the bare necessaries of life, and they are in fact partly chained to their needs and partly free. The average man is three and a half cubits tall, but he lives in a house that is much taller, and has plenty of room for the freedom of movement so essential for health and comfort. This applies equally to education. A boy should be allowed to read books of his own choice in addition to the prescribed text-books he must read for his school-work. His mental development is likely to be arrested if he is not allowed to do this, and he may grow into a man with the mind of a boy.

Unfortunately a boy in this country has very little time at his disposal. He must learn a foreign language, pass several examinations, and qualify himself for a job, in the shortest possible time. So, what can he do but cram up a few text-books with breathless speed? His parents and his teachers do not let him waste precious time by reading a book of entertainment, and they snatch it away from him the moment they see him with one.

An unkind fate has ruled that the Bengalee boy shall subsist on the lean diet of grammar, lexicon, geography. To see him in the class room, his thin legs dangling from his seat, is to see the most unfortunate child in the world. At an age when children of other countries are having all sorts of treats, he must digest his teacher's cane with no other seasoning that the teacher's abuse.

That sort of fare is sure to ruin anybody's digestive organs, and there can be no doubt that for lack of nourishment and recreation the Bengalee boy grows up without fully developing his physical and mental powers. That explains why, although many of us take the highest university degrees and write many books, we as a people have minds that are neither virile nor mature. We cannot get a proper hold on anything, cannot make it stand firm, cannot build it up from bottom to top. We do not talk, think, or act like adults, and we try to cover up the poverty of our minds with overstatement, ostentation and swagger.

This is due mainly to the joyless education our boys receive from childhood onwards, learning a few prescribed text-books by heart, and acquiring a working knowledge of a few subjects instead of mastering them. Human beings need food, and not air, to satisfy their hunger, but they also need air properly to digest their food. Many books of entertainment are likewise necessary for a boy properly to digest one text-book. When a boy

---

14. Rabindranath Tagore *Towards Universal Man* ed. Humayun Kabir, (Asia Publishing house, 1961) pp 39-48.

reads something for pleasure, his capacity for reading increases imperceptibly, and his powers of comprehension, assimilation and retention grow stronger in an easy and natural manner.

Language is our first difficulty. Because of the many grammatical and syntactical differences between English and our mother-tongue, English is very much a foreign language to us. Then there is the difficulty connected with the subject matter, which makes an English book doubly foreign to us. Utterly unfamiliar with the life it describes, all we can do is to get the text by rote without understanding it – with the same result as that of swallowing food without chewing it. Suppose a children's Reader in English contains a story about haymaking, and another about a quarrel that Charlie and Katie had when they were snowballing. These stories relate incidents familiar to English children, and are interesting and enjoyable to them; but they rouse no memories in the minds of our children, unfold no pictures before their eyes. Our children simply grope about in the dark when reading these books.

A further difficulty stems from the fact that the men who teach the lower forms of our schools are not adequately trained for their work. Some of them have only passed the Matriculation examination, some have not even done that, and all are lacking adequate knowledge of English language and literature, English life and thought. Yet these are the teachers to whom we owe our introduction to English learning. They know neither good English nor good Bengali, and the only work they can do is misteaching.

Nor can we really blame the poor men. Suppose I have to put the sentence 'The horse is a noble animal' into Bengali. How shall I do it? Shall I say the horse is a 'great' animal, a 'high class' animal, a 'very good' animal, or what? None of the Bengali words for 'noble' I can think of seem right, but in the end I shall probably resort to downright cheating. So I cannot really blame the teacher if in the end he resorts to a dodge.

The result is that the boy learns nothing. Had he been learning no other language than Bengali, he would at least have been able to read and appreciate the *Ramayana* and *Mahabharata*. Had he not been sent to school at all, he would have had all the time in the world to play games, climb trees, swim in the rivers and ponds, pluck flowers, and do a thousand damages to fields and woods. He would thus have fully gratified his youthful nature and developed a cheerful mind and a healthy body. But as he struggles with his English, neither does he learn it, nor does he enjoy himself; neither does he acquire the ability to enter the imaginary world of literature, nor does he get the time to step into the real world of nature.

Man belongs to two worlds, one of which lies within him and the other outside. They give him life, health and strength and keep him ever-flowering by ceaselessly breaking upon him in waves of form, colour and smell, movement and music, and love and joy. Our children are banished from both these worlds, as from two native lands, and are kept chained in a foreign prison. God has filled the hearts of parents with love so that children can have their fill of it, and He has made the breasts of mothers soft so that children can rest on them. Children have small bodies but all the empty spaces of the house do not give them enough room to play. And where do we make our sons and daughters spend their childhood? Among the grammars and lexicons of a foreign language; and within the narrow confines of a school work which is dull and cheerless, stale and unending.

A man's years are like links in a chain, and it will be somewhat superfluous to state anew the well-known fact that childhood grows into manhood by degrees. Certain mental qualities are indispensable to a grown-up man who has just entered the world of action. But these qualities are not instantly available; they have to be developed. Like our hands and feet our mental qualities grow at every stage of our life in answer to the call that is made on them. They are not like ready-made articles which can be bought in shops whenever needed.

The power of thought and the power of imagination are indispensable to us for discharging the duties of life. We cannot do without those two powers if we want to live like real men. And unless we cultivate them in childhood we cannot have them when we are grown up.

Our present system of education, however, does not allow us to cultivate them. We have to spend many years of our childhood in learning a foreign language taught by men not qualified for the job. To learn the English language is difficult enough, but to familiarize ourselves with English thought and feeling is even more difficult, and takes a long time during which our thinking capacity remains inactive for lack of an outlet.

To read without thinking is like accumulating building materials without building anything. After we have accumulated a mountainous pile of mortar, lime and sand, and of bricks, beams and rafters, we suddenly get an order from the University to do the roof of a three-storied house. So we instantly climb to the top of our pile and beat it down incessantly for two years, until it becomes level and somewhat resembles the flat roof of a house. But could this pile be called a house? Has it windows to let in air and light? Could a man make it his home for the whole of his life? Has it order, beauty, harmony?

There is no doubt that a great deal of material is now collected in our country for building the edifice of the mind, much greater than at any other time in its history. But we must not make the mistake of thinking that by learning to collect we have learnt to build. Good results follow only when accumulation and building are carried on, step by step, at the same time.

It follows, therefore, that if I want my son to grow up into a man, I should see that he grows up like a man right from his childhood. Otherwise he will always remain a child. He should be told not to rely entirely on memory, and be given plenty of opportunity to think for himself and use his imagination. To get a good crop it is necessary to water the field besides ploughing it and harrowing it, and rice in particular grows best on well-watered earth. Rain is essential to rice at a particular moment in its cultivation, and the crop will be ruined if there is no rain when it is needed most. When the moment is gone, even a lot of rain will not save the crop. Childhood and adolescence are the moments when the stimulus of literature is essential to the growth of a man. Quickened by that stimulus, the tender shoots of his mind and heart will come forth in the air and light, and continue to grow in health and strength. But they will remain undeveloped if the moment is wasted in studying dry and dusty grammars and lexicons. Even if the most vital truths, wonderful conceptions, and sublime thoughts of European literature are showered on the man for the rest of his life, he will never imbibe its inmost spirit.

In our lives that auspicious moment is wasted in joyless education. From childhood to adolescence, and again from adolescence to manhood, we are coolies of the goddess of learning, carrying loads of words on our folded backs. When at last we manage to enter the realm of English ideas, we find that we are not quite at home there. We find that although we can somehow understand those ideas, we cannot absorb them into our deepest nature; that although we can use them in our lectures and writings, we cannot use them in the practical affairs of our lives.

So the first twenty or twenty-two years of our lives are spent in picking up ideas from English books. But at no time are those ideas chemically fused with our lives. The result is that our minds present a most bizarre look, some of those ideas sticking to them like pieces of gummed paper while others have been rubbed off in course of time. After smearing ourselves with a European learning which has no connection with our inner lives, we strut about as proudly as those savages who ruin the natural brightness and loveliness of their skin by painting and tattooing it. Savage chiefs do not realize how ridiculous they look when they put on European clothes and decorate themselves with cheap European glass beads. We too do not realize what unconscious figures of farce we become when we parade the cheap smartness of the English words we know, and ruin some of the greatest European ideas by completely misapplying them. If we see anyone laughing at us, we immediately try to justify ourselves by speaking even more impressively.

Since our education bears no relation to our life, the books we read paint no vivid pictures of our homes, extol no ideals of our society. The daily pursuits of our lives find no place in those pages, nor do we meet there anybody or anything we happily recognize as our friends and relatives, our sky and earth, our mornings and evenings, or our cornfields and rivers. Education and life can never become one in such circumstances, and are bound to remain separated by a barrier. Our education may be compared to rainfall on a spot that is a long way from our roots. Not enough moisture seeps through the intervening barrier of earth to quench our thirst.

The barrier that separates education from life is really impenetrable in this country, so that their union is hard to attain. A growing hostility between the two is most often the result. We begin to develop a fundamental dislike and distrust of what we learn at school and college, since we find it contradicted in every detail by the conditions of the life around us. We begin to think that we are learning untruths and that European civilization is wholly based on them; that Indian civilization is wholly based on truth and our education is directing us to a land of enchanting falsehood. The real reason why European learning often fails us is not to be sought in any defect in that learning, but in the unfavourable conditions of our life. Yet we say that European learning fails us because failure is inherent in its nature. The stronger our dislike of this learning, the fewer the benefits it confers on us. And so the feud between our education and our life sharpens. As they draw further apart, our days become a stage where they mock and revile each other like two characters in a farce.

How to effect the union of education and life is today our most pressing problem. That union can be achieved only by Bengali language and literature. We all know that Bankimchandra Chatterji's periodical, *Bangadarshan*, appeared in the sky of Bengal like the dawn of a new day. Why was it that it gave the entire educated class such deep satisfaction? Did it publish any truth hitherto unknown to European history, philosophy or science? The answer is that *Bangadarshan* was the instrument with which a great genius broke down the barrier between our education and our life, and effected the joyous union of our head and heart. Until then, European culture had been an alien amongst us. As *Bangardarshan* brought it into our homes, we began to see ourselves in a new, revealing light. In the figures of Suryamukhi and Kamalmani, *Bangardarshan* showed our women as they really are; in the characters of Chandraesekhar and Pratap, it raised the ideal of Bengali manhood; and it cast a ray of glory on the petty affairs of our day-to-day life.

The pleasure we derived from *Bangadarshan* has had the effect of making educated Bengalees of today eager to write in their mother-tongue. They have realized that English can serve only their business, and not literary purposes; and they have noticed that, in spite of the great care with which English is learnt in this country, the books that are likely to live a long time are all being written in Bengali. The main reason for this is that a Bengalee can never acquire so close and intimate a knowledge of English as to make it the medium of a spontaneous literary expression. Even if he were a master of the English language, he would not be able to make it a live instrument of Bengali thought and feeling. The uncommon beauties and memories that impel us to creative activity can never assume their true form in a foreign language. Nor can those inherited qualities, which through generations have cast our minds in a special mould.

I have already said that our childhood and adolescence are spent in learning a language without gaining access to the underlying thought. The situation is reversed when we are older; we then lack a language with which to express our thoughts. I have also said that the reason why we are never on intimate terms with English literature is to be found in the dissociation of language and thought that takes place in us early in life. It is also the reason why many of our latter-day intellectuals feel dissatisfied with English literature. Turning to these intellectuals, we find that their thought is dissociated not only from English, but from Bengali as well. They have in fact become strangers to Bengali and developed an aversion for it. They do not, of course, openly admit that they do not know it, and they cry it down as unsuitable for thoughtful work and unworthy of cultivated people like themselves. It is the story of sour grapes over again.

From whatever angle we consider the matter, we find that our life, our thought and our language are not harmonized. Because of this fundamental disunity, we cannot stand on our two feet, cannot get what we want, cannot succeed in our efforts. I once read a story of a poor man who wanted to buy himself winter clothes for winter and summer clothes for summer. So he used to save up all the money he could get by begging. But he could not save up enough to buy summer clothes until summer was gone. This went on year after year until God, moved by pity, told the man that He would grant him a wish. 'All I ask for,' the man said, 'is this: let the vicissitudes of fortune end, so that I no longer get winter clothes in summer and summer clothes in winter.'

We too pray that God would end the vicissitudes of our education, and grant us winter clothes in winter and summer clothes in summer. God has put before us everything we need, but we cannot help ourselves to the right thing at the right moment. And that is why we live like that beggar in the story. So let us pray to God to give us food, when we are hungry, and clothes when we are cold. Let us pray that He would unite our language with our thought and our education with our life.

The Problem of Education (1906)[15]

WHAT WE NOW call a school in this country is really a factory, and the teachers are part of it. At half past ten in the morning the factory opens with the ringing of a bell; then, as the teachers start talking, the machines start working. The teachers stop talking at four in the afternoon when the factory closes, and the pupils then go home carrying with them a few pages of machine-made learning. Later, this learning is tested at examinations and labelled.

One advantage of a factory is that it can make goods exactly to order. Moreover, the goods are easy to label, because there is not much difference between what the different machines turn out.

But there is a good deal of difference between one man and another, and even between what the sane man is on different days.

Moreover, we can never get from the machines what we can get from human beings. A machine can hold a thing before us, but cannot give it to us. It can give us the oil with which to light a lamp, but it cannot light the lamp.

The school plays a minor part in the mental development of a European boy; the major part is played by the life of the country in which he grows up. Far from being divorced from life, European education is an integral part of it. It grows, develops and circulates in society, and leaves its imprint on what people say, think and do in their everyday life. The school is only a medium of the culture which society has acquired through its long history and the manifold activities of many people.

But the schools in our country, far from being integrated to society, are imposed on it from outside. The courses they teach are dull and dry, painful to learn, and useless when learnt. There is nothing in common between the lessons the pupils cram up from ten to four o'clock and the country where they live; no agreement, but many disagreements, between what they learn at school and what their parents and relatives talk about at home. The schools are little better than factories for turning out robots.

It is clear, therefore, that although we might succeed in copying to perfection the externals of the European school, we shall never get the real thing. We shall only be burdening ourselves with tables and benches, rules and curricula, which are but imitations, however, exact, of those in European schools.

Education in ancient India was in the charge of *gurus* who were moral and spiritual preceptors, and of teachers who were men rather than machines. It did not range over too wide a course, and was not in disagreement with

---

15. In Humayun Kabir, *Towards Universal Man* pp. 67-82.

the prevalent ideas and opinions of society. But to try to bring it back will mean useless revival of forms which will become a burden in the end.

If we at all understand the needs of the present day, we must see that any new schools founded by us fulfil the following conditions: that their courses are both lively and varied, and nourish the heart as well as the intellect; that no disunity or discord disrupts the minds of our young; and that education does not become something unreal, heavy and abstract with which the pupils are concerned only for those few hours when they are at school.

Boarding schools will be the result if we try to convert schools into homes. Boarding schools conjure up visions which are far from pleasant, and they are akin to army barracks, lunatic asylums, hospitals and prisons.

We must put the European model entirely out of our minds, if only for the reason that European history and European society are different from our history and our society. We must try properly to understand the ideals by which our country has been attracted and stimulated in the past.

This will present many difficulties. Because we have received English education, English models usurp the whole field of our vision and obscure the achievements of our own country. Even in our keenest struggles for freedom from British rule we remain fettered to Britain in so far as we seek no political models other than the British.

One of our difficulties arises from the fact that, lacking knowledge of Britain, we are unable to put English education in its proper perspective. Never having it in relation to the society to which it belongs, we fail to find the way by which its Indian counterpart can be harmonized with Indian life. Yet this is the most important question. To discuss such questions as the text-books that are studied, and the rules that are observed in some English school or college, is waste of time.

The idea seems to be bred in our bones that we can achieve anything by the mere act of founding an association and setting up a committee. In this respect we resemble the Tibetans who believe that they can acquire merit in heaven by hiring a lama to turn a prayer wheel on their behalf. After having founded a science association long ago, we have been lamenting for years on end that our country is not interested in science. As if to establish a science association is the same thing as making a people interested in science. To think that a country will produce thousands of scientists as soon as a science association has been founded show how addicted to machine worship we are in the present age.

The main thing is to get people interested. When that is done, our effort will be fully rewarded. How is it that ancient Indians were fully interested in the education they received? This is a question to be seriously considered. I know that some people study the calendars of foreign universities so assiduously as to give the impression of enjoying them immensely. I do not wish to spoil their enjoyment. It is certainly important to think about the subjects that should be taught in our schools; but the question how to get the pupils fully interested in their work is just as important.

The gurus of ancient India, so tradition says, lived in hermitages. We cannot form a clear picture of what they really were. But one thing is certain, and it is that the guru was a family man and his pupils lived with him as members of his household. The idea that a teacher and his pupils should live together has come down to the present day and is sometimes found in our *tols* and *chatuspathis*, schools and colleges that provide orthodox Hindu learning.

A glance at these *tols* and *chatuspathis* would also show that they do not regard book-learning as the most important part of education. They are surrounded by an atmosphere of culture, and the teachers are dedicated to their vocation. They live a simple life, without any material interest or luxury to distract their minds, and with plenty of time and opportunity for absorbing into their nature the things they learn. I would like to mention that this idea is also found in the great seats of learning in Europe.

In ancient India it was considered essential that the pupil should live at his teacher's home and that he should practise *brahmacharya*.

Brahmacharya should not be narrowly interpreted as austerity. A boy brought up in society is distracted by the impact of many people and many affairs, and his natural development is impeded. His feelings, while they are still in a formative stage, are aroused by false stimuli. Much waste of physical and mental power then follows. Young nature must be insulated from everything that might pervert it, and the object of *brahmacharya* is to protect growing manhood by disciplining it against the premature awakening of desire and its unhealthy gratification.

As a matter of fact, boys are happy to live in the discipline of nature. The discipline helps them to develop fully and taste the pleasure of real freedom, and it makes their bodies glow with the vigour of their sprouting minds.

Moral instruction has now displaced *brahmacharya* in our schools, and guardians want it to be given on every conceivable pretext. But it is a mechanical affair, like daily doses of sarsaparilla to an invalid, or prescribed diet for building up bonny babies, and it presents many difficulties. It cannot possibly be made attractive to a boy; it either hurts him or goes over his head, and it makes him feel like a criminal in the dock. I consider moral instruction an utter waste of time and effort and I am frightened that good people should be so keen on it. It is as futile as it is disagreeable, and I cannot think of anything that does more harm to society.

In a world where our standards are being daily pulled down by lies and distortions, it is too much to hope that everything will be put right by parroting a few copy-book maxims between the hours of ten and four at school. Pi jaws breed an awful lot of pretension and presumption, and destroy the freshness and naturalness of young minds.

Bramacharya gives power instead of mere instruction, and considers morality to be the essential ingredient, rather than the superficial ornament, of life. The person who practises it, far from regarding religion as something alien, takes to it easily and naturally as to a friend, and holds it close to his heart. It is not moral instruction that is needed for building up a boy's mind and character, but friendly guidance and congenial environment.

Besides practising *brahmacharya* a boy should live in the midst of nature. Towns are not our natural abodes, and have been built to supply our material needs. That we should be born in towns and be brought up in the lap of stone and brick was never intended by Providence. Towns snatch us away from the bosom of nature and consume us in their hungry furnace. People who live in them, and are absorbed by work, hardly feel that anything is missing from their lives, even though they have already strayed from nature and are daily getting further and further away from the great universe.

But nature's help is indispensable when we are still growing up, and still learning, and before we are drawn neck and crop into the whirlpool of affairs. Trees and rivers, and blue skies and beautiful views are just as necessary as benches and blackboards, books and examinations.

From ancient times the Indian mind has developed through close and unbroken contact with nature, and the desire to be one with animal and vegetable life has been inherent in the Indian spirit. The young hermits of ancient India used to chant:

> *To the God who resides in fire and water,*
> *in trees and plants,*
> *Immanent in the world and the universe,*
> *We bow, we bow.*

The four elements of earth, water, air and fire form a whole and are instinct with the universal soul – this knowledge cannot be gained at a school in town. A school in town is a factory which can only teach us to regard the world as a machine.

Practical people will dismiss an idea of this kind as mysticism or mystification. But even they will not be able to deny that blue sky and air, trees and flowers, are indispensable for the proper growth of the body and mind of a boy. We cannot be in close contact with nature when we have grown up into busy men of affairs working in an office in a crowded town. So, it is all the more necessary for us to be under nature's influence when we are young, our minds fresh and eager to learn, and our senses vigorous. We can grow into full manhood only if we have been nursed by earth and water, sky and air, and nourished by them as by our mother's breasts. So let the children play under the open sky which is the playground of sunlight and clouds. Let them not be taken away from *Bhuma*, the Supreme Spirit.

Let them see the six-act musical show nature puts on through the six seasons of the year. Let them hear the roar of thunder and see the massed clouds darken the woods before bursting into rain. When the rains are over, let the children see the green and dewy fields waving in the wind and overflowing with corn as far as the horizon.

Freedom is essential to the mind in the period of growth, and it is richly provided by nature. It is impossible for a boy to develop in a healthy way if he has to rush through a meal between the hours of half past nine and ten in the morning in order to present himself at roll-call at school like a suspicious character reporting himself at a police station. How we make the young suffer by walling education in, and shutting it up behind gates guarded by a porter! Are children to be blamed for not having learnt problems of algebra and dates of history before coming into this world? And is that any reason for depriving them of air and light, of freedom and joy, and turning their education into a punishment in every detail? Children are born ignorant in order that they may have the joy of growing into knowledge by degrees. We may be too incompetent to make education a thing of joy, but we need not be so cruel as to turn schools into prisons. God intended children to be educated in the freedom of nature, and we defeat ourselves by defeating his intention. So for pity's sake let us break down the prison walls. Let children be no longer sentenced to imprisonment with hard labour because they did not become *pundits* before being born.

My view is that we should follow the ancient Indian principles of education. Students and teachers should live together and in natural surroundings, and the students should complete their education by practising *brahmacharya*. Founded on the eternal truths of human nature, these principles have lost nothing of their significance, however much our circumstances might have altered through the ages.

If we had to build a school that would serve as a model, we should see that it was situated in a quiet spot far from the crowded city, and had the natural advantages of open sky, fields, trees and the like. It should be a retreat where teachers and students would live dedicated to learning.

If possible, there should be a plot of land which the students would help in cultivating, and which would provide food for the school. There should be cows for milk, and the students have a hand in tending them. When they are not engaged in study, the students should work in the garden, loosening the soil around the roots of trees, watering plants and training hedges. Their contact with nature would thus be both manual and mental.

In favourable weather the classes should be held in the shade of big trees. Part of the teaching should be in the form of discussion between teacher and student while they are walking between the rows of trees. In the evening recess the students should read the stars, cultivate music, and listen to legendary and historical tales.

A student who has done wrong should expiate for it in the ancient Indian manner. Punishment is the revenge of the wronged on the wrong-doer, but expiation is voluntarily undertaken by the wrong-doer himself. We should all learn early in life that expiation is a duty we owe to ourselves, and is the only way in which a wrong can be fully redressed. It is humiliating for a man to be punished by another man.

There is something else to be said in this connection. I see no reason why we must have tables, chairs and benches in our model school, and I hope I shall not be suspected of saying this out of prejudice against European ways. What I have in mind is the principle of dispensing with everything that is inessential, and I would like to see it upheld in every possible way in our school. Not all of us can afford to have tables, chairs and benches, but the ground is always there for all to sit on. Chairs and benches deprive us of the use of the ground. Ours is not a cold country and our clothes are not unsuitable for sitting on the ground, and yet we are so keen on aping foreign ways that we create furniture that is utterly superfluous. The more we regard as indispensable the things that are really useless, the more shall we be wasting our energy.

Our country has not got the resources of wealthy Europe, and things that are cheap to Europeans are very dear to us. When making plans for some work of public welfare that we have undertaken, we concentrate on the preliminaries, such as house and furniture, and we get many headaches over what they will cost, although they are mostly superfluous. Why do we not have the courage to say that we shall start work in a mud hut, and sit down on the floor when holding our meetings? That would cut our labour by a half without impairing the quality of our work. As things stand, we feel ashamed and dissatisfied unless we make ambitious plans on the model of European countries which have unlimited resources and are overflowing with wealth, with the result that we use up our meagre resources in providing the preliminaries, and have very little left over for the work in hand.

Our country had no lack of schools when a piece of chalk and the bare floor were all that a boy needed to learn to write; now it has a glut of slates and pencils but few schools. The tendency to care more for inessentials than for essentials is now seen in every aspect of our life. Our ancestors cared little for social formalities and much for social duties, but we do the opposite. They regarded furniture as part of wealth, but not of civilization. The guardians of civilization had very little furniture in their homes in those days, and they the country contentment by making poverty respectable. If we could be imbued with the ideal of plain living while we are young, we could at least acquire a few powers, if nothing else: the powers of sitting on the ground, putting on plain clothes, eating plain food, and of getting the best possible result with the least possible effort. These are not small powers, and they need a lot of effort to acquire.

Simplicity, naturalness and ease are the marks of the civilized, and excess and ostentation of the barbarian. Real greatness shines with its own native lustre, and loses nothing in humble surroundings. This is the simple truth, but it must be brought home to our boys in every possible way and instilled into their nature. They must learn it, not as a moral precept that can do them no good, but through the vivid example of plain living that they will see everywhere in their school. If they do not learn it, they will form a dislike of manual work, and think it demeaning to sit on the floor. Worse still, they will despise their fore-fathers and misunderstand the message of ancient India.

Assuming that we shall dispense with all externals, however glamorous, and concentrate wholly on inner worth, the question now arises whether the resources at our command will be adequate to our purpose. Our first duty as founders of a school should be to see that the teaching is in the charge of gurus. But how to get them? Gurus cannot be made to order, nor can we get them, as we can get schoolmasters, by advertising for them.

On this question I admit that we must cut the coat according to the cloth. It would be sheer folly to imagine that, because we needed a guru very badly, we would get a *Yajnavalkya*.[16] But we should also remember that under existing conditions a considerable part of our country's talent remains idle, like uninvested capital, because no attempt is made to turn it to full account. By using a large pail of water for sticking postage stamps on envelopes we leave most of the water unutilized, but we use it all up if we have it for a bath. This shows that the value of the pail of water increases or decreases according to use. The duties performed by a schoolmaster today do not call for more than a very small part of his mind and spirit and they can be performed almost as well by a gramophone with a bit of brain and a cane tied to it. But the same schoolmaster will devote his whole mind and spirit to the service of his students if he is called upon to undertake beyond his capacity, but he will also be ashamed to give less. It takes two to make a bargain, and we must ask for the best if we want to get it. Only a small part of our country's mental and spiritual powers is now in operation in the form of schoolmasters, but a much larger part will come into action in the form of gurus if our country earnestly desires it.

Economic forces compel the teacher of today to look for pupils, but in the natural order of things it is the pupils who should look for the teacher. The teacher is now a tradesman, a vendor of education in search of customers, and no one expects to find affection, regard, devotion or any other feeling in the list of goods he has for sale. After he has sold his goods, paid for in the form of a salary, he has no more to do with his pupils. But in spite of the unfavourable conditions of today, our country still possesses a few teachers who are able to

---

16. *Yajnavalkya* was a sage of Hinduism mentioned in the Vedas.

rise above financial considerations by virtue of their inner worth, and it is one these teachers who should be elevated to the position of the guru. Such a teacher will not fail to appreciate, when he is a guru, that he will do himself credit only if he can put life into his pupils with his own life, light their lamps with his own learning, and make them happy with his affection. By giving his pupils things that cannot be bought and sold and are really beyond all price, he will earn from them a devotion that owes nothing to the fear of being punished, and is deep enough to be called religious and genuine enough to be called natural. Although he will be obliged to take a salary for the sake of a livelihood, he will lend distinction to his position by giving much more than he is paid for.

Discussion of such details may seem useless to many of my readers who disagree with me on fundamentals, e.g., on the question whether it is good for boys to be sent away from home to be educated.

On this question I should say first that to give a boy what is now commonly regarded as education, our parents see no need to do anything more than send him to the nearest school and maybe, engage a private tutor. That sort of 'education' aims solely at helping a boy to grow into a moneymaker and, as I have already pointed out, it is unworthy of its name.

The world consists of people of different occupations, who live in homes varying in character and atmosphere and have children growing up with distinctive traits right from their infancy. Due to their occupations adults must attain different characteristics and fall into separate groups; it is not good for a boy, however, to be cast in the mould of his parents on the threshold of life.

Let us take a rich man's son as an example. He does not bring with him anything special when he comes into the world, anything that differentiates him from the son of the poor. It is the way he is brought up that gives him the marks of the rich.

So it is the duty of his parents first to build up his common humanity. Only after that has been done, and only to the extent that is compulsive, should they allow him to develop as a rich man's son. What actually happens is just the opposite. The boy is taught to act and behave like a rich man's son before he has fully learnt to act and behave like a human child; with the result that he is debarred from many of the fruitful experiences of childhood, and grows up with a rather limited range of feeling. For one thing, he is turned into a cripple, although he has hands and feet, by parents who themselves live like caged and pinioned birds. He must not walk, and must have a carriage. He must not carry the lightest load, and must have a porter. He must not do anything for himself, and must have a servant. Although healthy in every limb, he must behave like a paralytic. And he must do all this, not because he has any physical infirmities, but for fear of what people would think if he did not. The easiest things become difficult to him in consequence, the most natural things appear shameful. In deference to their social circle his parents shackle him with so many worthless conventions as to deprive him of almost all his natural rights as a human being. Should we say that such parents, who sow the cornfields of the earth with weeds, are the best people to be in charge of children?

It is not possible to forbid adults the luxury of snobbery, but children, if we understand what they really like, must not be forced into that kind of perversion. Children love the earth with its dust and its dirt, and they love the sun, the wind and the rain. They do not like to be dressed up, they enjoy themselves most when they are discovering the world with their senses, and they are not a bit ashamed to be their natural selves.

Many of our boys and girls are now being brought up in the way Europeans live in this country. They have nannies to look after them; they learn perverted Hindi and forget Bengali. They have been severed from the umbilical cord by which all children should remain tied to their native land and derive sustenance from it. Nor have they any access to European society. They have been uprooted from a forest and transplanted to a European flower-box. A grown-up Bengali is of course free to adopt European ways if he likes to do so, but why should Bengali parents go to such lengths in bringing up their children in the European way? I once heard a westernized boy cry out to his mother at the sight of some relatives of his who were dressed in the Indian style, 'Mamma, Mamma, look – a lot of babus are coming.' I can hardly imagine a worse degradation. Such youngsters, when they grow up, will be unfit for Bengali society and unacceptable to European society, and doomed to live as social outcasts.

In point of fact, those parents had no idea that they were bringing up their son in the wrong way; since people are blind to their own defects, they fail to see the harm they do to others. That is why they are unwilling to send their children away from home to be educated, even when the homes are hotbeds of evil passions, prejudices and superstitions. It must be laid down that parents who want their boys to become real men should consider it their duty to send them to schools where they would live with gurus in close communion with nature and under the discipline of *brahmacharya*.

Embryos and seeds grow in the seclusion of the womb and of the under-earth, drawing nourishment from their surroundings all day and night, until they are strong enough to come out in the air and the light. Nature keeps them in a congenial environment, taking care that they are not disturbed by forces from outside.

The human mind is in the embryo stage in childhood and schoolboys should live in surroundings which protect them from all disturbing forces. To acquire strength by absorbing knowledge both consciously and unconsciously should be their sole aim, and their environment should be adapted to this purpose.

The worm thinks it foolish that man does not eat his books,
Rabindranath Tagore

My School (1917)[17]

I STARTED A SCHOOL in Bengal when I was nearing forty. Certainly this was never expected of me, who had spent the greater portion of my life in writing, chiefly verses. Therefore people naturally thought that as a school it might not be one of the best of its kind, but it was sure to be something outrageously new, being the product of daring inexperience.

This is one of the reasons why I am often asked what is the idea upon which my school is based. The question is a very embarrassing one for me, because to satisfy the expectation of my questioners I cannot afford to be commonplace in my answer. However, I shall resist the temptation to be original and shall be content with being merely truthful.

In the first place, I must confess it is difficult for me to say what is the idea which underlies my institution. For the idea is not like a fixed foundation upon which a building is erected. It is more like a seed which cannot be separated and pointed out directly it begins to grow into a plant.

And I know what it was to which this school owes its origin. It was not any new theory of education, but the memory of my school-days.

That those days were unhappy ones for me I cannot altogether ascribe to my peculiar temperament or to any special demerit of the schools to which I was sent. It may be that if I had been a little less sensitive, I could gradually have accommodated myself to the pressure and survived long enough to earn my university degrees. But all the same schools are schools, though some are better and some worse, according to their own standard.

The provision has been made for infants to be fed upon their mother's milk. They find their food and their mother at the same time. It is complete nourishment for them, body and soul. It is their first introduction to the great truth that man's true relationship with the world is that of personal love and not that of the mechanical law of causation.

The introduction and the conclusion of a book have a similarity of features. In both places the complete aspect of truth is given. Only in the introduction it is simple because undeveloped, and in the conclusion it becomes simple again because perfectly developed. Truth has the middle course of its career, where it grows complex, where it hurts itself against obstacles, breaks itself into pieces to find itself back in a fuller unity of realization.

Similarly man's introduction to this world is his introduction to his final truth in a simple form. He is born into a world which to him is intensely living,

---

17. Sisir Kumar Das, ed *The English Writings of Rabindranath Tagore* (New Delhi: Sahitya Akademi, 1996) Vol 2 pp. 389-403.

where he as an individual occupies the full attention of his surroundings. Then he grows up to doubt this deeply personal aspect of reality, he loses himself in the complexity of things, separates himself from his surrounding, often in a spirit of antagonism. But this shattering of the unity of truth, this uncompromising civil war between his personality and his outer world, can never find its meaning in interminable discord. Thereupon to find the true conclusion of his life he has to come back through this digression of doubt to the simplicity of perfect truth, to his union with all in an infinite bond of love.

Therefore our childhood should be given its full measure of life's draught, for which it has an endless thirst. The young mind should be saturated with the idea that it has been born in a human world which is in harmony with the world around it. And this is what our regular type of school ignores with an air of superior wisdom, severe and disdainful. It forcibly snatches away children from a world full of the mystery of God's own handiwork, full of the suggestiveness of personality. It is a mere method of discipline which refuses to take into account the individual. It is a manufactory specially designed for grinding out uniform results. It follows an imaginary straight line of the average in digging its channel of education. But life's line is not the straight line, for it is fond of playing the see-saw with the line of the average, bringing upon its head the rebuke of the school. For according to the school life is perfect when it allows itself to be treated as dead, to be cut into symmetrical conveniences. And this was the cause of my suffering when I was sent to school. For all of a sudden I found my world vanishing from around me, giving place to wooden benches and straight walls staring at me with the blank stare of the blind. I was not a creation of the schoolmaster, - the Government Board of Education was not consulted when I took birth in the world. But was that any reason why they should wreak their vengeance upon me for this oversight of my creator?

But the legend is that eating of the fruit of knowledge is not consonant with dwelling in paradise. Therefore men's children have to be banished from their paradise into a realm of death, dominated by the decency of a tailoring department. So my mind had to accept the tight-fitting encasement of the school which, being like the shoes of a mandarin woman, pinched and bruised my nature on all sides and at every movement. I was fortunate enough in extricating myself before insensibility set in.

Though I did not have to serve the full penal term which men of my position have to undergo to find their entrance into cultured society, I am glad that I did not altogether escape from its molestation. For it has given me knowledge of the wrong from which the children of men suffer.

The cause of it is this, that man's intention is going against God's intention as to how children should grow into knowledge. How we should conduct our business is our own affair, and therefore in our offices we are free to create in the measure of our special purposes. But such office arrangement does not suit God's creation. And children are God's creation.

We have come to this world to accept it, not merely to know it. We may become powerful by knowledge, but we attain fullness by sympathy. The highest education is that which does not merely give us information but makes our life in harmony with all existence. But we find that this education of sympathy is not only systematically ignored in schools, but it is severely repressed. From our very childhood habits are formed and knowledge is imparted in such a manner that our life is weaned away from nature and our mind and the world are set in opposition from the beginning of our days. Thus the greatest of educations for which we came prepared is neglected, and we are made to lose our world to find a bagful of information instead. We rob the child of his earth to teach him geography, of language to teach him grammar. His hunger is for the Epic, but he is supplied with chronicles of facts and dates. He was born in the human world, but is banished into the world of living gramophones, to expiate for the original sin of being born in ignorance. Child-nature protests against such calamity with all its power of suffering subdued at last into silence by punishment.

We all know children are lovers of the dust; their whole body and mind thirst for sunlight and air as flowers do. They are never in a mood to refuse the constant invitations to establish direct communication which come to their senses from the universe.

But unfortunately for children their parents, in the pursuit of their profession, in conformity to their social traditions, live in their own peculiar world of habits. Much of this cannot be helped. For men have to specialize, driven by circumstances and by need of social uniformity.

But our childhood is the period when we have or ought to have more freedom – freedom from the necessity of specialization into the narrow bounds of social and professional conventionalism.

I well remember the surprise and annoyance of an experienced headmaster, reputed to be a successful disciplinarian, when he saw one of the boys of my school climbing a tree and choosing a fork of the branches for settling down to his studies. I had to say to him in explanation that 'childhood is the only period of life when a civilized man can exercise his choice between the branches of a tree and his drawing-room chair, and should I deprive this boy of that privilege because I, as a grown-up man, am barred from it?' What is surprising is to notice the same headmaster's approbation of the boy's studying botany. He believes in an impersonal knowledge of the tree because that is science, but not in a personal experience of it. This growth of experience leads to forming instinct, which is the result of nature's own method of instruction. The boys of my school have acquired instinctive knowledge of the physiognomy of the tree. By the least touch they know where they can find a foothold upon an apparently inhospitable trunk; they know how far they can take liberty with the branches, how to distribute their bodies' weight so as to make themselves least burdensome to branchlets. My boys are able to make the best possible use of the tree in the matter of gathering fruits, taking rest and hiding from undesirable pursuers. I myself was brought up in a cultured home in a town, and as far as my personal behaviour goes I have been obliged to act all through my life as if I were born in a world where there are no trees. Therefore I consider it as part of education for my boys to let them fully realize that they are in a scheme of existence where trees are a substantial fact not merely as generating chlorophyll and taking carbon from the air, but as living trees.

Naturally the soles of our feet are so made that they become the best instruments for us to stand upon the earth and to walk with. From the day we commenced to wear shoes we minimized the purpose of our feet. With the lessening of their responsibility they have lost their dignity, and now they lend themselves to be pampered with socks, slippers and shoes of all prices and shapes and misproportions. For us it amounts to a grievance against God for not giving us hooves instead of beautifully sensitive soles.

I am not for banishing foot-gear altogether from men's use. But I have no hesitation in asserting that the soles of children's feet should not be deprived of their education, provided for them by nature, free of cost. Of all the limbs we have they are the best adapted for intimately knowing the earth by their touch. For the earth has her subtle modulations of contour which she only offers for the kiss of her true lovers – the feet.

I have again to confess that I was brought up in a respectable household and my feet from childhood have been carefully saved from all naked contact with the dust. When I try to emulate my boys in walking barefoot, I painfully realize what thickness of ignorance about the earth I carry under my feet. I invariably choose the thorns to tread upon in such a manner as to make the thorns exult. My feet have not the instinct to follow the lines of least resistance. For even the flattest of earth-surfaces has its dimples of diminutive hills and dales only discernible by educated feet. I have often wondered at the unreasonable zigzag of footpaths across perfectly plain fields. It becomes all the more perplexing when you consider that a footpath is not made by the caprice of one individual. Unless most of the walkers possessed exactly the same eccentricity such obviously inconvenient passages could not have been made. But the real cause lies in the subtle suggestions coming from the earth to which our feet unconsciously respond. Those for whom such communications have not been cut off can adjust the muscles of their feet with great rapidity at the least indication. Therefore they can save themselves from the intrusion of thorns, even while treading upon them, and walk barefooted on a gravelly path without the least discomfort. I know that in the practical world shoes will be worn, roads will be metalled, cars will be used. But during their period of education should children not be given to know that the world is not all drawingroom, that there is such a thing as nature to which their limbs are made beautifully to respond?

There are men who think that by the simplicity of living, introduced in my school, I preach the idealization of poverty which prevailed in the mediaeval age. The full discussion of this subject is outside the scope of my paper, but seen from the point of view of education, should we not admit that poverty is the school in which man had his first lessons and his best training? Even a millionaire's son has to be born helplessly poor and to begin his lesson of life from the beginning. He has to learn to walk like the poorest of children, though he has means to afford to be without the appendage of legs. Poverty brings us into complete touch with life and the world, for living richly is living in a world of lesser reality. This may be good for one's pleasure and pride, but not for one's education. Wealth is a golden cage in which the children of the rich are bred into artificial deadening of their powers. Therefore in my school, much to the disgust of the people of expensive habits, I had to provide for this great teacher, - this bareness of furniture and materials, - not because it is poverty, but because it leads to personal experience of the world.

What I propose is that men should have some limited period of their life specially reserved for the life of the primitive man. Civilized busybodies have not been allowed to tamper with the unborn child. In the mother's womb it has leisure to finish its first stage of the vegetative life. But directly it is born, with all its instincts ready for the next stage, which is the natural life, it is at once pounced upon by the society of cultivated habits, to be snatched away from the open arms of earth, water and sky, from the sunlight and air. At first it struggles and bitterly cries, and then it gradually forgets that it had for its inheritance God's creation; then it shuts its windows, pulls down its curtains, loses itself among meaningless miscellanies and feels proud of its accumulations at the cost of its world and possibly of its soul.

The civilized world of conventions and things comes in the middle career of man's progress. It is neither in the beginning nor in the end. Its enormous complexity and codes of decorum have their uses. But when it takes these to be final, and makes it a rule that no green spot should be left in man's life away from its reign of smoke and noise, of draped and decorated propriety, then children suffer, and in the young men is produced world-weariness, while old men forget to grow old in peace and beauty, merely becoming dilapidated youths, ashamed of their shabbiness of age, full of holes and patchwork.

However, it is certain that children did not bargain for this muffled and screened world of decency when they were ready to be born upon this earth. If they had any idea that they were about to open their eyes to the sunlight, only to find themselves in the hands of the education department till they should lose their freshness of mind and keenness of sense, they would think twice before venturing upon their career of humanity. God's arrangements are never insolently special arrangements. They always have the harmony of wholeness and unbroken continuity with all things. Therefore what tortured me in my school-days was the fact that the school had not the completeness of the world. It was a special arrangement for giving lessons. It could only be suitable for grown-up people who were conscious of the special need of such places and therefore ready to accept their teaching at the cost of dissociation from life. But children are in love with life, and it is their first love. All its colour and movement attract their eager attention. And are we quite sure of our wisdom in stifling this love? Children are not born ascetics, fit to enter at once into the monastic discipline of acquiring knowledge. At first they must gather knowledge through their love of life, and then they will renounce their lives to gain knowledge, and then again they will come back to their fuller lives with ripened wisdom.

But society has made its own arrangements for manipulating men's minds to fit its special patterns. These arrangements are so closely organized that it is difficult to find gaps through which to bring in nature. There is a serial adjustment of penalties which follows to the end one who ventures to take liberty with some part of the arrangements, even to save his soul. Therefore it is one thing to realize truth and another to bring it into practice where the whole current of the prevailing system goes against you. This is why when I had to face the problem of my own son's education I was at a loss to give it a practical solution. The first thing that I did was to take him away from the town surroundings into a village and allow him the freedom of primeval nature as far as it is available in modern days. He had a river, noted for its danger, where he swam and rowed without check from the anxiety of his elders. He spent his time in the fields and on the trackless sand-banks, coming late for his meals without being questioned. He had none of those luxuries that are not only customary but are held as proper for boys of his circumstance. For which privations, I am sure, he was pitied and his parents blamed by the people for whom society has blotted out the whole world. But I was certain that luxuries are burdens to boys. They are the burdens of other people's habits, the burdens of the vicarious pride and pleasure which parents enjoy through their children.

Yet, being an individual of limited resources, I could do very little for my son in the way of educating him according to my plan. But he had the freedom of movement, he had very few of the screens of wealth and respectability between himself and the world of nature. Thus he had a better opportunity for a real experience of this universe than I ever had. But one thing exercised my mind as more important than anything else.

The object of education is to give man the unity of truth. Formerly when life was simple all the different elements of man were in complete harmony.

But when there came the separation of the intellect from the spiritual and the physical, the school education put entire, emphasis on the intellect and the physical side of man. We devote our sole attention to giving children information, not knowing that by this emphasis we are accentuating a break between the intellectual, physical and the spiritual life.

I believe in a spiritual world – not as anything separate from this world – but as its innermost truth. With the breath we draw we must always feel this truth, that we are living in God. Born in this great world, full of the mystery of the infinite, we cannot accept our existence as a momentary outburst of chance, drifting on the current of matter towards an eternal nowhere. We cannot look upon our lives as dreams of a dreamer who has no awakening in all time. We have a personality to which matter and force are unmeaning unless related to something infinitely personal, whose nature we have discovered, in some measure, in human love, in the greatness of the good, in the martyrdom of heroic souls, in the effable beauty of nature, which can never be a mere physical fact nor anything but an expression of personality.

Experience of this spiritual world, whose reality we miss by our incessant habit of ignoring it from childhood, has to be gained by children by fully living in it and not through the medium of theological instruction. But how this is to be done is a problem difficult of solution in the present age. For nowadays men have managed so fully to occupy their time that they do not find leisure to know that their activities have only movement but very little truth, that their soul has not found its world.

In India we still cherish in our memory the tradition of the forest colonies of great teachers. These places were neither schools nor monasteries in the modern sense of the word. They consisted of homes where with their families lived men whose object was the see the world in God and to realize their own life in him. Though they lived outside society, yet they were to society what the sun is to the planets, the centre from which it received its life and light. And here boys grew up in an intimate vision of eternal life before they were thought fit to enter the state of the householder.

Thus in ancient India the school was there where was the life itself. There the students were brought up, not in the academic atmosphere of scholarship and learning, or in the maimed life of monastic seclusion, but in the atmosphere of living aspiration. They took the cattle to pasture, collected firewood, gathered fruit, cultivated kindness to all creatures, and grew in their spirit with their own teachers' spiritual growth. This was possible because the primary object of these places was not teaching but giving shelter to those who lived their life in God.

That this traditional relationship of the masters and disciples is not a mere romantic fiction is proved by the relic we still possess of the indigenous system of education which has preserved its independence for centuries, to be about to succumb at last to the hand of the foreign bureaucratic control. These *chatuspathis*, which is the Sanskrit name for the university, have not the savour of the school about them. The students live in their master's home like the children of the house, without having to pay for their board and lodging or tuition. The teacher prosecutes his own study, living a life of simplicity, and helping the students in their lessons as a part of his life and not of his profession.

This ideal of education through sharing a life of high aspiration with one's master took possession of my mind. The narrowness of our caged-up future and the sordidness of our maimed opportunities urged me all the more towards its realization. Those who in other countries are favoured with unlimited expectations of worldly prospects can fix their purposes of education on those objects. The range of their life is varied and wide enough to give them the freedom necessary for development of their powers. But for us to maintain the self-respect which we owe to ourselves and to our creator, we must make the purpose of our education nothing short of the highest purpose of man, the fullest growth and freedom of soul. It is pitiful to have to scramble for small pittances of fortune. Only let us have access to the life that goes beyond death and rises above all circumstances, let us find our God, let us live for that ultimate truth which emancipates us from the bondage of the dust and gives us the wealth, not of things but of inner light, not of power but of love. Such emancipation of soul we have witnessed in our country among men devoid of book-learning and living in absolute poverty. In India we have inheritance of this treasure of spiritual wisdom. Let the object of our education be to open it out before us and to give us the power to make the true use of it in our life, and offer it to the rest of the world when the time comes, as our contribution to its eternal welfare.

I had been immersed in literary activities when this thought struck my mind with painful intensity. I suddenly felt like one groaning under the suffocation of nightmare. It was not only my own soul, but the soul of my country that seemed to be struggling for its breath through me. I felt clearly that what was needed was not any particular material object, not wealth or comfort or power, but our awakening to full consciousness in soul freedom, the freedom of the life in God, where we have no enmity with those who must fight, no competition with those who must make money, where we are beyond all attacks and above all insults.

Fortunately for me I had a place ready to my hand where I could begin my work. My father, in one of his numerous travels, had selected this lonely spot as the one suitable for his life of communion with God. This place, with a permanent endowment, he dedicated to the use of those who seek peace and seclusion for their meditation and prayer. I had about ten boys with me when I came here and started my new life with no previous experience whatever.

All round our *ashram* is a vast open country, bare up to the line of the horizon except for sparsely-growing stunted date-palms and prickly shrubs struggling with ant-hills. Below the level of the field there extend numberless mounds and tiny hillocks of red gravel and pebbles of all shapes and colours, intersected by narrow channels of rain-water. Not far away towards the south near the village can be seen through the intervals of a row of palm trees the gleaming surface of steel-blue water, collected in a hollow of the ground. A road used by the village people for their marketing in the town goes meandering through the lonely fields, with its red dust staring in the sun. Travellers coming up this road can see from a distance on the summit of the undulating ground the spire of a temple and the top of a building, indicating the Shanti-Niketan *ashram*, among its *amalaki* groves and its avenue of stately *sal* trees.

And here the school has been growing up for over fifteen years, passing through many changes and often grave crisis. Having the evil reputation of a poet, I could with great difficulty win the trust of my countrymen and avoid the suspicion of the bureaucracy. That at last I have been able to accomplish it in some measure is owing to my never expecting it, going on in my own way without waiting for outside sympathy, help or advice. My resources were extremely small, with the burden of a heavy debt upon them. But this poverty itself gave me the full strength of freedom, making me rely upon truth rather than upon materials.

Because the growth of this school was the growth of my life and not that of a mere carrying out of my doctrines, its ideals changed with its maturity like a ripening fruit that not only grows in its bulk and deepens in its colour, but undergoes change in the very quality of its inner pulp. I started with the idea that I had a benevolent object to perform. I worked hard, but the only satisfaction I had came from keeping count of the amount of sacrifice in money, energy and time; admiring my own untiring goodness. But the result achieved was of small worth. I went on building system after system and then pulling them down. It merely occupied my time, but at the heart my work remained vacant. I well remember when an old disciple of my father came and said to me, 'What I see about me is like a wedding hall where nothing is wanting in preparation only the bridegroom is absent.' The mistake I made was in thinking that my own purpose was that bridegroom. But gradually my heart found its centre. It was not in the work, not in my wish, but in truth. I sat alone on the upper terrace of the Shanti-Niketan house and gazed upon the tree tops of the *sal* avenue before me. I withdrew my heart from my own schemes and calculations, from my daily struggles, and held it up in silence before the peace and presence that permeated the sky; and gradually my heart was filled. I began to see the world around me through the eyes of my soul. The trees seemed to me like silent hymns rising from the mute heart of the earth, and the shouts and laughter of the boys mingling in the evening sky came before me like trees of living sounds rising up from the depth of human life. I found my messages in the sunlight that touched my inner mind and felt a fulness in the sky that spoke to me in the word of our ancient rishi – 'Ko hyevânyât, kah prânyât yadesha âkâsha ânando no syât' – 'Who could ever move and strive and live in this world if the sky were not filled with love?' Thus when I turned back from the struggle to achieve results, from the ambition of doing benefit to others, and came to my own innermost need; when I felt that living one's own life in truth is living the life of all the world, then the unquiet atmosphere of the outward struggle cleared up and the power of spontaneous creation found its way through the centre of all things. Even now whatever is superficial and futile in the working of our institution is owing to the distrust of the spirit, lurking in our mind, to the ineradicable consciousness of our self-importance, to the habit of looking for the cause of our failures outside us, and the endeavour to repair all looseness in our work by tightening the screws of organization. From my experience I know that where the eagerness to teach others is too strong, especially in the matter of spiritual life, the result becomes meagre and mixed with untruth. All the hypocrisy and self-delusion in our religious convictions and practices are the outcome of the goadings of over-zealous activities of mentorship. In our spiritual attainment gaining and giving are the same thing; as in a lamp, to light itself is the same as to impart light to others. When a man makes it his profession to preach God to others, then he will raise the dust more than give direction to truth. Teaching of religion can never be imparted in the form of lessons, it is there where there is religion in living. Therefore the ideal of the forest colony of the seekers of God as the true school of spiritual life holds good even in this age. Religion is not a fractional thing that can be doled out in fixed weekly or daily measures as one among various subjects in the school syllabus. It is the truth of our complete being, the consciousness of our personal relationship with the infinite; it is the true centre of gravity of our life. This we can attain during our childhood by daily living in a place where the truth of the spiritual world is not obscured by a crowd of necessities assuming artificial importance; where life is simple, surrounded by fullness of leisure, by ample space and pure air and profound peace of nature; and where men live with a perfect faith in the eternal life before them.

But the question will be asked whether I have attained my ideal in this institution. My answer is that the attainment of all our deepest ideals is difficult to measure by outward standards. Its working is not immediately perceptible by results. We have fully admitted the inequalities and varieties of human life in our *ashram*. We never try to gain some kind of outward uniformity by weeding out the differences of nature and training of our members. Some of us belong to the Brahma Samaj sect and some to other sects of Hinduism; and some of us are Christians. Because we do not deal with creeds and dogmas of sectarianism, therefore this heterogeneity of our religious beliefs does not present us with any difficulty whatever. This also I know, that the feeling of respect for the ideal of this place and the life lived here greatly varies in depth and earnestness among those who have gathered in this *ashram*. I know that our inspiration for a higher life has not risen far above our greed for worldly goods and reputation. Yet I am perfectly certain, and proofs of it are numerous, that the ideal of the *ashram* is sinking deeper and deeper into our nature every day. The tuning of our life's strings into purer spiritual notes is going on without our being aware of it. Whatever might be our original motive in coming here, the call sounds without ceasing through all our clamour of discords, the call of *shântam, shivam, advaitam,* - the All peace, the All Good, and the One. The sky here seems penetrated with the voice of the infinite, making the peace of its daybreak and stillness of its night profound with meaning, and sending through the white crowds of *shiuli* flowers in the autumn and *malati* in the summer, the message of self-dedication in the perfect beauty of worship.

It will be difficult for others than Indians to realize all the associations that are grouped round the word *ashram*, the forest sanctuary. For it blossomed in India like its own lotus, under a sky generous in its sunlight and starry splendour. India's climate has brought to us the invitation of the open air; the language of her mighty rivers is solemn in their chants; the limitless expanse of her plains encircles our homes with the silence of the world beyond; there the sun rises from the marge of the green earth like an offering of the unseen to the altar of the Unknown, and it goes down to the west at the end of the day like a gorgeous ceremony of nature's salutation to the External. In India the shades of the trees are hospitable, the dust of the earth stretches its brown arms to us, the air with its embraces clothes us with warmth. These are the unchanging facts that ever carry their suggestions to our minds, and therefore we feel it is India's mission to realize the truth of the human soul in the Supreme Soul through its union with the soul of the world. This mission had taken its natural form in the forest schools in the ancient time. And it still urges us to seek for the vision of the infinite in all forms of creation, in the human relationships of love; to feel it in the air we breathe, in the light in which we open our eyes, in the water in which we bathe, in the earth on which we live and die. Therefore I know – and I know it from my own experience, – that the students and the teachers who have come together in this *ashram* are daily growing towards the emancipation of their minds into the consciousness of the infinite, not through any process of teaching or outer discipline, but by the help of an unseen atmosphere of aspiration that surrounds the place and the memory of a devoted soul who lived here in intimate communion with God.

I hope I have been able to explain how the conscious purpose that led me to found my school in the *ashram* gradually lost its independence and grew into unity with the purpose that reigns in this place. In a word my work found its soul in the spirit of the *ashram*. But that soul has its outer form, no doubt, which is its aspect of the school. And in the teaching system of this school I have been trying all these years to carry out my theory of education, based upon my experience of children's minds.

I believe, as I suggested before, that children have their subconscious mind more active than their conscious intelligence. A vast quantity of the most important of our lessons has been taught to us through this. Experiences of countless generations have been instilled into our nature by its agency, not only without causing us any fatigue, but giving us joy. This subconscious faculty of knowledge is completely one with our life. It is not like a lantern that can be lighted and trimmed from outside, but it is like the light that the glow-worm possesses by the exercise of its life-process.

Fortunately for me I was brought up in a family where literature, music and art had become instinctive. My brothers and cousins lived in the freedom of ideas, and most of them had natural artistic powers. Nourished in these surroundings, I began to think early and to dream and to put my thoughts into expression. In religion and social ideals our family was free from all convention, being ostracized by society owing to our secession from orthodox beliefs and customs. This made us fearless in our freedom of mind, and we tried experiments in all departments of life. This was the education I had in my early days, freedom and joy in the exercise of my mental and artistic faculties. And because this made my mind fully alive to grow in its natural environment of nutrition, therefore the grinding of the school system became so extremely intolerable to me.

I had the experience of my early life to help me when I started my school. I felt sure that what was most necessary was the breath of culture and no formal method of teaching. Fortunately for me, Satish Chandra Roy, a young student of great promise, who was getting ready for his BA degree, became attracted to my school and devoted his life to carry out my idea. He was barely nineteen, but he had a wonderful soul, living in a world of ideas, keenly responsive to all that was beautiful and great in the realm of nature and of human mind. He was a poet who would surely have taken his place among the immortals of world-literature if he had been spared to live, but he died when he was twenty, thus offering his service to our school only for the period of one short year. With him boys never felt that they were confined in the limit of a teaching class; they seemed to have their access to everywhere. They would go with him to the forest when in the spring the *sal* trees were in full blossom and he would recite to them his favourite poems, frenzied with excitement. He used to read to them Shakespeare and even Browning, – for he was a great lover of Browning, – explaining to them in Bengali with his wonderful power of expression. He never had any feeling of distrust for boys' capacity of understanding; he would talk and read to them about whatever was the subject in which he himself was interested. He knew that it was not at all necessary for the boys to understand literally and accurately, but that their minds should be roused, and in this he was always successful. He was not like other teachers, a mere vehicle of text-books. He made his teaching personal, he himself was the source of it, and therefore it was made of life stuff, easily assimilable by the living human nature. The real reason of his success was his intense interest in life, in ideas, in everything around him, in the boys who came in contact with him. He had his inspiration not through the medium of books, but through the direct communication of his sensitive mind with the world. The seasons had upon him the same effect as they had upon the plants. He seemed to feel in his blood the unseen messages of nature that are always travelling through space, floating in the air, shimmering in the sky, tingling in the roots of the grass under the earth. The literature that he studied had not the least smell of the library about it. He had the power to see ideas before him, as he could see his friends, with all the distinctness of form and subtlety of life.

Thus the boys of our school were fortunate enough to be able to receive their lessons from a living teacher and not from text-books. Have not our books, like most of our necessaries, come between us and our world? We have got into the habit of covering the windows of our minds with their pages, and plasters of book phrases have stuck into our mental skin, making it impervious to all direct touches of truth. A whole world of bookish truths have formed themselves into strong citadel with rings of walls in which we have taken shelter, secured from the communication of God's creation. Of course, it would be foolish to underrate the advantages of the book. But at the same time we must admit that the book has its limitations and its dangers. At any rate during the early period of education children should come to their lesson truths through natural processes – directly through persons and things.

Being convinced of this, I have set all my resources to create an atmosphere of ideas in the *ashram*. Songs are composed, not specially made to order for juvenile minds. They are songs that poet writes for his own pleasure. In fact, most of my *Gitanjali* songs were written here. These, when fresh in their first bloom, are sung to the boys, and they come in crowds to learn them. They sing them in their leisure hours, sitting in groups, under the open sky on moonlight nights, in the shadows of the impending rain in July. All my latter-day plays have been written here, and the boys have taken part in their performance. Lyrical dramas have been written for their season-festivals. They have ready access to the room where I read to the teachers any new things that I write in prose or in verse, whatever the subject may be. And this they utilize without the least pressure put upon them, feeling aggrieved when not invited. A few weeks before leaving India I read to them Browning's drama 'Luria', translating it into Bengali as I went on. It took me two evenings, but the second meeting was as full as the first one. Those who have witnessed these boys playing their parts in dramatic performances have been struck with their wonderful power as actors. It is because they are never directly trained in the histrionic art. They instinctively enter into the spirit of the plays in which they take part, though these plays are no mere school-boy dramas. They require subtle understanding and sympathy. With all the anxiety and hyper-critical sensitiveness of an author about the performance of his own play I have never been disappointed in my boys, and I have rarely allowed teachers to interfere with the boy's own representation of the characters. Very often they themselves write plays or improvise them and we are invited to their performance. They hold meetings of their literary clubs and they have at least three illustrated magazines conducted by three sections of the school, the most interesting of them being that of the infant section. A number of our boys have shown remarkable powers in drawing and painting, developed not through the orthodox method of copying models, but by following their own bent and by the help of occasional visits from some artists to inspire the boys with their own work.

When I first started my school my boys had no evident love for music. The consequence is that at the beginning I did not employ a music teacher and did not force the boys to take music lessons. I merely created opportunities when those of us who had the gift could exercise their musical culture. It had the effect of unconsciously training the ears of the boys. And when gradually most of them showed a strong inclination and love for music I saw that they would be willing to subject themselves to formal teaching, and it was then that I secured a music teacher.

In our school the boys rise very early in the morning, sometimes before it is light. They attend to the drawing of water for their bath. They make up their beds. They do all those things that tend to cultivate the spirit of self-help.

I believe in the hour of meditation, and I set aside fifteen minutes in the morning and fifteen minutes in the evening for that purpose. I insist on this period of meditation, not, however, expecting the boys to be hypocrites and to make believe that they are meditating. But I do insist that they remain quiet, that they exert the power of self-control, even though instead of contemplating on God, they may be watching the squirrels running up the trees.

Any description of such a school is necessarily inadequate. For the most important element of it is the atmosphere, and the fact that it is not a school which is imposed upon the boys by autocratic authorities. I always try to impress upon their minds that it is their own world, upon which their life ought fully and freely to react. In the school administration they have their place, and in the matter of punishment we mostly rely upon their own court of justice.

In conclusion I warn my hearers not to carry away with them any false or exaggerated picture of this *ashram*. When ideas are stated in a paper, they appear too simple and complete. But in reality their manifestation through the materials that are living and varied and ever changing is not so clear and perfect. We have obstacles in human nature and in outer circumstances. Some of us have a feeble faith in boys' minds as living organisms, and some have the natural propensity of doing good by force. On the other hand, the boys have their different degrees of receptivity and there are a good number of inevitable failures. Delinquencies make their appearance unexpectedly, making us suspicious as to the efficacy of our own ideals. We pass through dark periods of doubt and reaction. But these conflicts and waverings belong to the true aspects of reality. Living ideals can never be set into a clockwork arrangement, giving accurate account of its every second. And those who have firm faith in their idea have to test its truth in discords and failures that are sure to come to tempt them from their path. I for my part believe in the principle of life, in the soul of man more than in methods. I believe that the object of education is the freedom of mind which can only be achieved through the path of freedom – though freedom has its risk and responsibility as life itself has. I know it for certain, though most people seem to have forgotten it, that children are living beings – more living than grown-up people, who have built their shells of habit around them. Therefore it is absolutely necessary for their mental health and development that they should not have mere schools for their lessons, but a world whose guiding spirit is personal love. It must be an ashram where men have gathered for the highest end of life, in the peace of nature; where life is not merely meditative, but fully awake in its activities, where boys' minds are not being perpetually drilled into believing that the ideal of the self-idolatry of the nation is the truest ideal for them to accept; where they are bidden to realize man's world as God's Kingdom to whose citizenship they have to aspire; where the sunrise and sunset and the silent glory of stars are not daily ignored; where nature's festivities of flowers and fruit have their joyous recognition from man; and where the young and the old, the teacher and the student, sit at the same table to partake of their daily food and the food of their eternal life.

The Centre of Indian Culture (1919)[18]

I

INDIA HAS PROVED that it has its own mind, which has been deeply concerned to solve according to its light the problems of existence. India's aim in education is to enable this mind to fulfil its quest in its own individual way.

For this purpose the mind of India must become organized and self-aware; then only will it accept education from its teachers in the right spirit, assess it by its own standard of values, and make use of it by its own creative power. The fingers must be held close to take as well as to give. When we bring scattered minds into co-ordinated activity, they will become receptive as well as creative; and the waters of life will cease to slip through the gaps and sodden the ground beneath.

In education the most important factor is an atmosphere of creative activity, in which the work of intellectual exploration may find full scope. The teaching should be like the overflow water of a spring of culture, spontaneous and inevitable. Education becomes natural and wholesome only when it is the fruit of a living and growing knowledge.

Further, our education should be in constant touch with our complete life, economic, intellectual, aesthetic, social and spiritual; and our schools should be at the very heart of our society, connected with it by the living bonds of varied co-operation. For, true education is to realize at every step how our training and knowledge have an organic connection with our surroundings.

II

All over India there is a vague feeling of discontent about our prevalent system of education. There have recently been many signs of a desire for change – there seems to be an urge of life in the subsoil of our national mind, which sends forth new institutions and gives rise to new experiments. But it often happens that, because man's wish is so immediate and so strong, it becomes difficult to locate accurately the exciting cause, to make sure of the object towards which it aspires.

The current system of education, in which our mind has been nurtured, is as tangible to us as our physical body, so that we cannot think that it can change. Our imagination dare not soar beyond its limits; we are unable to see it and judge it from outside. We have neither the courage nor the heart to say that it has to be replaced by something else, because our own intellectual life, for which we have a natural bias, is a product of this system.

---

18. In *Towards Universal Man*, pp. 202-230.

And yet there lurks behind our complacence a thorn which does not let us sleep in comfort. As the secret pricking goes on, we in our fretfulness ascribe the cause of our irritation to some outside intrusion. We say that the only thing wrong in our education is that it is not in our absolute control; that the boat is sea-worthy, only the helm has to be in our hands to save it from wreckage. Lately, most of our attempts to establish national schools and universities were made with the idea that it was external independence which was needed. We forget that the same weakness in our character or circumstance which inevitably draws us on to the slippery slope of imitation, will pursue us when our independence is merely of the outside. For our freedom will then become the freedom to imitate the foreign institutions, thus bringing our evil fortune under the influence of the conjunction of two malignant planets – those of imitation and the badness of imitation – producing a machine-made university, which is made with a bad machine.

It often happens that the partners in a beaten team ascribe their defeat to each other's incompetence. In our discredited system of education, the two partners – our foreign rulers and ourselves – are following the same course of mutual recrimination. It is very likely that the blame can be justly apportioned between us; yet I always think it is merely academic to wrangle with one another about our respective responsibility for the common failure. What is of practical use is for us to know the extent of our own contribution to the deficiency.

Let us forget the other part in this concern. Let us blame our own weakness in being obsessed with the idea that we must have some artificial wooden legs of an education of foreign make just because we imagine we have no legs of our own. I have heard of a similar case of a man who got drowned in shallow water because he imagined he had gone off his depth.

The trouble is that as soon as we think of a university, the idea of Oxford, Cambridge, and a host of other European universities rushes in and fills our mind. We then imagine that our salvation lies in selecting the best points of each, patched together in an eclectic perfection. We forget that European universities are organic parts of the life of Europe, and each found its natural birth. Grafting a patch of skin from a foreign limb is allowed in modern surgery; but to build up a whole man by that process is beyond the resources of science, not only today, but let us fervently hope, for all time to come.

The European university rises full grown before our vision today. That is why we cannot think of a university except as a fully developed institution. The sight of my neighbour with a sturdy son to help and support him may naturally make me wish to have a son for myself. But if I am intent on having a full-grown son all at once, then in my hurry I may stumble upon someone who is full-grown but is no son to me at all. An impatient craving for results and an unfortunate weakness for imitation have led us to cherish just such an unnatural desire for a National university, full-fledged from its very birth;

hence, our endeavours become fruitless, or else the only fruit they produce is an **ersatz** one. Even if it is like the real thing in size and shape and colour, one has to beware of biting it, still more of swallowing it. These solidly complete universities, over which our country is brooding, are like hard-boiled eggs from which you cannot expect chicks.

Not only ourselves, but our European schoolmaster himself seems to have forgotten that his university has grown with the nation to which it belongs, and that its material magnificence does not relate to its early stages. He can well afford to forget that it was the indigent monks who were the early providers of his education and that most of the students at one time were poor. But when he affects to ignore the fact that in a poor country like India the material aspects of a university must not have more importance than is warranted, when he callously forgets that our inadequate schools and colleges must not be made still narrower in scope by cutting down facilities and increasing furniture, then it becomes disastrous for our people.

I quite understand that man needs both food and the utensils out of which to eat. But when there is a shortage of food itself, economy in regard to utensils becomes even more necessary. To make the paraphernalia of education so expensive that education itself becomes difficult to attain would be like squandering all one's money to buy money-bags.

We in the East have had to arrive at our own solution of the problems of life. We have, as far as possible, made our food and clothing unburdensome; our climate has taught us to do so. We require the openings in walls more than the walls themselves. Light and air have more to do with our clothes than the weaver's loom. The sun produces in us the energy which elsewhere is gained from food. All these natural advantages have moulded our life to a particular shape, which I cannot believe it will be profitable to ignore in the case of our education.

I do not seek to glorify poverty. But simplicity is of greater value than the appendages of luxury. The simplicity of which I speak is not the effect of a lack of superfluity; it is one of the signs of perfection. When this dawns on mankind, the unhealthy fog which now besmirches civilization will be lifted. It is for lack of this simplicity that the necessaries of life have become so rare and costly.

Most things in the civilized world, such as eating and merry-making, education and culture, administration and litigation, occupy more than their legitimate space. Much of their burden is needless; and in bearing it civilized man may be showing great strength, but little skill. To the goods, viewing this from on high, it must seem like the floundering of a giant who has gone out of his depth and does not know how to swim; who, as he keeps muddying the whole pool by his futile thrashings, cannot be rid of the idea that there must be some virtue in this display of strength.

III

All organic beings live like a flame, a long way beyond themselves. They have thus a smaller and a larger body. The former is visible to the eye; it can be touched, captured and bound. The latter is indefinite; it has no fixed boundaries, but is widespread both in space and time. When we see a foreign university, we see only its smaller body – its buildings, its furniture, its regulations, its syllabus; its larger body is not visible to us. But as the kernel of the cocoanut is in the whole cocoanut, so the university, in the case of Europeans, is in their society, in their parliament, in their literature, in the numerous activities of their corporate life. Their thoughts have their being in books, as well as in the living men who think those thoughts and criticize, compare and disseminate them. One common medium of mind connects their teachers and students in a relationship which is living and luminous. In short, their education has its permanent vehicle in their minds, its permanent source in their spring of culture, and its permanent field for irrigation in their social life. This organic unity of mind and life and culture has enabled them to absorb truth from all lands and from all times, making it an essential element in their own culture.

On the other hand, those who, like Indian students today, have to rely on books, not for their mental sustenance but for some external advantage, are sure to become anaemic in intellect, like babies fed solely with artificial food. They do not have intellectual courage because they never see in the right perspective the environment and the process of growth of those thoughts which they are compelled to learn. They are hypnotized by the sharp black and white of the printed words but forget their human genesis. They not only borrow a foreign culture but also a foreign standard of judgement. Their education is a chariot that does not carry them in it but drags them behind it. The sight is pitiful and often comic. Modern European culture, whose truth and strength lie in its mobility, comes to us rigidly fixed, almost like our own Shastras, about which our minds have to be passive and uncritical because of their supposed divine origin.

So we have missed the dynamic character of living truth. The English mind, from the early Victorian to the post-Victorian period of its growth, has been passing through different moods and standards. But we, who take our lessons from the English, can only accept some one or other of these moods and standards as fixed; we cannot naturally move with the moving mind of our teacher, but only hop from point to point and miss the modulations of life. We securely confine all our intellectual faith, either within the utilitarianism of Bentham and Mill, or the spiritualism of Carlyle and Ruskin, or the paradoxicalism, startling lazy minds into truth, in which Chesterton and Bernard Shaw excel; and we fail to notice their inevitable action and reaction. We boast of the up-to-dateness of our education. We forget that the mission of all education is to lead us beyond the present.

IV

Communication of life is possible only through a living agency. And culture, which is the life of the mind, can be imparted only through man to man. Book-learning simply turns us into pedants. It is static and quantitative; it accumulates and is hoarded under strict guard. Culture grows and moves and multiplies itself in life.

The students of European universities not only have, in society, their human environment of culture, but they also make gains by their close contact with their teachers. They have their sun to give them light; it is the human relationship between teachers and students. We have our hard flints which give us disconnected sparks after they have been struck hard. The noise is a great deal more than the light. These flints are the abstractions of learning; they are solid methods, inflexible and cold.

To our misfortune we have in our country all the furniture of the European university – except the living teacher. We have instead purveyors of book-lore in whom the paper god of the bookshop seems to have made himself vocal. As a natural result we find our students to be 'untouchables' even to our own professors. These teachers distribute doles of mental food, gingerly and from a dignified distance, with walls of notebooks between themselves and their students. This kind of food is not palatable, nor does it give nourishment. It is a famine ration, strictly regulated, and saves us, not from emaciation but only from death. It holds out no hope of that culture which is far in excess of man's mere necessity; it is certainly less than enough, and far less than a feast.

Until we are in a position to prove that the world has need of us and cannot afford to do without us, that we are not merely hangers-on-beggars who cannot repay – so long must our sole hope lie in gaining other's favours. And these we must get by lamentation, flattery, and constitutional methods of wagging tails.

No one will feel any concern about us if we can offer nothing that is worthy of being reverently accepted. But whom are we to blame? Where is space enough, lying fallow on this earth, for men who merely live and do not produce? How can they build an infirmary as big as the country itself? The hard fact must be grasped that we cannot make a thing our own only because it is given to us. It is only the lake, and not the desert, which can accept and retain a contribution from heaven's clouds because, in its depth, the receiving and the giving have become one. Only to him who hath is given; otherwise the gift is insulted and he, also, who receives it.

V

Let me give an illustration of a university which was born and grew on national soil, and of how it failed with the turn in its history.

In that age of Europe which is called dark, when the lamp of Rome was extinguished by the attack of barbarians, Ireland, almost alone among the countries of the West, kept up its heritage of culture. Students from many parts of Europe came there for education. They had their board, lodging and books free, as in our own Sanskrit *pathasalas*. The Irish monks revived all over Europe the bedimmed light of Christian religion and culture. Charlemagne took the help of Clemens, a learned Irishman, in founding the University of Paris. There are many other instances of the glory which Irish culture of the time attained. Though its origin was in Rome, in course of a long period of segregation it became imbued with the life and mind of the people and acquired a genius which was characteristically Irish. And this culture had for its medium the Irish language.

When the Danes and the English invaded Ireland, they set fire to Irish colleges, destroyed libraries, and killed or scattered the monks and students. Nevertheless, in those parts of the country which still remained independent and free from outrage, the work of education was carried on in the mother-tongue, until in the time of Queen Elizabeth Ireland was wholly conquered and its indigenous universities were lost. Deprived of the atmosphere of culture and study, the Irish language fell into contempt and was regarded as fit only for the lower classes. Then, in the nineteenth century, the National School movement was set afoot, and the Irish, with their ingrained love of learning, welcomed it with uncritical enthusiasm.

The idea of the so-called national school was to mould the Irish on the Anglo-Saxon pattern. But, whether for good or for evil, Providence has fashioned each race on a different pattern, and to put one into the coat of another results in a misfit. When the National School movement was started, eighty per cent of Irishmen were using their own language. But the Irish boys, under threats of punishment, were forced to give up their own language and the ban was also extended to the study of their history.

The result was just what could be expected. Mental numbness spread all over the country. Irish-speaking boys, who entered the schools with their intelligence and curiosity alive, left them as mental cripples, with a distaste for all study. The reason was that the method was machine-like and the result had to be parrot-like.

VI

For the proper irrigation of learning, a foreign language cannot be the right medium. This is a truism which would bore men to sleep everywhere, except in our own country, where it would sound as dangerous heresy. Rousing us into active hostility, it would indeed act on us like a tonic! Platitudes have an even better effect, and so I repeat that when we are compelled to learn through the medium of English, the knocking at the gate and turning of the key take away the best part of our life. The feast may be waiting for us inside the room, but the difficulty and delay of admission spoils our appetite and the long privation permanently injures our stomach. The ideas come late and the tedious grinding over grammar, and a system of spelling which is devoid of all rationale, take away our relish for the food when it does come at last.

If we want to grow a tree on the sandy soil of a rainless desert, we must not only borrow the seed from some distant land, but also the soil itself and the water. Yet, after the immense trouble we have taken, the tree remains stunted. Even if it does bear fruit, the seeds do not mature. The education which we receive from our universities takes it for granted that it is for filling the arid land, and that not only the mental outlook and the knowledge, but also the whole language must bodily be imported from across the sea. And this makes our education so nebulous, distant and unreal, so detached from all association of life, so terribly costly to us in time, health and means, and yet so meagre in results.

So far as my own experience of teaching goes, a good proportion of the pupils are naturally deficient in the power of learning languages. They find it barely possible to matriculate with an insufficient understanding of the English language, while in the higher stages disaster is inevitable. There are, moreover, other reasons why English cannot be mastered by a large majority of Indian boys. First of all, to accommodate this language in their minds, whose imagined habit has been to think in an eastern tongue, is as much a feat as fitting an English sword into the scabbard of a scimitar. Then again, very few boys have the means of getting anything like a proper grounding in English at the hands of a competent teacher. The sons of the poor certainly have not.

I know what the counter-argument will be. 'You want to give higher education through Indian languages, but where are the text-books?' I am aware that there are none. But unless higher education is given in our own languages, how are text-books to come into existence? We cannot expect a mint to go on working if the coins are refused circulation.

VII

Another lesson to be learnt from the Irish example is that, in the natural course of things, the water comes first and then the fish. It is the presence of the learned men which draws the students around them.

In an age of great mental vitality, when there were men whose minds overflowed with thought and learning, the culture centres of Nalanda and Taxila were naturally formed in India. But, accustomed as we have been merely to branding institutions, even in our attempts to found national universities we begin from the wrong end. The students come first, and then we cast about for the teachers. It is like the vagary of an absent-minded Creator who takes great pains in making a tail and then suddenly finds that the head is missing. We seat our guests at the table, and afterwards discover that the cooking has not even started.

For the sanity of our mind and reasonableness of our purpose, let us for once throw to the winds all anxiety as to syllabuses and students. Let us drive out of our thoughts the fixed images of our existing educational institutions. And then let us pray that those who have successfully passed through the discipline of cultivating their minds, who are ready to produce and therefore to import, may come together and take up their seats of studious striving, doing intently their own work of exploration and discovery in the region of knowledge. In this way will be concentrated the power which shall be adequate for the spontaneous creation of a university, from within ourselves, in all the truth of life.

We must know that this concentration of intellectual forces in the country is the most important mission of a university, for it is like the nucleus of a living cell, the centre of the creative life of the national mind.

VIII

To bring about an intellectual unity in India is, I am told, difficult and almost impossible, because of the fact that India has so many different languages.

But every nation in the world must solve its own problems or else accept defeat and degradation. All true civilizations have been built upon the bedrock of difficulties. Men who have rivers for their water supply are to be envied, but those who have not must dig wells and find water in the depths of the soil. But let us never imagine that dust can be made to do the duty of water only because it is more easily available. We must bravely accept the inconvenient fact of the diversity of our languages, and at the same time admit that a foreign language, like foreign soil, may be good for hothouse culture, but not for that cultivation which is necessary for the maintenance of life.

Let us admit also that India is not like any one of the great countries of Europe, which has its one language, but like the whole of Europe with her different peoples and languages. And yet Europe has a common civilization with an intellectual unity which is not based upon linguistic uniformity.

In the earlier stage of her culture all Europe had Latin for her language of learning. It was her intellectual bud-time, when all her petals of self-expression closed into one point. But the perfection of her mental unfolding was not represented by the oneness of her literary vehicle. When the great European countries found their individual languages, then only the true federation of cultures became possible in the West. The very differences of the channels made the commerce of ideas in Europe so richly copious and so variedly active. In fact, when natural differences find their harmony, then it is true unity; but artificial uniformity leads to lifelessness. We can well imagine what the loss to European civilization would be, if France, Italy, Germany and England, through their separate agencies did not contribute to the common coffer their individual earnings. And we know why, when German culture tried to assert its dominance, it was repelled by all Europe as a calamity.

There was a time when India also had her common language of culture in Sanskrit. But, for the completeness of her commerce of thought, all her languages must attain their full power through which each of her peoples will manifest its distinctive genius. This can never be done through a language which is foreign, containing its own peculiar associations which are sure to hamper our freedom of thought and creation. The use of English inevitably tends to turn our mind for its source of inspiration towards the West, with which we can never be in intimate contact; and therefore our education will remain sterile, or produce incongruities. The diversity of our languages should not frighten us; but we should beware of the futility of borrowing the language of our culture from a far-away land, and making the moving stream we have stagnant and shallow.

IX

The seat of our Indian learning must accordingly be quite apart from the existing university-controlled schools and colleges. Let these lumbering machines be allotted a place among our law courts, our offices, our prisons, asylums, and other paraphernalia of civilization.

If our country wants fruit and shade, let it abandon brick-and-mortar erections. Why do we not boldly avow that we shall tend our life-force as naturally as the pupils who used to gather around the teachers in the forest retreats of the Vedic age; or at Nalanda and Taxila during the Buddhist era; or, as they gather even now, in our day of decadence, at the *tols* and *chatuspathis*?

We must beware even of calling it a university. For the name itself is bound to create an irrepressible tendency to comparison and feeble imitation. My suggestion is that we should generate somewhere a centripetal force which will attract and group together from different parts of our land and from different ages all our own materials of learning, and thus create a complete and moving orb of Indian culture.

X

A pupil at an Anglo-Vernacular school in Allahabad was asked to define a river. The clever little fellow gave a correct definition. But when he was asked what river he had seen, this boy, living at the confluence of the Ganges and the Jumna, replied that he had not seen any. He had a dim idea that his familiar world (which so easily came to him through the medium of his own direct consciousness) could never be the great learned world of geography.

In later life he must have learnt that even his own country had its place in geography and actually had its rivers. Suppose this news did not reach him until some foreign traveller told him one day that his was a big country, that the Himalayas were big mountains, that the Indus, Ganges and Brahmaputra were great rivers. The shock of it could not but upset his mental balance, and by way of reaction against the self-contempt he had nursed so long, he would lose no time in making himself hoarse by shouting that other countries were merely countries while his was heaven itself! His earlier understanding of the world was wrong, due to his ignorance. His subsequent understanding was worse – its falsehood all the more ridiculous because of sophisticated stupidity.

The same thing happens with our Indian culture. Because of gaps in our course of study we take it for granted that India had no culture, or next to none. Then, as we hear some foreign scholar laud Indian culture, we can no longer contain ourselves; we rend the sky with the shout that all other cultures are merely human, but ours is divine!

We should remember that the doctrine of special creation is out of date, and the idea of a favoured race belongs to a barbaric age. We have come to understand in modern times that any special culture, which is wholly dissociated from the universal, cannot be true. Only the prisoner condemned to a solitary cell is isolated from the world. He who declares that India has condemned by Providence to intellectual solitary confinement does not glorify her.

It can be easily pointed out that our culture has its superstitions and its shortcomings. So, too, has European culture – its politics and science are full of them. But, then, those do not become fatal because they move and change just like Europe's caste distinctions, which are not so oppressive because they are in a constant state of flux.

Only a few years ago, Europe began to see the whole world through the mist of one scientific shibboleth, 'the struggle for existence'. This coloured her vision and decided her point of view. We, also, like an obedient pupil, took the phrase from her and not to believe in it became to us a sign of deficient education. But there is already an indication of change in this view; it is being proved that the positive force which works at the basis of natural selection is the power of sympathy, the power to combine. In the nineteenth century, the message of political economy was unrestrained competition; in the twentieth, it is beginning to change into co-operation.

There was a time when we in India worked at the problem of life; we freely made experiments; the solutions we arrived at cannot be ignored just because they are different from those of Europe. But they must not be static; they have to join the procession of man's discoveries and march to the drumbeat of life.

XI

Far too long have we kept our culture outcast in the confines of our indigenous Sanskrit *pathasalas* – undue respect creates untouchability no less than undue contempt.

There was a time when the excess of dignity of the Mikado of Japan kept him a virtual prisoner in his palace, with the result that not he, but the Shogun, was the real ruler. When it became necessary for him to reign in fact, he had to be brought forth from his seclusion into the public view. So was the culture of our Sanskrit *pathasala* confined within itself, disdainfully ignoring all other cultures. It was belauded, as having come straight from Brahma's mouth, or Shiva's matted locks, so that it was unlike anything else in the world, and had to be kept apart and guarded, lest it be contaminated by the touch of the common people. Thus it became the Mikado of our country, while foreign culture, gaining strength from its perfect freedom of movement and growth and its humanness, dominated the situation like the Shogun. Our reverence is reserved for the one, but all our taxes are paid to the other. We may hurl invectives at the latter in private, we may lament over our subjection to it; all the same, we sell our wife's ornaments and mortgage our ancestral homes to send our sons to its durbar.

It will not do to keep our culture so reverently shackled with chains of gold. The age has come when all artificial fences are breaking down. Only that will survive which is basically consistent with the universal. That which seeks safety in the out-of-the way hole of the special will perish. The nursery of the infant should be secluded, its cradle safe. But the same seclusion, if continued after the infant has grown up, makes it weak in body and mind.

There was a time when China, Persia, Egypt, Greece and Rome had, each of them, to nurture its civilization in comparative seclusion. Each had its measure of the universal and grew strong within its protective sheath of individuality. Now has come the age for co-ordination and co-operation. The seedlings that were reared within their enclosures must now be transplanted in open fields. They must pass the test of the world-market, if their maximum value is to be obtained.

So we prepare the grand field for the co-ordination of the cultures of the world, the field of give-and-take. This adjustment of knowledge through comparative study, this progress in intellectual co-operation, is to be the key-note of the coming age. We may seek to shield our holy aloofness in the imagined security of a sheltered corner, but the world will prove stronger than our refuge.

But before we are in a position to face other world cultures, or co-operate with them, we must build up our own by the synthesis of the diverse elements that have come to India. When we take our stand at such a centre and turn towards the West, our gaze shall no longer be timid and dazed, our heads shall remain erect. For, we shall then be able to look at truth from our own vantage ground and open out a new vista of thought before the grateful world.

XII

All great countries have their vital centres for intellectual life. There is a high standard of learning is maintained, the minds of the people find a genial atmosphere and prove their worth. They contribute to the country's culture, and kindle a sacrificial fire of intellect which radiates the sacred light in all directions.

Athens was such a centre, so was Rome, and so is Paris today. Banaras has been and still continues to be centre of our Sanskrit culture. But Sanskrit learning does not exhaust all the elements of culture that exist in India.

If we take for granted what some people maintain, the European culture is the only one worth the name in our modern age, then the question comes to our mind: Has it any natural centre in India? Has it any vital, ever-flowing connection with her life? The answer is that not only has it none, but it never can have any; for the perennial centre of European culture is sure to be in Europe. If we must accept it as the only source of life today it would be like depending not on our sun but upon some alien star for our daybreak. Such a star may give us light, but not the day; it may give us direction in our voyage of exploration, but it can never open the full view of truth before us. In fact, we can never use this starlight for stirring sap in our invisible depths and giving colour and bloom to our life.

This is why European education has become for India mere school learning and not culture, a box of matches good for various uses, but not the morning light in which utility and grace and the subtle mystery of life have blended in one.

And this is why the inner spirit of India is calling to us to establish in this land centres where all her intellectual forces will gather for the purpose of creation, and all resources of knowledge and thought, Eastern and Western, will unite in perfect harmony. She is seeking her modern Brahmavarta, her Mithila of Janaka's time, her Ujjaini of the time of Vikramaditya. She is seeking the glorious opportunity when she will know her mind and give freely to the world, when she will be released from the chaos of scattered power and the inertness of borrowed acquisition.

XIII

Let me state clearly that I have no distrust of any culture because of its foreign character. On the contrary, I believe that the shock of outside forces is necessary for maintaining the vitality of our intellect. It is admitted that much of the spirit of Christianity runs counter, not only to the classical culture of

Europe, but to the European temperament. And yet this alien movement, constantly running against the natural tendencies of Europe, has been the most important factor in strengthening and enriching her civilization. In fact, the very antagonism of its direction has made it the more effective. The European languages first woke to life and fruitful vigour under the impact of this foreign thought with all its oriental forms and feelings. The same thing is happening in India. European culture has come to us not only with its knowledge but with its speed. Even when our assimilation is imperfect and aberrations follow, it is rousing our intellectual life from the inertia of formal habits. The contradiction it offers to our traditions makes our consciousness glow.

What I object to is the artificial arrangement by which this foreign education tends to occupy all the space of our national mind and thus kills, or hampers, the great opportunity for the creation of new thought by a new combination of truths. It is this which makes me urge that all the elements in our own culture have to be strengthened; not to resist the culture of the West, but to accept and assimilate it. It must become for us nourishment and not a burden. We must gain mastery over it and not live on sufferance as hewers of texts and drawers of book-learning.

XIV

The main river of Indian culture has flowed in four streams – the Vedic, the Puranic, the Buddhist, and the Jain. It had its source in the heights of the Indian consciousness.

But a river belonging to a country is not fed by its own waters alone. The Tibetan Brahmaputra mingles its water with the Indian Ganges. Contributions have similarly found their way to India's original culture. The Muslim, for example, has repeatedly come into India from outside, laden with his own stores of knowledge and feeling and his wonderful religious democracy, bringing freshet after freshet to swell the current. In our music, our architecture, our pictorial art, our literature, the Muslims have made their permanent and precious contribution. Those who have studied the lives and writings of our medieval saints, and all the great religious movements that sprang up in the time of Muslim rule, know how deep is our debt to this foreign current that has so intimately mingled with our life.

And then has descended upon us the later flood of western culture, which bids fair to break through all banks and bounds, covering all the other streams in its impetuous rush. If only we can provide a channel through which it may flow, we shall be saved from a deluge which otherwise may overwhelm us.

At our centre of Indian learning we must provide for the co-ordinate study of all these different cultures – the Vedic, the Puranic, the Buddhist, the

Jain, the Islamic, the Sikh, and the Zoroastrian. And side by side with them the European – for only then shall we be able to assimilate it. A river flowing within banks is truly our own, but our relations with a flood are fraught with disaster.

It is needless to add that, along with the languages in which lies stored our ancestral wealth of wisdom, we must make room for the study of all the languages which carry the living stream of the mind of modern India. Along with this study of our living languages, we must include our folk literature in order truly to know the psychology of our people and the direction towards which our underground current of life is moving.

There are some who are insularly modern, who believe that the past is bankrupt, that it has left no assets for us but only a legacy of debts. They refuse to believe that the army that is marching forward can be fed from the rear. It is well to remind them that the great ages of renaissance in history were those when men suddenly discovered the seeds of thought in the granary of the past.

The unfortunate people who have lost the harvest of their past have lost their present age. They have missed their seeds for cultivation, and go begging for their bare livelihood. We must not imagine that we are one of those disinherited peoples of the world. The time has come for us to break open the treasure-trove of our ancestors and use it for our commerce of life. Let us, with its help, make our future secure, and cease to live as the eternal rag-picker at other peoples' dustbins.

XV

So far I have dwelt only on the intellectual aspect of education. That is because, like the moon, we in modern India present to the sun of world-culture only one side of our life, which is the intellectual side. We do not yet fully realize that our other sides also require the same light for their illumination. From the educational point of view, we know Europe where it is scientific, or at best literary. So our notion of modern culture is limited within the boundary lines of grammar and the laboratory. We almost completely ignore the aesthetic life of man and leave it uncultivated, allowing weeds to grow there.

So, again, I have to repeat a truism and say that music and the fine arts are among the highest means of national self-expression, that without them the people remain inarticulate.

Our conscious mind occupies only a superficial layer of our life; the sub-conscious mind is almost fathomless in its depth. There the wisdom of countless ages grows up beyond our ken. Our conscious mind finds its expression in activities which pass and repass before our view. Our sub-conscious, where dwells our soul, must also have its adequate media of expression. These media are poetry and music and the arts; here the complete personality of man finds its expression.

The timber merchant may think that flowers and foliage are only frivolous decorations for a tree, but he will know to his cost that if these are eliminated, the timber follows them.

During the Mughal period, music and art in India found a great impetus from the rulers. This was because their whole life was in this land, not merely their official life. It is the wholeness of a man from which Art originates. Our English teachers are birds of passage; they cackle to us but do not sing; their true heart is not in this land of their exile. The natural place for their art and music is in Europe. There they are so deep in the soil that they cannot be transferred to a distant land, unless the soil itself is removed.

We in India see the European, where he is learned, where he is masterful, where he is busily constructive in his trade and politics, but not where he is artistically creative. That is why modern Europe has not been revealed to us her complete personality, but only in her intellectual power and utilitarian activities; and therefore she has only touched our intellect and evoked our utilitarian ambitions.

The mutilation of life owing to this narrowness of culture must no longer be encouraged. In the proposed centre of our culture, music and art must have prominent seats of honour, and not merely a tolerant nod of recognition.

A real standard of aesthetic taste will thus develop; and with its help our own art will grow in strength and riches, enabling us to judge all foreign arts with soberness and appropriate from them ideas and forms without incurring the charge of plagiarism.

XVI

We are faced with two stupendous problems; one is our poverty of intellectual life; the other, the poverty of our material life.

The first I have discussed in some detail in this paper. I have come to the conclusion that for the perfection of our mental life the co-ordination of all our cultural resources is necessary. I have found that our present education is, for our minds, a kind of food which contains only one particular ingredient needed for our sustenance, and even that not fresh but dried and packed in tins. For a balanced meal, we must have co-ordination of different ingredients – and most of these, not as laboratory products, or in a dehydrated condition, but as organic things, similar to our own living tissues.

Our material poverty, likewise, can be removed only by the co-operation of our individual powers. And our institution should be based on this economic co-operation. It must not only instruct, but live; not only think, but produce. Our tapovanas, which were our natural universities, were not isolated from life. There the masters and students lived their full life; they gathered fruit and fuel; they took their cattle to graze; and the spiritual education, which the students had, was a part of the spiritual life itself which comprehended all life. Our centre of culture should not only be the centre of the intellectual life of India, but the centre of her economic life as well. It must cultivate land, breed cattle, to feed itself and its students it must produce all necessaries, devising the best means and using the best materials, calling science to its aids. Its very existence would depend on the success of its industrial ventures carried out on the co-operative principle, which will unite the teachers and students in a living and active bond of necessity. This will also give us a practical, industrial training, whose motive force is not profit.

Such an institution must group around it all the neighbouring villages and unite them with itself in all its economic endeavours. The improvement of their housing and sanitation, besides their moral and intellectual life should be the object of the social side of its activity. In a word, it should never be like a meteor – a stray fragment of a world – but a complete world, self-sustaining, rich with ever-renewing life, radiating light across space and time, attracting and maintaining round it a planetary system of dependent bodies, and imparting life-breath to the complete man, who is intellectual as well as economic, bound by social bonds and aspiring towards spiritual freedom.

XVII

Before I conclude, a delicate question has to be considered. What must be the religious teaching to be given at our centre of Indian culture which I may name Visva-Bharati? The question has been generally shirked in the case of the schools which we call national. A National University, in our minds, has been only another name for a Hindu University. Whenever we think over the question, we think of the Hindu religion alone. Unable to rise to the conception of the Great India, we divide it, in culture, as in religious rites and social customs. In other words, the idea of such unity as we are capable of achieving for ourselves not only fails to stir enthusiasm in all hearts, but gives rise to antipathy in some.

Be that as it may, it has to be admitted that the world is full of different religious sects and will probably always remain so. It is no use lamenting over, or quarrelling, with this fact. There is a private corner for me in my house with a little table, which has its special fittings of pen and ink-stand and paper, and here I can best do my writing and other work. There is no reason to run down, or run away from, this corner of mine, because in it I cannot invite and provide seats for all my friends and guests. It may be that this corner is too narrow, or too close, or too untidy, so that my doctor may object, my friends remonstrate, my enemies sneer; but all that has nothing to do with the present case. My point is that if all the rooms in my house be likewise solely for my own special convenience, if there be no reception room for my friends or accommodation for my guests, then indeed I may be blamed. Then with bowed head I must confess that in my house no great meeting of friends can ever take place.

Religious sects are formed in every country and every age owing to historical causes. There will always be many who, by tradition and temperament, find solace in belonging to a particular sect. Also, there will be others who think that such solace can only be allowed as legitimate within the pale of their own. Between such, there must be quarrels. Allowing for the possibility of squabbles, can there be no wide meeting place, where all sects gather together and forget their differences? Has India, in her religious ideals, no space for the common light of day and open air for all humanity? The vigour with which the sectarian fanatic will shake his head, makes one doubt it; the bloodshed which so frequently occurs for trivial causes makes one doubt it; the cruel and insulting distinctions between man and man which are kept alive under the sanction of religion make one doubt it. Even so, when I look back to India's culture – in those ages when it flourished in its truth – I am emboldened to assert that it is there. Our forefathers did spread a single carpet on which all the world was cordially invited to take its seat in amity and good fellowship. No quarrel could have arisen there; for He, in whose name the invitation went forth, for all time to come, was *Santam, Sivam, Advaitam* – the Peaceful, in the heart of all conflicts; the God, who is revealed through all losses and sufferings; the One, in all diversities of creation. And in His name was this eternal truth declared in ancient India:

He alone sees, who sees all beings as himself.

– 1919

Leaves are masses of silence
round flowers which are their words
              Rabindranath Tagore

An Eastern University (1921)[19]

IN THE MIDST of much that is discouraging in the present state of the world, there is one symptom of vital promise. Asia is awakening. This great event, if it be but directed along the right lines, is full of hope, not only for Asia herself, but for the whole world.

On the other hand, it has to be admitted that the relationship of the West with the East, growing more and more complex and widespread for over two centuries, far from attaining its true fulfilment, has given rise to a universal spirit of conflict. The consequent strain and unrest have profoundly disturbed Asia, and antipathetic forces have been accumulating for years in the depth of the Eastern mind.

The meeting of the East and the West has remained incomplete, because the occasions of it have not been disinterested. The political and commercial adventures carried on by Western races – very often by force and against the interest and wishes of the countries they have dealt with – have created a moral alienation, which is deeply injurious to both parties. The perils threatened by this unnatural relationship have long been contemptuously ignored by the West. But the blind confidence of the strong in their apparent invincibility has often led them, from their dream of security, into terrible surprises of history.

It is not the fear of danger or loss to one people or another, however, which is most important. The demoralising influence of the constant estrangement between the two hemispheres, which affects the baser passions of man – pride, greed and hypocrisy on the one hand; fear, suspiciousness and flattery on the other, - has been developing, and threatens us with a world-wide spiritual disaster.

The time has come when we must use all our wisdom to understand the situation, and to control it, with a stronger trust in moral guidance than in any array of physical forces.

In the beginning of man's history his first social object was to form a community, to grow into a people. At that early period, individuals were gathered together within geographical enclosures. But in the present age, with its facility of communication, geographical barriers have almost lost their reality, and the great federation of men, which is waiting either to find its true scope or to break asunder in a final catastrophe, is not a meeting of individuals, but of various human races. Now the problem before us is of

---

19. In Das, ed. Vol 2 pp. 556-570.

one single country, which is this earth, where the races as individuals must find both their freedom of self-expression and their bond of federation. Mankind must realize a unity, wider in range, deeper in sentiment, stronger in power than ever before. Now that the problem is large, we have to solve it on a bigger scale, to realize the God in man by a larger faith and to build the temple of our faith on a sure and world-wide basis.

The first step towards realization is to create opportunities for revealing the different peoples to one another. This can never be done in those fields where the exploiting utilitarian spirit is supreme. We must find some meeting-ground, where there can be no question of conflicting interests. One of such places is the University, where we can work together in a common pursuit of truth, share together our common heritage, and realize that artists in all parts of the world have created forms of beauty, scientists discovered secrets of the universe, philosophers solved the problems of existence, saints made the truth of the spiritual world organic in their own lives, not merely for some particular race to which they belonged, but for all mankind. When the science of meteorology knows the earth's atmosphere as continuously one, affecting the different parts of the world differently, but in a harmony of adjustments, it knows and attains truth. And so, too, we must know that the great mind of man is one, working through the many differences which are needed to ensure the full result of its fundamental unity. When we understand this truth in a disinterested spirit, it teaches us to respect all the differences in man that are real, yet remain conscious of our oneness; and to know that perfection of unity is not in uniformity, but in harmony.

This is the problem of the present age. The East, for its own sake and for the sake of the world, must not remain unrevealed. The deepest source of all calamities in history is misunderstanding. For where we do not understand, we can never be just.

Being strongly impressed with the need and the responsibility, which every individual to-day must realize according to his power, I have formed the nucleus of an International University in India, as one of the best means of promoting mutual understanding between the East and the West. This Institution, according to the plan I have in mind, will invite students from the West to study the different systems of Indian philosophy, literature, art and music in their proper environment, encouraging them to carry on research work in collaboration with the scholars already engaged in this task.

India has her renaissance. She is preparing to make her contribution to the world of the future. In the past she produced her great culture, and in the present age she has an equally important contribution to make to the culture of the New World which is emerging from the wreckage of the Old. This is a momentous period of her history pregnant with precious possibilities, when any disinterested offer of co-operation from any part of the West will have an immense moral value, the memory of which will become brighter as the regeneration of the East grows in vigour and creative power.

The Western Universities give their students an opportunity to learn what all the European peoples have contributed to their Western culture. Thus the intellectual mind of the West has been luminously revealed to the world. What is needed to complete this illumination is for the East to collect its own scattered lamps and offer them to the enlightenment of the world.

There was a time when the great countries of Asia had, each of them, to nurture its own civilization apart in comparative seclusion. Now has come the age of co-ordination and co-operation. The seedlings that were reared within narrow plots must now be transplanted into the open fields. They must pass the test of the world-market, if their maximum value is to be obtained.

But before Asia is in a position to co-operate with the culture of Europe, she must base her own structure on a synthesis of all the different cultures which she has. When, taking her stand on such a culture, she turns toward the West, she will take, with a confident sense of mental freedom, her own view of truth, from her own vantage-ground, and open a new vista of thought to the world. Otherwise, she will allow her priceless inheritance to crumble into dust, and, trying to replace it clumsily with feeble imitations of the West, make herself superfluous, cheap and ludicrous. If she thus loses her individuality and her specific power to exist, will it in the least help the rest of the world? Will not her terrible bankruptcy involve also the Western mind? If the whole world grows at last into an exaggerated West, then such an illimitable parody of the modern age will die, crushed beneath its own absurdity.

In this belief, it is my desire to extend by degrees the scope of this University on simple lines, until it comprehends the whole range of Eastern cultures – the Aryan, Semitic, Mongolian and others. Its object will be to reveal the Eastern mind to the world.

Of one thing I felt certain during my travels in Europe, that a genuine interest has been roused there in the philosophy and the arts of the East, from which the Western mind seeks fresh inspiration of truth and beauty. Once the East had her reputation of fabulous wealth, and the seekers were attracted from across the sea. Since then, the shrine of wealth has changed its site. But the East is famed also for her storage of wisdom, harvested by her patriarchs from long successive ages of spiritual endeavour. And when, as now, in the midst of the pursuit of power and wealth, there rises the cry of privation from the famished spirit of man, an opportunity is offered to the East, to offer her store to those who need it.

Once upon a time we were in possession of such a thing as our own mind in India. It was living. It thought, it felt, it expressed itself. It was receptive as well as productive. That this mind could be of any use in the process, or in the end, of our education was overlooked by our modern educational dispensation. We are provided with buildings and books and other magnificent burdens calculated to suppress our mind. The latter was treated like a library-shelf solidly made of wood, to be loaded with leather-bound volumes of second-hand information. In consequence, it has lost its own colour and character, and has borrowed polish from the carpenter's shop. All this has cost us money, and also our finer ideas, while our intellectual vacancy has been crammed with what is described in official reports as Education. In fact, we have bought our spectacles at the expense of our eyesight.

In India our goddess of learning is *Saraswati*. My audience in the West, I am sure, will be glad to know that her complexion is white. But the signal fact is that she is living and she a woman, and her seat is on a lotus-flower. The symbolic meaning of this is that she dwells in the centre of life and the heart of all existence, which opens itself in beauty to the light of heaven.

The Western education which we have chanced to know is impersonal. Its complexion is also white, but it is the whiteness of the white-washed classroom walls. It dwells in the cold-storage compartments of lessons and the ice-packed minds of the schoolmasters. The effect which it had on my mind when, as a boy, I was compelled to go to school, I have described elsewhere. My feeling was very much the same as a tree might have, which was not allowed to live its full life, but was cut down to be made into packing-cases.

The introduction of this education was not a part of the solemn marriage ceremony which was to unite the minds of the East and West in mutual understanding. It represented an artificial method of training specially calculated to produce the carriers of the white man's burden. This want of ideals still clings to our education system, though our Universities have latterly burdened their syllabus with a greater number of subjects than before. But it is only like adding to the bags of wheat the bullock carries to market; it does not make the bullock any better off.

Mind, when long deprived of its natural food of truth and freedom of growth, develops an unnatural craving for success; and our students have fallen victims to the mania for success in examinations. Success consists in obtaining the largest number of marks with the strictest economy of knowledge. It is a deliberate cultivation of disloyalty to truth, of intellectual dishonesty, of a foolish imposition by which the mind is encouraged to rob itself. But as we are by means of it made to forget the existence of mind, we are supremely happy at the result. We pass examinations, and shrivel up into clerks, lawyers and police inspectors, and we die young.

Universities should never be made into mechanical organizations for collecting and distributing knowledge. Through them the people should offer their intellectual hospitality, their wealth of mind to others, and earn their proud right in return to receive gifts from the rest of the world. But in the whole length and breadth of India there is not a single university established in the modern time where a foreign or an Indian student can properly be acquainted with the best products of the Indian mind. For that we have to cross the sea, and knock at the doors of France and Germany. Educational institutions in our country are India's alms-bowl of knowledge; they lower our intellectual self-respect; they encourage us to make a foolish display of decorations composed of borrowed feathers.

This it was that led me to found a school in Bengal, in face of many difficulties and discouragements, and in spite of my own vocation as a poet, who finds his true inspiration only when he forgets that he is a schoolmaster. It is my hope that in this school a nucleus has been formed, round which an indigenous University of our own land will find its natural growth – a University which will help India's mind to concentrate and to be fully conscious of itself; free to seek the truth and make this truth its own wherever found, to judge by its own standard, give expression to its own creative genius, and offer its wisdom to the guests who come from other parts of the world.

Man's intellect has a natural pride in its own aristocracy, which is the pride of its culture. Culture only acknowledges the excellence whose criticism is in its inner perfection, not in any external success. When this pride succumbs to some compulsion of necessity or lure of material advantage, it brings humiliation to the intellectual man. Modern India, through her very education, has been made to suffer this humiliation. Once she herself provided her children with a culture which was the product of her own ages of thought and creation. But it has been thrust aside, and we are made to tread the mill of passing examinations, not for learning anything, but for notifying that we are qualified for employments under organisations conducted in English. Our educated community is not a cultured community, but a community of qualified candidates. Meanwhile the proportion of possible employments to the number of claimants has gradually been growing narrower, and the consequent disaffection has been widespread. At last the very authorities who are responsible for this are blaming their victims. Such is the perversity of human nature. It bears its worst grudge against those it has injured.

It is as if some tribe which had the primitive habit of decorating its tribal members with birds' plumage were some day to hold these very birds guilty of the crime of being extinct. There are belated attempts on the part of our governors to read us pious homilies about disinterested love of learning, while the old machinery goes on working, whose product is not education but certificates. It is good to remind the fettered bird that its wings are for soaring; but it is better to cut the chain which is holding it to its perch. The most pathetic feature of the tragedy is that the bird itself has learnt to use its chain for its ornament, simply because the chain jingles in fairly respectable English.

In the Bengali language there is a modern maxim which can be translated, 'He who learns to read and write rides in a carriage and pair'. In English there is a similar proverb, 'Knowledge is power'. It is an offer of a prospective bribe to the student, a promise of an ulterior reward which is more important than knowledge itself. Temptations, held before us as inducements to be good or to pursue uncongenial paths, are most often flimsy lies or half-truths, such as the oft-quoted maxim of respectable piety, 'honesty is the best policy', at which politicians all over the world seem to laugh in their sleeves. But unfortunately, education conducted under a special providence of purposefulness, of eating the fruit of knowledge from the wrong end, does lead one to that special paradise on earth, the daily rides in one's own carriage and pair. And the West, I have heard from authentic sources, is aspiring in its education after that special cultivation of worldliness.

Where society is comparatively simple and obstructions are not too numerous, we can clearly see how the life-process guides education in its vital purpose. The system of folk-education, which is indigenous to India, but is dying out, was one with the people's life. It flowed naturally through the social channels and made its way everywhere. It is a system of widespread irrigation of culture. Its teachers, specially trained men, are in constant requisition, and find crowded meetings in our villages, where they repeat the best thoughts and express the ideals of the land in the most effective form. The mode of instruction includes the recitation of epics, expounding of the scriptures, reading from the Puranas, which are the classical records of old history, performance of plays founded upon the early myths and legends, dramatic narration of the lives of ancient heroes, and the singing in chorus of songs from the old religious literature. Evidently, according to this system, the best function of education is to enable us to realize that to live as a man is great, requiring profound philosophy for its ideal, poetry for its expression, and heroism in its conduct. Owing to this vital method of culture the common people of India, though technically illiterate, have been made conscious of the sanctity of social relationships, entailing constant sacrifice and self-control, urged and supported by ideals collectively expressed in one word, *Dharma*.

Such a system of education may sound too simple for the complexities of modern life. But the fundamental principle of social life in its different stages of development remains the same; and in no circumstance can the truth be ignored that all human complexities must harmonize in organic unity with life, failing which there will be endless conflict. Most things in the civilized world occupy more than their legitimate space. Much of their burden is needless. By bearing this burden civilized man may be showing great strength, but he displays little skill. To the gods, viewing this from on high, it must seem like the flounderings of a giant who has got out of his depth and knows not how to swim.

The main source of all forms of voluntary slavery is the desire of gain. It is difficult to fight against this when modern civilization is tainted with such a universal contamination of avarice. I have realized it myself in the little boys of my own school. For the first few years there is no trouble. But as soon as the upper class is reached, their worldly wisdom – the malady of the aged – begins to assert itself. They rebelliously insist that they must no longer learn, but rather pass examinations. Professions in the modern age are more numerous and lucrative than ever before. They need specialization of training and knowledge, tempting education to yield its spiritual freedom to the claims of utilitarian ambitions. But man's deeper nature is hurt; his smothered life seeks to be liberated from the suffocating folds and sensual ties of prosperity. And this is why we find almost everywhere in the world a growing dissatisfaction with the prevalent system of teaching, which betrays the encroachment of senility and worldly prudence over pure intellect.

In India, also, a vague feeling of discontent has given rise to numerous attempts at establishing national schools and colleges. But, unfortunately, our very education has been successful in depriving us of our real initiative and our courage of thought. The training we get in our schools has the constant implication in it that it is not for us to produce but to borrow. And we are casting about to borrow our educational plans from European institutions. The trampled plants of Indian corn are dreaming of recouping their harvest from the neighbouring wheat fields. To change the figure, we forget that, for proficiency in walking, it is better to train the muscles of our own legs than to strut upon wooden ones of foreign make, although they clatter and cause more surprise at our skill in using them than if they were living and real.

But when we go to borrow help from a foreign neighbourhood we are apt to overlook the real source of help behind all that is external and apparent. Had the deep-water fishes happened to produce a scientist who chose the jumping of a monkey for his research work, I am sure he would give most of the credit to the branches of the trees and very little to the monkey itself. In a foreign University we see the branching wildernesses of its buildings, furniture, regulations, and syllabus, but the monkey, which is a difficult creature to catch and more difficult to manufacture, we are likely to treat as a mere accident of minor importance. It is convenient for us to overlook the fact that among the Europeans the living spirit of the University is widely spread in their society, their parliament, their literature, and the numerous activities of their corporate life. In all these functions they are in perpetual touch with the great personality of the land which is creative and heroic in its constant acts of self-expression and self-sacrifice. They have their thoughts published in their books as well as through the medium of living men who think those thoughts, and who criticise, compare and disseminate them. Some at least of the drawbacks of their academic education are redeemed by the living energy of the intellectual personality pervading their social organism. It is like the stagnant reservoir of water which finds its purification in the showers of rain to which it keeps itself open. But, to our misfortune, we have in India all the furniture of the European University except the human teacher. We have, instead, mere purveyors of book-lore in whom the paper god of the bookshop has been made vocal.

A most important truth, which we are apt to forget, is that a teacher can never truly teach unless he is still learning himself. A lamp can never light another lamp unless it continues to burn its own flame. The teacher who has come to the end of his subject, who has no living traffic with his knowledge, but merely repeats his lessons to his students, can only load their minds; he cannot quicken them. Truth not only must inform but inspire. If the inspiration dies out, and the information only accumulates, then truth loses its infinity. The greater part of our learning in the schools has been wasted because, for most of our teachers, their subjects are like dead specimens of once living things, with which they have a learned acquaintance, but no communication of life and love.

The educational institution, therefore, which I have in mind has primarily for its object the constant pursuit of truth, from which the imparting of truth naturally follows. It must not be a dead cage in which living minds are fed with food artificially prepared. It should be an open house, in which students and teachers are at one. They must live their complete life together, dominated by a common aspiration for truth and a need of sharing all the delights of culture. In former days the great master-craftsmen had students in their workshops where they co-operated in shaping things to perfection. That was the place where knowledge could become living – that knowledge which not only has its substance and law, but its atmosphere subtly informed by a creative personality. For intellectual knowledge also has its aspect of creative art, in which the man who explores truth expresses something which is human in him – his enthusiasm, his courage, his sacrifice, his honesty, and his skill. In merely academical teaching we find subjects, but not the man who pursues the subjects; therefore the vital part of education remains incomplete.

For our Universities we must claim, not labelled packages of truth and authorized agents to distribute them, but truth in its living association with her lovers and seekers and discoverers. Also we must know that the concentration of the mind-forces scattered throughout the country is the most important mission of a University, which, like the nucleus of a living cell, should be the centre of the intellectual life of the people.

The bringing about of an intellectual unity in India is, I am told, difficult to the verge of impossibility owing to the fact that India has so many different languages. Such a statement is as unreasonable as to say that man, because he has a diversity of limbs, should find it impossible to realize life's unity in himself, and that only an earthworm composed of a tail and nothing else could truly know that it had a body.

Let us admit that India is not like any one of the great countries of Europe, which has its own separate language; but is rather like Europe herself, branching out into different peoples with many different languages. And yet Europe has a common civilization, with an intellectual unity which is not based upon uniformity of language. It is true that in the earlier stages of her culture the whole of Europe had Latin for her learned tongue. That was in her intellectual budding time, when all her petals of self-expression were closed in one point. But the perfection of her mental unfolding was not represented by the singularity of her literary vehicle. When the great European countries found their individual languages, then only the true federation of cultures became possible in the West, and the very differences of the channels made the commerce of ideas in Europe so richly copious and so variedly active. We can well imagine what the loss to European civilization would be if France, Italy and Germany, and England herself, had not through their separate agencies contributed to the common coffer their individual earnings.

There was a time with us when India had her common language of culture in Sanskrit. But, for the complete commerce of her thought, she required that all her vernaculars should attain their perfect powers, through which her different peoples might manifest their idiosyncrasies; and this could never be done through a foreign tongue.

In the United States, in Canada and other British Colonies, the language of the people is English. It has a great literature which had its birth and growth in the history of the British Islands. But when this language, with all its products and acquisitions, matured by ages on its own mother soil, is carried into foreign lands, which have their own separate history and their own life-growth, it must constantly hamper the indigenous growth of culture and destroy individuality of judgement and the perfect freedom of self-expression. The inherited wealth of the English language, with all its splendour, becomes an impediment when taken into different surroundings, just as when lungs are given to the whale in the sea. If such is the case even with races whose grandmother-tongue naturally continues to be their own mother-tongue, one can imagine what sterility it means for a people which accepts, for its vehicle of culture, an altogether foreign language. A language is not like an umbrella or an overcoat that can be borrowed by unconscious or deliberate mistake; it is like the living skin itself. If the body of a draught-horse enters into the skin of a race-horse, it will be safe to wager that such an anomaly will never win a race, and will fail even to drag a cart. Have we not watched some modern Japanese artists imitating European art? The imitation may sometimes produce clever results; but such cleverness has only the perfection of artificial flowers which never bear fruit.

All great countries have their vital centres for intellectual life, where a high standard of learning is maintained, where the minds of the people are naturally attracted, where they find their genial atmosphere, in which to prove their worth and to contribute their share to the country's culture. Thus they kindle, on the common altar of the land, that great sacrificial fire which can radiate the sacred light of wisdom abroad.

Athens was such a centre in Greece, Rome in Italy; and Paris is such today in France. Benares has been and still continues to be the centre of our Sanskrit culture. But Sanskrit learning does not exhaust all the elements of culture that exist in modern India.

If we were to take for granted, what some people maintain, that Western culture is the only source of light for our mind, then it would be like depending for daybreak upon some star, which is the sun of a far distant sphere. The star may give us light, but not the day; it may give us direction in our voyage of exploration, but it can never open the full view of truth before our eyes. In fact, we can never use this cold starlight for stirring the sap in our branches, and giving colour and bloom to our life. This is the reason why European education has become for India mere school lessons and no culture; a box of matches, good for the small uses of illumination, but not the light of morning, in which the use and beauty, and all the subtle mysteries of life are blended in one.

Let me say clearly that I have no distrust of any culture because of its foreign character. On the contrary, I believe that the shock of such extraneous forces is necessary for the vitality of our intellectual nature. It is admitted that much of the spirit of Christianity runs counter, not only to the classical culture of Europe, but to the European temperament altogether. And yet this alien movement of ideas, constantly running against the natural mental current of Europe, has been a most important factor in strengthening and enriching her civilization, on account of the sharp antagonism of its intellectual direction. In fact, the European vernaculars first woke up to life and fruitful vigour when they felt the impact of this foreign thought-power with all its oriental forms and affinities. The same thing is happening in India. The European culture has come to us, not only with its knowledge, but with its velocity.

Then, again, let us admit that modern Science is Europe's great gift to humanity for all time to come. We, in India, must claim it from her hands, and gratefully accept it in order to be saved from the curse of futility by lagging behind. We shall fail to reap the harvest of the present age if we delay.

What I object to is the artificial arrangement by which foreign education tends to occupy all the space of our national mind, and thus kills, or hampers, the great opportunity for the creation of a new thought-power by a new combination of truths. It is this which makes me urge that all the elements in our own culture have to be strengthened, not to resist the Western culture, but truly to accept and assimilate it; to use it for our sustenance, not as our burden; to get mastery over this culture, and not to live on its outskirts as the hewers of texts and drawers of book-learning.

The main river in Indian culture has flowed in four streams, – the Vedic, the Puranic, the Buddhist, and the Jain. It has its source in the heights of the Indian consciousness. But a river, belonging to a country, is not fed by its own waters alone. The Tibetan Brahmaputra is a tributary to the Indian Ganges. Contributions have similarly found their way to India's original culture. The Muhammadan, for example, has repeatedly come into India from outside, laden with his own stores of knowledge and feeling and his wonderful religious democracy, bringing freshet after freshet to swell the current. To our music, our architecture, our pictorial art, our literature, the Muhammadans have made their permanent and precious contribution. Those who have studied the lives and writings of our medieval saints, and all the great religious movements that sprang up in the time of the Muhammadan rule, know how deep is our debt to this foreign current that has so intimately mingled with our life.

So, in our centre of Indian learning, we must provide for the co-ordinate study of all these different cultures, – the Vedic, the Puranic, the Buddhist, the Jain, the Islamic, the Sikh and the Zoroastrian. The Chinese, Japanese, and Tibetan will also have to be added; for, in the past, India did not remain isolated within her own boundaries. Therefore, in order to learn what she was, in her relation to the whole continent of Asia, these cultures too must be studied. Side by side with them must finally be placed the Western culture. For only then shall we be able to assimilate this last contribution to our common stock. A river flowing within banks is truly our own, and it can contain its due tributaries; but our relations with a flood can only prove disastrous.

There are some who are exclusively modern, who believe that the past is the bankrupt time, leaving no assets for us, but only a legacy of debts. They refuse to believe that the army is marching forward to believe that the army which is marching forward can be fed from the rear. It is well to remind such persons that the great ages of renaissance in history were those when man suddenly discovered the seeds of thought in the granary of the past.

The unfortunate people who have lost the harvest of their past have lost their present age. They have missed their seed for cultivation, and go begging for their bare livelihood. We must not imagine that we are one of these disinherited peoples of the world. The time has come for us to break open the treasure-trove of our ancestors, and use it for our commerce of life. Let us, with its help, make our future our own, and not continue our existence as the eternal rag-pickers in other people's dustbins.

So far I have dwelt only upon the intellectual aspect of Education. For, even in the West, it is the intellectual training which receives almost exclusive emphasis. The Western universities have not yet truly recognized that fullness of expression is fullness of life. And a large part of man can never find its expression in the mere language of words. It must therefore seek for its other languages, – lines and colours, sounds and movements. Through our mastery of these we not only make our whole nature articulate, but also understand man in all his attempts to reveal his innermost being in every age and clime. The great use of Education is not merely to collect facts, but to know man and to make oneself known to man. It is the duty of every human being to master, at least to some extent, not only the language of intellect, but also that personality which is the language of Art. It is a great world of reality for man, – vast and profound, – this growing world of his own creative nature. This is the world of Art. To be brought up in ignorance of it is to be deprived of the knowledge and use of that great inheritance of humanity, which has been growing and waiting for every one of us from the beginning of our history. It is to remain deaf to the eternal voice of Man that speaks to all men the messages that are beyond speech. From the educational point of view we know Europe where it is scientific, or at best literary. So our notion of its modern culture is limited within the boundary lines of grammar and the laboratory. We almost completely ignore the aesthetic life of man, leaving it uncultivated, allowing weeds to grow there. Our newspapers are prolific, our meeting-places are vociferous; and in them we wear to shreds the things we have borrowed from our English teachers. We make the air dismal and damp with the tears of our grievances. But where are our arts, which, like the outbreak of spring flowers, are the spontaneous overflow of our deeper nature and spiritual magnificence?

Through this great deficiency of our modern education, we are condemned to carry to the end a dead load of dumb wisdom. Like miserable outcasts, we are deprived of our place in the festival of culture, and wait at the outer court, where the colours are not for us, nor the forms of delight, nor the songs. Ours is the education of a prison-house, with hard labour and with a drab dress cut to the limits of minimum decency and necessity. We are made to forget that the perfection of colour and form and expression belongs to the perfection of vitality, – that the joy of life is only the other side of the strength of life. The timber merchant may think that the flowers and foliage are mere frivolous decorations of a tree; but if these are suppressed, he will know to his cost that the timber too will fail.

During the Moghal period, music and art in India found a great impetus from the rulers, because their whole life – not merely their official life – was lived in this land; and it is the wholeness of life from which originates Art. But our English teachers are birds of passage; they cackle to us, but do not sing – their true heart is not in the land of their exile.

Construction of life, owing to this narrowness of culture, must no longer be encouraged. In the centre of Indian culture which I am proposing, music and art must have their prominent seats of honour, and not be given merely a tolerant nod of recognition. The different systems of music and different schools of art which lie scattered in the different ages and provinces of India, and in the different strata of society, and also those belonging to the other great countries of Asia, which had communication with India, have to be brought there together and studied.

I have already hinted that Education should not be dragged out of its native element, the life-current of the people. Economic life covers the whole width of the fundamental basis of society, because its necessities are the simplest and the most universal. Educational institutions, in order to obtain their fullness of truth, must have close association with this economic life. The highest mission of education is to help us to realize the inner principle of the unity of all knowledge and all the activities of our social and spiritual being. Society in its early stage was held together by its economic co-operation, when all its members felt in unison a natural interest in their right to live. Civilization could never have been started at all if such was not the case. And civilization will fall to pieces if it never again realizes the spirit of mutual help and the common sharing of benefits in the elemental necessaries of life. The idea of such economic co-operation should be made the basis of our University. It must not only instruct, but live; not only think, but produce.

Our ancient *tapovanas*, or forest schools, which were our natural universities, were not shut off from the daily life of the people. Masters and students gathered fruit and fuel, and took their cattle out to graze, supporting themselves by the work of their own hands. Spiritual education was a part of the spiritual life itself, which comprehended all life. Our centre of culture should not only be the centre of the intellectual life of India, but the centre of her economic life also. I must co-operate with the villages round it, cultivate land, breed cattle, spin cloths, press oil from oil-seeds; it must produce all the necessaries, devising the best means, using the best materials, and calling science to its aid. Its very existence should depend upon the success of its industrial activities carried out on the co-operative principle, which will unite the teachers and students and villagers of the neighbourhood in a living and active bond of necessity. This will give us also a practical industrial training, whose motive force is not the greed of profit.

Before I conclude my paper, a delicate question remains to be considered. What must be the religious ideal that is to rule our centre of Indian culture? The one abiding ideal in the religious life of India has been *mukti*, the deliverance of man's soul from the grip of self, its communion with the Infinite Soul through its union in *ânanda* with the universe. This religion of spiritual harmony is not a theological doctrine to be taught, as a subject in the class, for half an hour each day. It is the spiritual truth and beauty of our attitude towards our surroundings, our conscious relationship with the Infinite, and the lasting power of the Eternal in the passing moments of our life. Such a religious ideal can only be made possible by making provision for students to live in intimate touch with nature, daily to grow in an atmosphere of service offered to all creatures, tending trees, feeding birds and animals, learning to feel the immense mystery of the soil and water and air.

Along with this, there should be some common sharing of life with the tillers of the soil and the humble workers in the neighbouring villages; studying their crafts, inviting them to the feasts, joining them in works of co-operation for communal welfare; and in our intercourse we should be guided, not by moral maxims or the condescension of social superiority, but by natural sympathy of life for life, and by the sheer necessity of love's sacrifice for its own sake. In such an atmosphere students would learn to understand that humanity is a divine harp of many strings, waiting for its one grand music. Those who realize this unity are made ready for the pilgrimage through the night of suffering, and along the path of sacrifice, to the great meeting of Man in the future, for which the call comes to us across the darkness.

Life, in such a centre, should be simple and clean. We should never believe that simplicity of life might make us unsuited to the requirements of the society of our time. It is the simplicity of the tuning-fork, which is needed all the more because of the intricacy of strings in the instrument. In the morning of our career our nature needs the pure and the perfect note of a spiritual idea in order to fit us for the complications of our later years.

In other words, this institution should be a perpetual creation by the co-operative enthusiasm of teachers and students, growing with the growth of their soul; a world in itself, self-sustaining, independent, rich with ever-renewing life radiating life across space and time, attracting and maintaining round it a planetary system of dependent bodies. Its aim should lie in imparting life-breath to the complete man, who is intellectual as well as economic, bound by social bonds, but aspiring towards spiritual freedom and final perfection.

A Poet's School (1926)[20]

FROM QUESTIONS THAT have often been put to me, I have come to feel that the public claims an apology from the poet for having founded a school, as I in my rashness have done. One must admit that the silkworm which spins and the butterfly that floats on the air represent two different stages of existence, contrary to each other. The silkworm seems to have a cash value credited in its favour somewhere in Nature's accounting department, according to the amount of work it performs. But the butterfly is irresponsible. The significance which it may possess has neither weight nor use and is lightly carried on its pair of dancing wings. Perhaps it pleases someone in the heart of the sunlight, the Lord of colours, who has nothing to do with account books and has a perfect mastery in the great art of wastefulness.

The poet may be compared to that foolish butterfly. He also tries to translate in verse the festive colours of creation. Then why should he imprison himself in duty: Why should he make himself accountable to those who would assess his produce by the amount of profit it would earn?

I suppose this poet's answer would be that, when he brought together a few boys, one sunny day in winter, among the warm shadows of the tall straight *sal* trees with their branches of quiet dignity, he started to write a poem in a medium not of words.

In these self-conscious days of psycho-analysis clever minds have discovered the secret spring of poetry in some obscure stratum of repressed freedom, in some constant fretfulness of thwarted self-realization. Evidently in this instance they were right. The phantom of my long-ago boyhood did come to haunt its early beginning; it sought to live in the lives of other boys, and to build its missing paradise with ingredients which may not have any orthodox material, prescribed measure, or standard value.

This brings to my mind Kalidasa, a poet of ancient India. Happily for the scholars, Kalidasa, has left behind him no clear indication of his birth-place, and there is ample scope for endless disagreement. My scholarship does not pretend to go deep, but I remember having read somewhere that he was born in beautiful Kashmir. Since then I have given up reading discussions about his birth-place lest I find some learned contradiction equally convincing. Anyhow, it is in the fitness of things that Kalidasa – should have been born in Kashmir and I envy him, for I was born in Calcutta.

---

20. In Kabir, pp. 285-301.

But psycho-analysis need not be disappointed, for he was banished to a city in the plains and *Meghaduta* vibrates with the music of sorrow that has its keynote 'in the remembrance of happier things.' It is significant that in this poem the lover's errant fancy, in quest of the beloved who dwelt in the paradise of eternal beauty, lingered with enjoyment about every hill, stream, or forest over which it passed; watched the grateful dark eyes of the peasant girls welcoming the rain-laden clouds of June; listened to some village elder reciting under the banyan tree a familiar love legend fresh with the tears and smiles of simple-souled generations. We feel in all this the prisoner of the stony-hearted city revelling in a vision of joy that, in his imaginary journey, followed him from hill to hill, waited at every turn of the path which bore the finger-posts of heaven for separated lovers banished on the earth.

It was not a physical home-sickness from which the poet suffered, it was something far more fundamental – the nostalgia of the soul. We feel in almost all his works the oppressive atmosphere of the King's palaces of those days, thick with luxury and the callousness of self-indulgence, and yet an atmosphere of refined culture, of an extra-vagrant civilization.

The poet in the royal court lived in exile, as it were. It was, he knew, not merely his own exile but that of the whole age to which he was born, the age that had amassed wealth and well-being, and lost its background of the great universe. What was the image in which his desire of perfection persistently appeared in his poems and dramas? It was *tapovana*, the forest resort of the patriarchal community of ancient India. Those who are familiar with Sanskrit literature know that this was not a colony of people with a primitive culture. They were seekers of truth, for the sake of which they lived in purity but not puritanism; they led a simple life, but not one of self-mortification. They did not advocate celibacy and were in close touch with people who pursued worldly interests. Their aim was briefly suggested in the Upanishad in these lines:

Te sarvagam sarvatah prapya dhira
Yuktatmanah sarvamevavisanti.

Those men of serene mind enter into the All, having realised and being everywhere in union with the omnipresent Spirit.

It was no negative philosophy of renunciation. Kalidasa, living in the prosperous city of Ujjaini in the glorious days of Vikramditya, his mind oppressed by material objects and by its own demands, let his thoughts escape to the vision of *tapovana*, and into life, light and freedom.

It was no deliberate copying but natural coincidence, that a poet of modern India should have a like vision when he felt within him the misery of a spiritual exile. In Kalidasa's time the people strongly believed in the ideal of *tapovana*, the forest colony, and there can be no doubt that even in that late age there were communities of men living in the heart of nature – not ascetics intent on a slow suicide but men of serene intellect who sought to realize the inward meaning of their life. When Kalidasa sang of the *tapovana*, his verses instantly touched the living faith of his listeners. But today the idea of the *tapovana* has lost all semblance with reality and has slipped into legend; therefore, in a modern poem, it would merely be 'literary'. Then again, the *tapovana* concept would be a fantastic anachronism in the present age, unless recast under the current conditions of life. That, indeed, was the reason why the poet of today had to compose his verse in a plausible language.

But I must give that history in some detail.

Civilized man has come far away from the orbit of his normal life. He has gradually formed and intensified some habits, like those of the bees, for adapting himself to his hive-world. We so often see modern men suffering from world-weariness, from a sense of revolt against their environment. Social revolutions are ushered in with a suicidal violence that is rooted in our dissatisfaction with our hive-wall arrangement – the too exclusive enclosure that deprives us of the perspective needed in our art of living. All this is an indication that man has not really been moulded in the model of the bee, and therefore he becomes recklessly anti-social when his freedom to be more than social is ignored.

In our highly complex modern conditions, mechanical forces are organized with such efficiency that the materials produced grow far in advance of man's capacity to select and assimilate them to suit his nature and needs. Such an overgrowth, like the rank vegetation of the tropics, creates confinement for man. The nest is simple. It has an easy relationship with the sky; the cage is complex and costly, it is too much itself, excommunicating whatever lies outside. And modern man is busy building his cage. He is always occupied in adapting himself to its dead angularities, limiting himself to its limitations, and so he becomes a part of it.

This talk may seem too oriental to some of my listeners. I am told that they believe in a constant high pressure of living produced by an artificially cultivated hunger for material objects. This according to them generates and feeds the energy driving civilization upon its endless journey. Personally, I do not believe that this has ever been the main driving force behind any great civilization. But I have touched on this theme in order to explain the conduct of a poet trespassing into a region reserved for experts and for those who have academic distinction.

I was born in what was then the metropolis of British India. Our ancestors came floating to Calcutta upon the earliest tide of the fluctuating fortune of the East India Company. The code of life for our family became composed of three cultures, Hindu, Muslim, and British. My grandfather belonged to that period when an extravagance in dress and courtesy and a generous leisure were gradually being clipped and curtailed into Victorian manners. I came to a world in which the modern city-bred spirit of progress had just triumphed over the lush green life of our ancient village community.

Though the trampling process was almost complete around me, something of the past lingered over the wreckage. In my boyhood days I often listened to my eldest brother dwelling regretfully on a society that had been hospitable, kindly, and filled with a simple faith and the ceremonial poetry of life. All that was a vanishing shadow in the twilight haze of the horizon; the all-pervading fact was the modern city, newly built by a Company of western traders, and the spirit of the new times striking upon our life, even if it had to face countless anomalies. But it has always been a surprise to me that while this hard crust of a city was my only experience of the world, I was constantly haunted by the nostalgic fancies of an exile.

It seems that the sub-conscious remembrance of some primeval dwelling-place, where in our ancestors' minds were figured and voiced the mysteries of the inarticulate rocks, the rushing water and the dark whispers of the forest, was constantly stirring my blood with its call. (Some living memory in me seemed to ache for the playground it had once shared with the primal life in the illimitable magic of land, water and air.) The thin, shrill cry of the high-flying kite in the blazing sun of a dazed Indian midday sent to a solitary boy the signal of a dumb distant kinship. The few coconut palms growing by the boundary wall of our house, like some war captives from an older army of invaders of this earth, spoke to me of the eternal companionship which the great brotherhood of trees have ever offered to man. They made my heart thrill to the invitation of the forest. I had the good fortune of answering this invitation when as a boy of ten I stood alone on the Himalayas under the shade of great *deodars*, awed by the dark dignity of life's first-born aristocracy, by its sturdy fortitude that was terrible as well as courteous.

Looking back upon those moments of my boyhood when all my mind seemed to float poised upon a large feeling of the sky, of the light, I cannot help believing that my Indian ancestry has left deep in my being the legacy of its philosophy, the philosophy which speaks of fulfilment through harmony with nature. It arouses in us a great desire to seek our freedom, not in the man-made world but in the depth of the universe; and it makes us offer our reverence to the divinity inherent in fire, water and trees, in everything moving and growing. The founding of my school had its origin in the memory of that longing for freedom, the memory which seems to go back beyond the sky-line of my birth.

Freedom in the mere sense of independence is meaningless. Perfect freedom lies in the harmony of relationship which we realize not through *knowing*, but in *being*. Objects of knowledge maintain an infinite distance from us who are the knowers. For knowledge is not union. We attain the world of freedom only through perfect sympathy.

Children with the freshness of their senses come directly to the intimacy of this world. This is the first great gift they have. They must accept it naked and simple and never lose their power of quick communication. For our perfection we have to be at once savage and civilized; we must be natural with nature and human with human society. The misery which I felt was due to the crowded solitude in which I dwelt in a city where man was everywhere, with no gap for the immense non-human. My banished soul, in the isolation of town-life, cried within me for new horizons. I was like the torn-away line of a verse, always in a state of suspense, the other line with which it rhymed and which could give it fullness, having been smudged. The easy power to be happy which, along with other children, I brought with me to this world, was being constantly worn away by friction with the brick-and-mortar arrangement of life, the mechanical habits and the customary code of respectability.

In the usual course I was sent to school, but possibly my suffering was unusual, greater than that of most other children. The non-civilized in me was sensitive; it had a great thirst for colour, for music, for the movements of life. Our city-built education took no heed of that living fact. It has its luggage-van waiting for branded bales of marketable result. The non-civilized and the civilized in man should be in the same proportion as water and land on our globe, the former predominating. But the school had for its object a continual reclamation of the non-civilized. Such a drain of the living water causes an aridity which may not be considered deplorable in a city, but my nature never became accustomed to those conditions. The non-civilized triumphed in me too soon and drove me away from school when I had just entered my teens. I found myself stranded on a solitary island of ignorance and had to rely solely on my own instincts to build up my education from the very beginning.

This reminds me that when I was young I had the great good fortune of coming upon a Bengali translation of *Robinson Crusoe*. I still believe that it is one of the best books for boys ever written. I have already spoken in this paper about my longing when young to run away from my own self and be one with everything in nature. I have described this mood as particularly Indian, the outcome of traditional desire for the expansion of consciousness. One has to admit that such a desire is too subjective, but this is inevitable in our geographical circumstances. We live under the tyranny of the tropics, paying heavy toll every moment for the barest right of existence. The heat, the damp, the unspeakable fecundity of minute life feeding upon big life, the perpetual sources of irritation, visible and invisible, leave little margin of capital for extravagant experiments.

Excess of energy seeks obstacles to fight with and overcome. That is why we find so often in western literature a constant emphasis on the malignant aspect of nature; in her the people of the West discover an enemy, for the sheer pleasure of challenging her to fight. The same reason which made Alexander wish for other worlds to conquer when his conquest of this world was complete made these enormously vital people go out of their way and spread their coat-tails in other peoples' thoroughfares, claiming indemnity when these are trodden upon. To enjoy the risk of hurting themselves they are ready to hurt others who are inoffensive; the birds which know how to fly away, the timid beasts which inhabit inaccessible regions, and ... I shall avoid the discourtesy of mentioning higher races.

Life needs hurdles on its path for its advance. The stream would lose the speed of its flow without the resistance of the soil through which it must cut its way. The spirit of combat is part of the genius of life. The tuning of an instrument helps music to be perfectly realized. Let us rejoice that, in the West, life's instrument is being tuned in all its chords through the contest with obstacles. The creativeness in the heart of the universe will never let obstacles be completely removed. It is only because there is an ideal of perfection to attain that the spirit of combat is great.

In *Robinson Crusoe*, the delight in union with nature finds its expression in a story of adventure where the solitary man is face to face with solitary nature, coaxing her, co-operating with her, exploring her secrets, using all his faculties to win her help. The pleasure I felt in reading this book was not in sharing the pride of human success against the closed fist of a parsimonious nature, but in the harmony with nature attained through intelligent dealings. And this is the heroic love-adventure of the West, the active wooing of the earth.

I remember how in my youth, in the course of a railway journey across Europe from Brindisi to Calais, I watched with keen delight and wonder that continent glowing with richness under the age-long attention of her chivalrous lover, western humanity. He had gained her, made her his own, unlocked the inexhaustible generosity of her heart. And I had intently wished that the introspective vision of the universal soul which an eastern devotee experiences in the solitude of his mind could be united with this spirit of service.

I remember a morning when a beggar woman in a Bengal village gathered in the loose end of her sari the stale flowers that were about to be thrown away from the vase on my table; and with a look of ecstatic tenderness she buried her face in them, exclaiming, 'Beloved of my heart!' Her eyes could easily pierce the veil of the outward form and reach the realm of the infinite in these flowers where she found the intimate touch of her beloved. But in spite of it all she lacked that energy of worship, the western form of direct divine service, which helps the earth to bring out her flowers and spread the reign of beauty on the desolate dust. I refuse to think that the twin spirits of East and West, the Mary and the Martha, can never meet to make perfect the realization of truth. And in spite of our material poverty and the antagonism of time I wait patiently for this meeting.

Robinson Crusoe's island comes to my mind when I think of an institution where the first great lesson in the perfect union of man and nature, not only through love but through active communication, may be learnt unobstructed. We have to keep in mind the fact that love and action are the only media through which perfect knowledge can be obtained, for the object of knowledge is not pedantry but wisdom. An institution of this kind should not only train up one's limbs and mind to be ready for all emergencies, but to be attuned to the response between life and the world, to find the balance of their harmony which is wisdom. The first important lesson for children in such a place would be that of improvisation, the ready-made having been banished in order to give the constant occasion to explore one's capacity through surprise achievements. I must make it plain that this implies a lesson not in simple life, but in creative life. For life may grow complex, and yet, if there is a living personality at its centre, it will have the unity of creation, it will carry its own weight in perfect grace, and will not be a mere addition to the number of facts that only go to swell a crowd.

I wish I could say that we have fulfilled this dream in our school. We have only made a beginning. We have given the children an opportunity to find their freedom in nature by being able to love it. For love is freedom; it saves us from paying with our soul for objects that are all too cheap. I know men who preach the cult of the simple life by glorifying the spiritual merit of poverty. I refuse to imagine any special value in poverty when it is a mere negation. Only when the mind is sensitive to the deeper call of reality is it weaned away from the lure of the fictitious. It is callousness which robs us of our simple power to enjoy and dooms us to the indignity of snobbish pride in furniture and the foolish burden of expensive things. But to pit the callousness of asceticism against the callousness of luxury is to fight one evil with another, inviting the pitiless demon of the desert in place of the indiscriminate demon of the jungle.

With the help of literature, festive ceremonials and religious teachings I tried to develop in the children of my school their feeling for nature as also a sensitiveness to their human surroundings. I prepared for them a real home-coming into this world. Among the subjects they learnt in the open air, in the shade of trees, were music and painting, and they had their dramatic performances.

But this was not sufficient, and I waited for men and the means to be able to introduce into our school activities that would build up character. I felt the need of the western genius for imparting to my educational ideal the strength of reality which knew how to achieve a definite end of practical good.

The obstacles were numerous. The tradition of the community which calls itself educated, the parents' expectations, the upbringing of the teachers themselves, the claim and the constitution of the official University, were all overwhelmingly arrayed against the idea I cherished. In addition, we attracted hardly any contributions from my countrymen as our funds were inadequate to support an institution in which the number of boys had necessarily to be small.

Fortunately, help came to us from an English friend who took the leading part in creating and guiding the rural organization connected with Visva-Bharati. He believes, as I do, in an education which takes count of the organic wholeness of human individuality, needing a general stimulation of all faculties, bodily and mental. In order to have the freedom to give effect to this idea, we started our work with a few boys who were orphans or whose parents were too poor to be able to send them to any kind of school.

Before long we discovered that minds actively engaged in constructive work fast developed energies which sought eager outlet in the pursuit of knowledge, even to the extent of undertaking extra tasks. The minds of these boys became so alert that a very simple fact made them at once see the advantage of learning English, which was not in their course of studies. The idea came to them one day when they were posting some letters: on the envelopes the post-master wrote in English the addresses that had already been written in Bengali. Immediately they went to their teacher asking that they be taught English in an additional hour. These boys never regretted their rash request. Yet I remember to this day what criminal thoughts used to fill my young mind when my own teacher of English showed himself at the bend of the lane leading to our house!

For these boys vacation has no meaning. Their studies, though strenuous, are not a task, being permeated by a holiday spirit which takes shape in activities in their kitchen, their vegetable garden, their weaving, their work of small repairs. It is because their classwork has not been separated from their normal activities but forms a part of their daily current of life, that it easily carries itself by its own onward flow.

Most of our boys when they first came were weak in body and mind; the ravages of malaria and other tropical diseases had been their fatal inheritance. They brought with them an intolerable mental perversity; the Brahmin was supercilious, the non-Brahmin pitiable in his shrinking self-abasement. They hated to do any work of common good lest others besides themselves should get the least advantage. They sulked when they were asked to do for their own benefit the kind of work that, they thought, should be done by a paid servant. They were not averse to living on charity but were ashamed of self-help.

It might have been thought that this meanness and moral lethargy were inherent in their nature. But within a very short time all that changed. The spirit of sacrifice and comradeship which these boys have developed is rare even in children who have had better opportunities. It was the active, healthy life which brought out all that was good in them and the accumulated rubbish of impurities was swept off. The daily work which they were doing gave rise to problems which demanded a solution. The logic of facts showed to them the reality of moral principles in life, and now they feel astonished when other boys do not understand such principles. They take great pleasure in cooking, weaving, gardening, improving their surroundings, and in rendering services to other boys, very often secretly, lest they should feel embarrassed. The members of a mess usually clamour for more than is provided for them, but these boys willingly simplify their needs. They have developed a sense of responsibility. Instead of grumbling at deficiencies, they think and manage for themselves. To improve their dietary they must apply extra zest on their vegetable patches. Even if they get poor results, these have a value not to be assessed in terms of market price.

To give an artistic touch to my description, I wish I could speak of some break-down in our plan, of some unexpected element of misfit trying to wreck the symmetry of our arrangements. I have to confess, however, that it has not yet happened. Perhaps our tropical climate is accountable for this dull calm in our atmosphere, for the lack of that excess energy which often loves to upset things. Maybe it is not too late to hope that this experiment of ours is not going to be a model paradise for harmless boys. Some incalculable problems, I am sure, will presently arise, challenging our theories and our faith in our ideal.

Meanwhile, having realized that this daily practice in the adaptation of mind and body to life's necessities has made these boys intellectually alert, we have mustered courage to extend the system to the primary section of our school. The children of that section, under an ideal teacher who believes that to teach is to learn, have just finished constructing their first hut of which they are absurdly proud. They have apparently begun to think that education is a permanent part of the adventure of life; it is not like a painful hospital treatment for curing them of the congenital malady of their ignorance, but is a function of health, the natural expression of their mind's vitality. Thus, I have just had the good fortune to watch the first shoot of life peeping out in a humble corner of our organization. My idea is to allow this creeper to grow, with no special label of learned nomenclature attached to it; grow till it completely hides the dead pole that bears no natural flower or fruit, but flourishes the parchment flag of examination success.

Before I stop I must say a few more words about a most important item on our educational programme.

Children have their active sub-conscious mind which, like the tree, has the power to draw food from the surrounding atmosphere. For them the atmosphere is a great deal more important than rules and methods, equipment, text-books and lessons. The earth has her mass of substance in her land and water; but, if I may use figurative language, she finds her stimulus in her atmosphere. It evokes from her responses in colour and perfume, music and movement. In his society man has about himself a diffuse atmosphere of culture. It keeps his mind sensitive to his racial inheritance, to the current of influences that come from tradition; it enables him to imbibe unconsciously the concentrated wisdom of ages. But in our educational organizations we behave like miners, digging only for things and not like the tillers of the earth whose work is a perfect collaboration with nature.

I tried to create an atmosphere in my school – this was the main task. In educational institutions our faculties have to be nourished in order to give our mind its freedom, to make our imagination fit for the world which belongs to art, and to stir our sympathy for human relationships. This last is even more important than learning the geography of foreign lands.

The minds of the children of today are almost deliberately made incapable of understanding other people with different languages and customs. The result is that, later, they hurt one another out of ignorance and suffer from the worst form of the blindness of the age. The Christian missionaries themselves help in this cultivation of contempt for alien races and civilizations. Led by sectarian pride while they profess brotherhood for all, they use school text-books to corrupt young susceptible minds. I have tried to save our children from such aberrations, and here the help of friends from the West, with their sympathetic hearts, has been of the greatest service.

> Children run out of the temple
> and play in the dust.
> God watches their games
> and forgets the priest.

—*Rabindranath Tagore*

The Parrot's Training (1918)[21]

ONCE UPON A TIME there was a bird. It was ignorant. It sang all right, but never recited scriptures. It hopped pretty frequently, but lacked manners.

Said the Raja to himself: 'Ignorance is costly in the long run. For fools consume as much food as their betters, and yet give nothing in return.' He called his nephews to his presence and told them that the bird must have a sound schooling. The pundits were summoned, and at once went to the root of the matter. They decided that the ignorance of birds was due to their natural habit of living in poor nests. Therefore, according to the pundits, the first thing necessary for this bird's education was a suitable cage.

The pundits had their rewards and went home happy.

A golden cage was built with gorgeous decorations. Crowds came to see it from all parts of the world. 'Culture, captured and caged!' exclaimed some, in a rapture of ecstasy, and burst into tears. Others remarked: 'Even if culture be missed, the cage will remain, to the end, a substantial fact. How fortunate for the bird!'

The goldsmith filled his bag with money and lost no time in sailing homewards.

The pundit sat down to educate the bird. With proper deliberation he took his pinch of snuff, as he said: 'Text-books can never be too many for our purpose!'

The nephews brought together an enormous crowd of scribes. They copied from books, and copied from copies, till the manuscripts were piled up to an unreachable height. Men murmured in amazement: 'Oh, the tower of culture, egregiously high! The end of it lost in the clouds!'

The scribes, with light hearts, hurried home, their pockets heavily laden. The nephews were furiously busy keeping the cage in proper trim. As their constant scrubbing and polishing went on, the people said with satisfaction: 'This is progress indeed!'

Men were employed in large numbers, and supervisors were still more numerous. These, with their cousins of all different degrees of distance, built a palace for themselves and lived there happily ever after. Whatever may be its other deficiencies, the world is never in want of fault-finders; and they went about saying that every creature remotely connected with the cage flourished beyond words, excepting only the bird.

---

21. In Das, ed. Vol 2 pp. 272-274.

When this remark reached the Raja's ears, he summoned his nephews before him and said: 'My dear nephews, what is this that we hear?'

The nephews said in answer: 'Sire, let the testimony of the goldsmiths and the pundits, the scribes and the supervisors, be taken, if the truth is to be known. Food is scarce with the fault-finders, and that is why their tongues have gained in sharpness.'

The explanation was so luminously satisfactory that the Raja decorated each one of his nephews with his own rare jewels. The Raja at length, being desirous of seeing with his own eyes how his Education Department busied itself with the little bird, made his appearance one day at the great Hall of Learning. From the gate rose the sounds of conch-shells and gongs, horns, bugles and trumpets, cymbals, drums and kettle-drums, tomtoms, tambourines, flutes, fifes, barrel-organs and bagpipes. The pundits began chanting *mantras* with their topmost voices, while the goldsmiths, scribes, supervisors, and their numberless cousins of all different degrees of distance, loudly raised a round of cheers.

The nephews smiled and said: 'Sire, what do you think of it all?'

The Raja said: 'It does seem so fearfully like a sound principle of Education?' Mightily pleased, the Raja was about to remount his elephant, when the fault-finder, from behind some bush, cried out:

'Maharaja, have you seen the bird?'

'Indeed, I have not!' exclaimed the Raja, 'I completely forgot about the bird.' Turning back, he asked the pundits about the method they followed in instructing the bird. It was shown to him. He was immensely impressed. The method was so stupendous that the bird looked ridiculously unimportant in comparison. The Raja was satisfied that there was no flaw in the arrangements. As for any complaint from the bird itself, that simply could not be expected. Its throat was so completely choked with the leaves from the books that it could neither whistle nor whisper. It sent a thrill through one's body to watch the process.

This time, while remounting his elephant, the Raja ordered his State ear-puller to give a thorough good pull at both the ears of the fault-finder.

The bird thus crawled on, duly and properly, to the safest verge of inanity. In fact, its progress was satisfactory in the extreme. Nevertheless, nature occasionally triumphed over training, and when the morning light peeped into the bird's cage it sometimes fluttered its wings in a reprehensible manner. And, though it is hard to believe, it pitifully pecked at its bars with its feeble beak.

'What impertinence!' growled the kotwal.

The blacksmith, with his forge and hammer, took his place in the Raja's Department of Education. Oh, what resounding blows! The iron chain was soon completed, and the bird's wings were clipped.

The Raja's brothers-in-law looked black, and shook their heads, saying: 'These birds not only lack good sense, but also gratitude.' With text-book in one hand and baton in the other, the pundits gave the poor bird what may fitly be called lessons!

The kotwal was honoured with a title for his watchfulness, and the blacksmith for his skill in forging chains.

The bird died.

Nobody had the least notion how long ago this had happened. The fault-finder was the first man to spread the rumour. The Raja called his nephews and asked them,

'My dear nephews, what is that we hear?'

The nephews said: 'Sire, the bird's education has been completed.'

'Does it hop?' the Raja enquired.

'Never!' said the nephews.

'Does it fly?'

'No.'

'Bring me the bird,' said the Raja.

The bird was brought to him, guarded by the kotwal and the sepoys and the sowars. The Raja poked its body with his finger. Only its inner stuffing of book-leaves rustled.

Outside the window, the murmur of the spring breeze amongst the newly budded *asoka* leaves made the April morning wistful.

Sriniketan (1924)[22]

[...] THE ATTAINMENT OF FREEDOM is the object of man. Freedom is in truth; this truth we must realise in all its aspects–all our endeavours in educationmust always keep that in view.

As individuals each of us is a living organism having unity of its own, as social beings we are a part of a complex organism called humanity, as aspiritual being we belong to an all comprehensive infinite reality.

The individual living organism has its needs and its faculties for self-preservation. As the man has to maintain it in order to exist he must beeducated how to feed, clothe and house himself. Otherwise not only he becomeshelpless but the faculties that are for his self-preservation become atrophied, the exercise of which gives him joy of life. Generally speaking in our educationthe training as to how to live is neglected and therefore we miss the joy of self-reliantfreedom in the region of existence.

As social beings the adjustment of our life with the vast life of man needsfor its training the spirit of mutual responsibility. In our educational institutionsthis hardly finds its place. The discipline of self control and good behaviour, to some extent is recognized in our education but social service which needsinformation, experience and exercise of a number of physical, moral andintellectual faculties is ignored. The result of such a deficiency we seeeverywhere in our surroundings, in our villages in the form of poverty, diseaseand ignorance. Owing to this lack of Education we suffer from the lack oftrue freedom in our social life which comes from general welfare and mutualsympathy and cooperation.

As spiritual beings we find our highest pleasure when we realise our unityof kinship with a supreme truth of unity. I have said that the world viewed as amere fact does not satisfy us; unless we know that it has a fullness of reality for its background and foundation our relationship with it becomes merely utilitarian; the consciousness of our own spiritual being not finding its harmony in the universe loses faith in itself urging us to put all our resources in the pursuit of self-interest. This is the worst form of bondage for us, the bondage of self, the bondage of existence which is alien to us because unspiritual. Ordinarily our education does nothing to train our mind to realise our spiritual relationship with the supreme truth. Through this want our life loses its depth and dignity, we fail to develop spirit of detachment,

---

22. In *Rabindranath Tagore: A Miscellany*, ed. Nityapriya Ghosh (New Delhi: Sahitya Akademi, 2007, rpt. 2011), 6 February 1924, Vol 4, pp. 488-492. This is an edited version of the text.

the detachment which is the large atmosphere of freedom in which our inner being must find its dwelling and the leisure and space for its creation. In this atmosphere he builds his own world in the joy of his freedom. Our science, philosophy, arts and literature have had their fullness of growth in this sky of detachment. The creative genius has always worked in the bosom of a mental space which is not crowded with the tangled web of necessities, where the creations are judged by a standard of perfection that is final. It may be said that such creations are abstract; that may be so. The miscellaneous voices of the concrete life is not music – it grows apart from it, in its own disinterested realm of delight. Because of that aloofness itself it enriches life. The vapour that forms clouds because of its distance and freedom can send its rain back to the earth to make the air sweet and the soil fertile. Our knowledge, feelings and experience in one of their stages are abstracted from life, taken into the bosom of the eternal and then purged of all that is nonessential come back to life bringing anew the message of the infinite and the velocity of a new impact needed for the rousing up of latent forces.

Those who constantly cling close to the soil of life grow dull in mind and uncreative; mind for its health and strength and freedom of outlook must soar in the upper air of abstraction, swim in the heart of the infinite for the mere joy of it, and then come back to its nest. In all great civilisations there is this cycle of sending up the adventurous mind into the upper and wider space thence to establish its path of return journey into the solid earth. The solid earth is suffocated to death if it loses its atmosphere which is unsubstantial through which it must receive its air and light. This atmosphere is the atmosphere of detachment which never has for its immediate object the production of necessities but the creations that give expression to the unlimited in man in the provinces of his thought and feeling and will.

Our ideal is to make ample provision in our education for training our personality to realise its spiritual relationship with Supreme Truth, for our freedom in all departments of life finds its reality in it, which divested from the touch of the infinite breeds hidden brood of slavery under the appearance of liberty. I can only quote in this connection what I have said elsewhere while discussing my plan of an ideal educational institution:
[*incomplete*]

The First Anniversary of Sriniketan (1924)[23]
(*The Visva-Bharati Department of Rural Reconstruction*)

President's Opening Address

THE IDEAL WHICH is in the heart of the spiritual endeavour in India is *mukti*, freedom. On the occasion of the anniversary of Sriniketan I take this opportunity to explain it.

The meditation text which was given to me when I was a boy is composed of three different sentences from three Upanishads. It has been the guiding light in my own spiritual path towards the attainment of inner freedom. At first it was only for recitation and its meaning was merely philological. With the growth and experience of life its deeper significance is being gradually unfolded to me. The text is:

Satyam Jnanam Anantam Brahma, Anandarupamamritam Yadvibhati; Shantam Shivam Advaitam. Brahma is Truth, He is Wisdom, He is infinite; He is revealed in deathless forms of Joy; He is peaceful, good; He is one.

We are born with the consciousness of one truth which for us is the background of our knowledge of all truths. It is the truth about *myself* which consists of an inner reality having its outer manifestations. The manifestations can be proved and measured, but not the inner reality which gives them their unity. There have been some according to whom the diverse facts of the movements of *myself* areall that is real, and not the truth in me which is one. But for me, it does not require any help from logic for realizing the *satyam*, for proving the *One* which comprehends all the facts of my life and transcends them.

By the indwelling light of this truth I know that the world to which I belong, and which consists of endless series of movements, has its Truth which is one, and which gives reality to the innumerable facts of the universe. When we realise this Truth we have our joy, for in it we find the eternal harmony of our own reality...

[...]As individuals, each of us has the unity of a living organism, distinct in himself. As social beings we are parts of a complex organism called humanity.

---

23. In Ghosh, 2007, 2011, 6 February 1924, Vol 4, pp.493-498. This is an edited version of the full text.

As spiritual being we belong to a Reality which is *anandam* (Joy) which is love, which is all-comprehensive.

The individual living organism has its need and its faculties for self-preservation. In the education of man there should be room for training him for the perfect maintenance of his individual life. Otherwise not only does he become helpless but the faculties atrophy that are for his self-preservation, the exercise of which gives him the true enjoyment of life. Generally speaking, in our education this training of how to live our physical life is neglected; therefore we miss the *Shantam* (the peaceful) in the self-reliant freedom of a well organised existence.

The adjustment of our individual with our social life, and these with the vast life of man, needs for its training the spirit of mutual responsibility. In our educational institutions this hardly finds its place. The discipline of self-control and good behaviour is no doubt recognised, but the service of society requires information, experience and the exercise of a number of physical, moral and intellectual faculties. The result of such deficiency in our education we find everywhere in our surroundings in the form of poverty, disease, ignorance, feebleness of intellect and will, and also in that aggressive spirit of egotism and self-assertion, associated with the cultivation of sectarianism, institutionalism and nationalism, that creates in the human world the worst form of dissension and spiritual blindness. Owing to this lack of training in sympathy, man suffers from that lack of true freedom in his social life which comes from a general welfare with a widespread atmosphere of mutual sympathy and co-operation.

I have said before that the world viewed as a mere external fact does not delight us; that unless we know that it has a fullness of reality for its background and foundation, our relation with it becomes merely utilitarian. When the conscious of our own spiritual being does not find its harmony in the universe it loses faith in itself and urges us to put all our resources into the pursuit of self-interest. Ordinarily our education does nothing to train our mind for realising our spiritual relationship with the supreme Truth. For want of this training we fail to develop the spirit of detachment which gives us that large atmosphere wherein our inner being finds its dwelling, and space and leisure for its fulfilment in creation. Our creations of science, philosophy, art and literature can have their fullness of growth only under this sky of detachment.

It is sometimes objected that such creations are mere abstractions. That may be so. But music is none the less valuable because of the fact that it is not the voice of concrete life. It grows apart from life's noises in its own disinterested realm of delight. By reason of that abstraction, that aloofness, it acquires the power to enrich life. Owing to its distance and freedom the vapour that forms clouds can send its rain back to earth, making its air sweet and soil fertile. Our knowledge, feelings and experience, at one stage of their progress, are abstracted from life, transported into the bosom of the eternal, and there purged of all that is non-essential, sent back to life with the velocity of new impact needed for the rousing of latent forces. The minds of those, who in the pursuit of immediate needs constantly cling close to the soil of life, grow dull. Mind in order to discover its freedom of outlook must soar into the upper air of abstraction, swim in the very heart of the infinite for the mere joy of it, and then come back to its world nest.

In all great civilisations there is the cycle of sending up the adventurous mind into the upper and wider space and then bringing it down back to solid ground. The solid earth is suffocated to death if it loses its atmosphere, indefinite and unsubstantial though it be, through which it must have its communication with air and light. So also must the human world have its atmosphere of detachment, which never has for its immediate object the production of necessities, but the function of giving life to the creations that express the unlimited in man in the province of his thought, emotion and will.

Our ideal should be to make ample provision in our bringing up for the development of our spiritual relationship with the Supreme Being which gives us freedom in all departments of life knowing full well that life divested of its consciousness of the infinite breeds only slavery in diverse forms under the appearance of liberty. Allow me to quote in this connection what I have said elsewhere while discussing my plan of an ideal Educational Institution:

The one abiding ideal in the religious life of India has been *Mukti*, the deliverance of man's soul from the grip of self, its communion with the Infinite Soul through its union in *ananda* with the universe. This religion of spiritual harmony is not a theological doctrine to be taught, as a subject in the class, for half an hour each day. It is the spiritual truth and beauty of our attitude towards our surroundings, our conscious relationship with the Infinite, and the lasting power of the Eternal in the passing moments of our life. Such a religious idea can only be made possible by making provision for students to live in infinite touch with nature, daily to grow in an atmosphere of service offered to all creatures, tending trees, feeding birds and animals, learning to feel the immense mystery of the soil and water and air.

Along with this, there should be some common sharing of life with the tillers of the soil and the humble workers in the neighbouring villages; studying their crafts, inviting them to the feasts, joining them in works of co-operation for communal welfare; and in our intercourse we should be guided, not by moral maxims or the condescension of social superiority, but by natural sympathy of life for life, and by the sheer necessity of love's sacrifice for its own sake. In such an atmosphere students would learn to understand that humanity is a divine harp of many strings, waiting for its one grand music. Those who realise this unity are made ready for the pilgrimage through the night of suffering, and along the path of sacrifice, to the great meeting of Man in the future, for which the call comes to us across the darkness.

Life, in such a centre, should be simple and clean. We should never believe that simplicity of life might make us unsuited to the requirements of the society of our time. It is the simplicity of the tuning-fork, which is needed all the more because of the intricacy of strings in the instrument. In the morning of our career our nature needs the pure and the perfect note of a spiritual ideal in order to fit us for the complications of our later years.

In other words, this institution should be a perpetual creation by the cooperative enthusiasm of teachers and students growing with the growth of their soul; a world in itself, self-sustaining, independent, rich with ever-renewing life, radiating life across space and time, attracting and maintaining round it a planetary system of dependent bodies. Its aim should lie in imparting life-breath to the complete man, who is intellectual as well as economic, bound by social bonds, but aspiring towards spiritual freedom and final perfection.

Patrick Geddes on Education

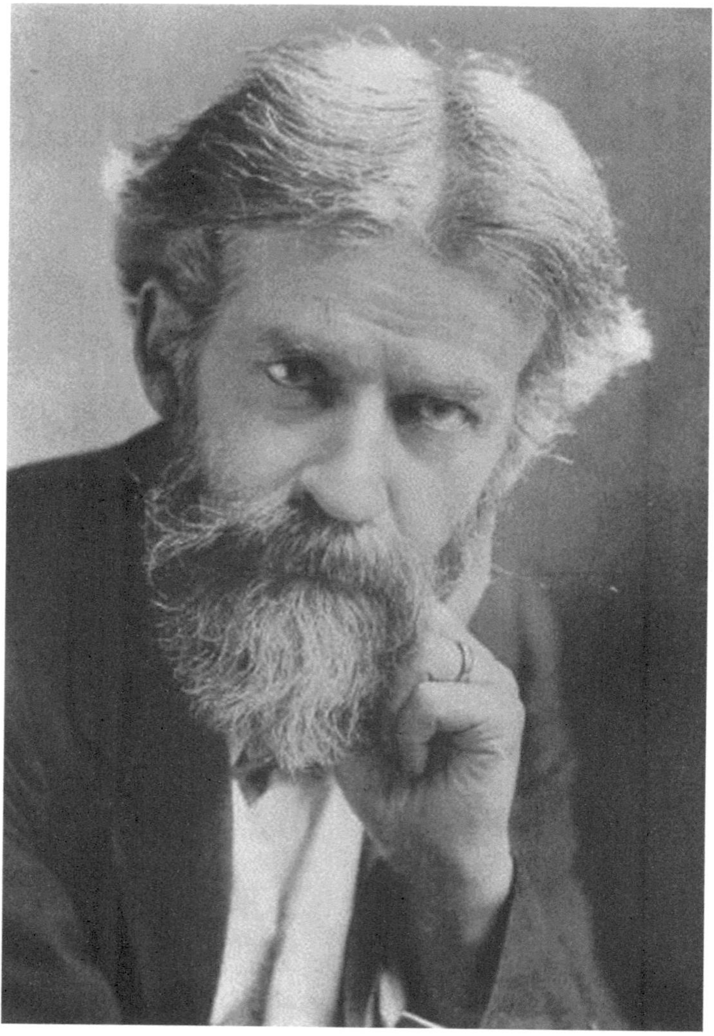

The World Without and the World Within (1905)[24]

HERE IS SUNDAY MORNING; and we can have a quiet hour together. What shall we do with it? What would you like? A lesson?

'No.'

'Yes. A Thinking Lesson.' Well, what shall we think about?

'What is Sunday?'

'What should people do with it?'

Suppose we try to understand some of the differences between week-days and Sunday? And since there are more week-days than Sundays, let us ask first, What do you do on them?

'Work, and play, and lessons.' Yes; mostly that. Play we know. What is work?

'What we do in the house and in the garden, and for our pets.'

'Yes, and basket-work.' And lessons?

'What we do at books and piano.'

Well, what we call work is in this every-day outer world, the 'Out-world', let us call it; while schools and lessons are meant at least to open up the thinking-world, the inner world – the 'In-world', let us say. Out-world and In-world thus make up our whole world; so let us enter them each in turn, and learn to travel in them both. For there have been two sorts of great travellers. First, of course, those who sail round the world, or climb higher and higher upon its mountain peaks, who venture farther into the icy North, deeper into the tropical forest than any who have gone before. Yet the other kind travel also, and that far further, in their chairs and in their dreams. For which has been the greater traveller – Nansen, or Shakespeare? Who has seen most – Sir John Murray from the deck of the world-circling 'Challenger', or blind Milton in his Paradise? Look up Keats' sonnet:-

> Oft have I travelled in the
> realms of gold,
> And many godly states and
> kingdoms seen –

You will see how the poet's world needs all the traveller's, yet englobes it. Both worlds then are well worth seeing – yet 'we only see what we bring the means of seeing'. Hitherto education has been too often trying to fit people to live mostly in the one world or in the other; seldom in both. That is how in old days it formed the soldier or the monk; and how nowadays it trains

---

24. Patrick Geddes, *The World Without and the World Within: Sunday Talks with my Children* (Bournville: St. George Press and London: George Allen, 1905) Part 1 pp.1-21.

the man of business or the student. But the true, the complete education, the coming education – yours, therefore, I hope in some measure – must fit for both; its educated man will again be like the Admirable Crichton, in the picture you know, standing with book and sword in either hand, and with his eyes looking forward above them both, resolute yet serene.

First, then, the Out-world: What do we know about that? Out we go from home and garden, through village and town, country and city; over the Border and beyond the Channel; and when we have travelled Europe, Asia, and Africa, America and Australia are still to see.

Next the In-world. This has never been seen with bodily eye, yet is no imaginary world for all that. In a very true and thorough sense it is more familiar, more real than the other; for all we know, or can ever know of the Out-world, or of each other, is in our minds. 'I think, therefore I am', said a great philosopher long ago; while another is famous for having puzzled people by seeming to deny that there was any matter at all. But when you think a little, you see something of what he meant – that all we know of matter is in mind.

In your Out-world, for instance the garden, what can you do in it? 'Work in it, and play in it.' Yes; but when play means simply ball, or hide and seek and run, the field and the lawn, the hedges and the wood would do better; indeed, they are what you mostly use. To *play* in the garden, as a garden – that is *with* a garden, and with what it gives you – takes a lot of looking at it, does it not? 'Yes, as we did this morning.' Quite so, watching still some late things grow, seeing the buds already formed, and finding here and there a green nose peeping, the last flowers opening – our friend the robin, too, not far away.

What do you do with me in the garden so often on week-day afternoons? 'We work; and on Sunday we rest and play.' Yes. Your Sunday in this sense is a real Sabbath. It ends the week. When we have laboured, then, like the Creator, we look around and see that it is very good.

What can we do with our garden beside working in it and looking at it? What becomes of the garden for you when we come in in the evening and pull down the blinds, or when you go to bed? 'We can still see it.' Yes, and again the sun shines, the flowers open, and the birds sing; all in some ways more beautifully than before. That is another sort of looking, is it not? The garden has come in with you; it is in your In-world now.

What else can we do about the garden? 'We can think about what we'll do next; and design and plan.' Yes; you remember, for instance, how we looked at our garden early last spring, and saw it was very poor in bulbs, so we dreamed of it rich and bright with snowdrops, crocuses, and daffodils for another year. Then as autumn came on we planned how to arrange these. Gradually the plan developed in our heads, with its patches of white and lines of gold, with its circles and groups of varied colours, its dotting over the lawns and its massing under the trees. And so we planted them, and in spring they will begin to come. Indeed, they are already coming; scrape away a little earth, and you see there is the crocus-bud piercing its way already.

Here you see is a whole circle of operations, which we may put down in its two halves, and still better in its four quarters:

Out-world	1	4	Facts	Acts
In-world	2	3	Memories	Plans

First, the outer world we see; second, the inner world we remember. But we are not content merely with seeing nor with remembering: we went deeper into the In-world. We made a new step in this when we began actively thinking and planning; and then in carrying out our plan we came back into the Out-world once more. So with this coming Spring the new garden-scene you have prepared will begin for you. You see the need then of being able to live and be active in the In-world as well as the Out-world; not merely to dream there, but to be awake and all alive, if you ever mean to do anything. From the hard World of Facts to the no less real World of Acts, you can only travel by this In-world way. In school (and in college too) we stay too much, I think, in its first division – the second of our fourfold scheme. So my thinking lessons are largely intended to help you on into the next, the third. From this is the true way up into the world of action again: those who stay behind, in the house of memory, may become more and more learned, but they will never do very much. That, in fact, is what is wrong with too many educated people; that is why they feel paralysed, and can neither speak nor act though the occasion calls.

Some people are rich in one world, some in the other. Everybody who is great in history has been rich in one or other way, or both. Sometimes people have great extremes between their two worlds. Not so many years ago we used to hear of a king who was enormously rich, and who was always building new castles, planting forests, laying out pleasure grounds and lakes. He had beautiful horses, splendid feasts and pageants, the greatest musician in the world, and the finest singers, sometimes all to himself. Yet this poor King went out of his mind (perhaps always thinking of himself alone had something to do with that – I believe it generally has); anyhow, one day he was found drowned in his lake. His Out-world was rich and beautiful; but in his inner world – once rich also – he had become poor: in that way many a kingship has ended sadly.

Now remember your *Pilgrim's Progress*. 'A splendid book!' Yes, indeed. From the Slough of Despond to the Delectable Mountains, from the Valley of the Shadow of Death to the Celestial City – no explorer of the Out-world has ever ranged so far as that. Yet this traveller, who was his own Pilgrim, was all the time in a dingy, dirty, little jail, in a dull little country town. He had not even leisure from hard work to read, or often to write; for he had to earn his own living by making shoelaces: yet he travelled all the time. Another of the great travellers in this kind of In-world – that of the poet-saints (when we don't understand them we call them 'mystics') – was a poor cobbler, who had always stuck to his last – one Jacob Behmen[25] – who to many has seemed the great prose poet of all the religious world. So Mohammed went farther than in any of his long caravan journeys across the deserts – sometimes as far as the seventh heaven: and Dante found his way there too, and, by a longer road, all the way through Hell and Purgatory.

In this way you see there are not simply 'rich' and 'poor'. There are some who are poor in the midst of riches, the poor Rich. Happily also there are some rich people of the right sort, the rich Rich; rich as we should all like to be; as, indeed, so far we are with our garden and the wood and water beyond to look at; and as every year's work may more and more make us.

Happily, also, there are rich Poor men like Bunyan; although, alas, the poor Poor are everywhere too common. In the same way you can think out for yourselves the strong and the weak, the great and the small, in the Out-world and the In-world of both ranks. And then the idea: - that is, what you would most like – the best of all – what is it? You would wish to be strong, beautiful, rich in all, if you would not be poor, weak, ugly. How are we to think out and realise these first? how avoid the second?

Read in the story of St. Peter how the angel took him out of prison. That angel is ready to come for anyone who can call him in the right way. And were I in prison, though I do not say I know St. Peter's secret, I would make thinking-ladders of my prison-bars, and so climb away up into the skies of thought, and away down into its strange dim depths, where no jailer, himself a prisoner, could ever follow. For it is literally true that

> 'Stone walls do not a prison make,
> Nor iron bars a cage.'

Some day I must tell you how I first learned this, and found out for myself how to make thinking-machines – (inventors will come to these after flying-machines – they are a better sort), in weary months of literal darkness, to which I now look back as the worst yet best experience of life.

You know parents are anxious to do their best for their children. Some work hard and save money to leave to them when they die; and others give their children what is called 'a good education', generally when they are almost grown up. Others are more inclined to give them a good time when they are

---

25. Also known as Jakob Boehme.

young, to help them to have an Out-world to live in and work in, and an In-world to think in with the best. And this is what your mother and I want for you. Even though we shall some of these days have to leave this bonny garden, and go back and live in town, you will be able to take it with you in your In-world more fully than we older ones can do. The garden that has made my life what it is, is my father's garden – the one I lived in as a boy. This one, much bigger, much nicer though it really is – much though I value and enjoy it, can never be the same to me – it can never mean half what that did. Make the most of this one then while you can a – happy world complete in all the four quarters; that is, lovely in sight, and therefore bright in memory; yet brighter still in the hope and the purpose of the coming year; then glorious again in its assured fulfilment.

You know the ten commandments, and the eleventh. Yet long before there was need for ten, there was one; and after these and the eleventh it remains also. What was that? 'To dress the garden and keep it' – *Il faut cultiver son jardin.*' This, too, is a commandment with promise – to the gardener the happiest of promises. 'Whatsoever a man soweth, that shall he also reap.' Town-bred parsons, and their people too, seem generally to think this a curse; and no doubt when one has sown the wrong thing it is so – and the most terrible – that which includes all others; yet I want you to remember it in its elementary practical sense as the most assured of blessings; as true alike for daily bread and for higher life, for Out-world and for In-world both.

So much for Out and In-world; now 'growing bigger', 'growing up', 'being educated' – what is that? At any rate, what should it be? 'Learning to be more at home in them both' – 'in them all four.'

Recall the Camera Obscura, where you have been so often. What does it show you? 'Picture of the Out-world.' And the little curtained cell beside it, empty of everything but a single low high-backed chair, and with no windows to look out of, only a light from the roof – what is that? 'A way into the In-world.' From the high garden, or from one of your tree-top castles, you look out upon everything, you see for miles and miles; but in your dark little caves in the ivy-bank you can sit and dream. Up in your tree-castle you often sit dreaming, of course; and from your hidden cave, through its ivy curtain, you love to peep; still, in the main, one is the Out-World's Watch-tower, the other the In-world's Gate.

You wonder sometimes why so many grown-ups look unhappy? There are many reasons no doubt; but one great reason is that too many have fallen from the first of these, or have lost their way to the other.

The Fifth Talk from my Outlook Tower: Our City of Thought[26]

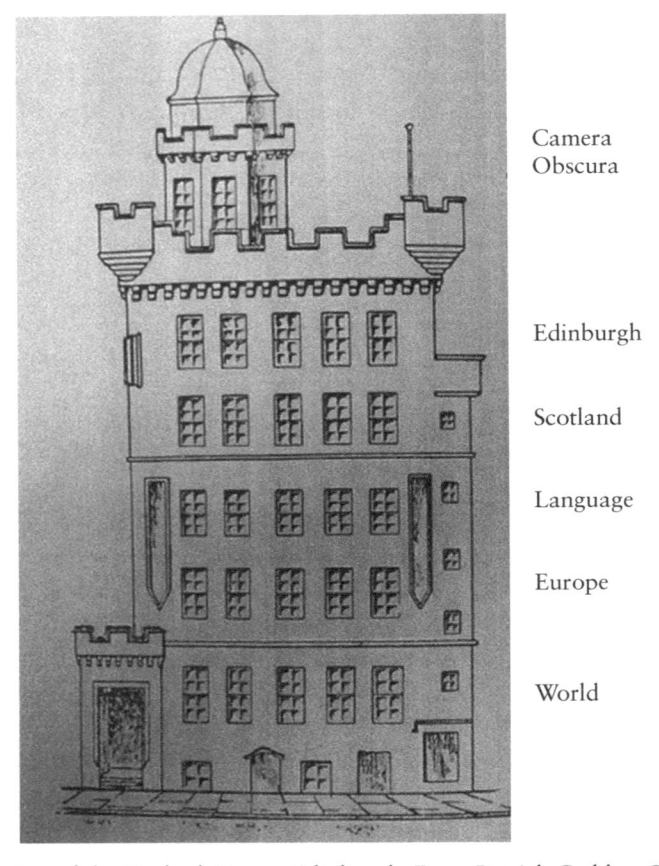

Diagrammatic elevation of the Outlook Tower, Edinburgh. From Patrick Geddes, *Cities in Evolution* (London: Williams & Norgate, 1915). Courtesy of the New York Public Library.

The venerable profession of the church, though we may trace its pastoral origins, nowadays thinks of these in a very abstract, and even metaphorical sense. So the law, with its parchment records of land-tenure, and crop-dues, etc. has similarly risen in the social scale far above the original farmer. These two leading faculties of our universities have long acquired their patrician status, with freedom from contamination by the vulgarities of 'mere labor.' The medical profession, as harbinger of the scientists, has been longer and

---

26. Patrick Geddes, *Our City of Thought (No. 5 in Talks from my Outlook Tower)* in M. Stalley, *Patrick Geddes: Spokesman for Man & Environment*, Rutgers University Press, 1972) pp. 349-364.

slower in obtaining its third place in precedence; since 'leech-craft' is after all a plebeian sort of work; pharmacy, with its herbs and salts, is only a remove or two from the soil; and the surgeon long lagged behind all these, as but late relieved of his humble original task, of barber.

Science, the youngest of studies, and until lately the least prosecuted, is hardly yet considered of full professional status. On the whole its votaries still seem plebeian; and they look so because they are so; since for the most part we are skilled artisans, men of our hands. For with these organs we have to do our experiments: and thus we dirty them – instead of voicing the high discourse of the really dignified professions, with gestures decently robed, and these with hands of the whitest. Still, as we have shown at times a certain efficiency in 'delivering the goods' – and these fresh and new ones, sometimes of value even to our 'pecuniary culture' – the status of the pioneers of science has in the last generation or two been rising.

I

Thus – though to the horror of 'Society' – Kelvin and Lister in time became heard of by respectable Londoners, as new 'Lords'; a little lower than the brewers, of course, but Lords anyhow. Educated Londoners (for there are such), knew of them as successive Presidents of the Royal Society. Their colleagues in that society, and in the university, knew of them as a professor of Physics and of Surgery respectively. But to the plebeian eye of the occupational sociologist, Kelvin becomes more intelligible than in any of these descriptions, as the first-rate Glasgow mechanic who was able to continue the job of instrument-maker, which was occupied in the same university and department two generations before by James Watt. Only this new man was even more skilled with electrical devices than was his predecessor with steamy ones. And then, recalling him to memory yet more closely, as the very type of the worthy old Glasgow mechanic in his Sunday clothes, we see him also as the modern avatar of the great god Hephaestus; as Vulcan, striking new sparks from his mighty forge: and also limping along somewhat lamed by his toil – thus true to the very life. Watt himself was indeed avatar of Prometheus, again bringing new, and dangerous as well as invaluable powers.

So now Lister. Relieving him successively of peer's robes, president's mace, and professor's gown, we have the good old Quaker surgeon. Getting him out of his long frock-coat, we have a look at him as barber – indeed of the record 'clean shave.' See him next with apron off, he is now 'the shepherd with his tar-box by his side' of old English pastoral poetry; and indeed of immemorial and worldwide practice. For when the sheep has had a scratch, and the blowflies lay their eggs in it, and the maggots have hatched and begin to eat the living flesh (so that the poor creature goes off its feed in agony), the noticing shepherd brushes the maggots off, dips his finger or stick in his little tarpot, and covers the sore spot; whereupon the sheep is peacefully browsing again in quarter of an hour. That is the elemental and central usage of antiseptic surgery, little though modern townsfolk may remember it, or much else of rural life and significance.

But Lister had chemical knowledge of his stuff; hence his carbolic acid, an extract of tar; and also microscopic knowledge of the infecting germs, smaller than maggots, and incomparably deadlier. This latter he learned from his father, a handyman at fixing up two spectacle-glasses to multiply one another as an 'eye-piece,' and two more or so near the object, as an 'objective', the two bits of apparatus being conveniently held in a tube, and then known as a microscope. Of this old Lister was one of the notable improvers.

Meantime too, a keen youth, the son of a village tanner in the Jura (a very low-caste job, in India in fact quite 'untouchable') had been puzzling to understand how oak-bark on hides prevented their decay – in fact, was literally anti-septic. Microscopic germs had already been discovered in decaying things; and he pondered and studied these. He saw that you might either kill the germs by antiseptics, and so prevent decay; or – better still, though more difficult try to keep out germs altogether; in which case no putrefaction would occur. Besides thus thinking out the practice of his tanner father, he essayed kindred experiments on his own; and having evidently had a tidy mother, with 'an eye for dirt', he went into the milk-house, and the cheese-making, and the baking, and the brewing; and by and by, the wine-making too – in fact all round these homely arts – henceforth revolutionized and purified throughout the world. Then, too, he found out how to clean up silk-worms, and get rid of their disease – so saving a main French industry, though he overworked himself into a paralytic seizure with that. But he pulled himself together, and went on, with a big experimental sort of tannery and germ-testing place, since called the Pasteur Institute, and next reproduced over the world. Among all these rural endeavors he had an indirect adventure with a mad dog: for he saved the man the dog bit, and next others. In course of all this, he started many younger workers, of whom not a few have also done illustriously; none more than the before-mentioned young surgeon, who specialized upon the human wound. Before that the frequent surgeon's story was that 'the operation was successful, but the patient died': while hospitals, especially maternity hospitals, with all their skill and care, had a far bigger death-rate than patients left in the slums. But Lister put an end to all that, as the world knows.

Knows, yes, but how tardily! The story is worth recalling, as full of significance, for the psychological survey of cities. First, let me preface it by another, one of James Watt, whose Birmingham firm only got to the point of selling its first engine twenty years after he had invented it. So very naturally, this enterprising and tenacious firm went bankrupt. There was the usual meeting of creditors, first valuing buildings, real estate, and materials.

Coming to the firm's patents, the lawyer-person began, 'Patent for – for what – something called a 'steam-engine!' What's that? What value am I to assign?' At once spoke out the practical man (true to his type in every generation). 'Yah! Put it down at a farthing!' And so, accordingly, this supreme and central invention of modern times was put down at one farthing – half a cent; and thus, we may presume, the firm by and by was able to buy it back again.

And if it be supposed that such 'practical' minds are no longer so sure of themselves, I may here recall the '*Daily Mail*,' a chief 'organ' of London mentality, so long, widely and deeply depressed by and to the level of its chief newsboy, one Harmsworth, alias Lord Northcliffe, whose professional boast was 'I buy paper, and sell it – inked!' It may be remembered that Marconi's first wireless message across the Atlantic, yielded only the letter S – 'Yah – what's the use of signalling S?' was the substance of next morning's press comment; not seeing that to get anything across at all was the main solution of Marconi's problem; so that he might get T and more across on the morrow, which of course he did.

Return now to Lister's struggle. Like many another good apprentice before him, he had married the daughter of his master, Syme, then the greatest surgeon of his day; and who, though he loved him as son-in-law, never could quite bring himself to believe the boy much of a surgeon (and of course so far truly, for as an operator Lister was but as others). After various fights, however, he got the hospital clean, and showed healings which silenced his local critics; indeed, soon converted them to followers. London surgeons, however, for a time continued to have nothing to do with 'the Scotch fad', as they called it; but Pasteur sent him a bright young military surgeon for a pupil. On 4th July 1870, there came for this last a telegram, 'War declared – return for the front'. Before taking the night train southward for Paris, the young surgeon spent the day in buying up all the carbolic acid and dressings he could take with him, and on the second day he proudly reported himself to his Surgeon-General with his life-saving burden. 'Bah! What's this!' railed his military superior. 'Nonsense – send it back to Paris!' So back it all went; thus condemning untold number of wounded soldiers to die of rotten wounds in the good old-fashioned way. Thirty years later, to the Boer War (with its colossal mortality, not from Boers' bullets, but from germs of all kinds) an experienced London surgeon was sent out at length, whose report was that the army's stock of surgical appliances was only in place in an archaeological museum. (The British volunteers, perhaps more fortunate, got no appliances at all.) It was not until the Russo-Japanese war a few years later that the work of Pasteur and Lister took root in military practice and then, thanks to Oriental hands. The Japanese soldiers not only had a bath before each battle, but washed their shirts as well, and so got clean wounds, easily dressed; but the poor Russians still went in dirty, and got germ-laden wounds accordingly, and these mostly left undressed – a potent factor in the result we know. So the late Great War was really the first in which ordinary skill of antiseptics and bacteriology was in use by all combatants.

So slow is it for a scientific advance to make head against the self-satisfied stupefactions of habit and routine. 'Practical' has thus become a word commonly used to boast the absence of that very occupational knowledge, and courage of application, from which it is derived. A new idea, when of any large complexity or breadth of application, but without alluring economic return, generally needs about a generation-length to work its way into the great world's practice.

Last of all, Lister has left to his old University his portrait and his honors, henceforth a glory of Edinburgh. Some day however, we shall make from this portrait a stained glass window – of this old Quaker saint of his great craft, and with its gentlest old patriarchal face – that of a good shepherd indeed.

II

But – returning to the hard struggle of new ideas or methods – it is rather in the social and political field that mental conductivity is most sluggish, even in our would- be progressive West. Thus the amazing candour, not to say brutality, of General Bernhardi and his fellows, before, during and after 1914, can only be explained or understood as their vigorous re-statement of the doctrine of survival, in struggle for existence, and at its very crudest – the Darwinism of 1860, and too long surviving. The subsequent outbursts of bolshevism in Russia must also be seen not as any sudden and new spectre, but as the tardy coming into power of ardent disciples of Karl Marx, a thinker of much the same time. Or again, everyone in the West has heard of Gandhi; and mostly of his leadership along new and revolutionary lines. When you come to know him, however, the strata of his ideology are plainly exposed. His ancient idealism and asceticism, and his deep respect for life is all rooted in his religion of Jainism, as old as Buddhism itself, viz. six centuries B.C. But what are the characteristic ideas he has expounded in his political career? Essentially four, and avowedly all western ones – (1) Mazzini's idealistic nationalism, (2) Thoreau's simplification of life, (3) Ruskin's criticism of the machine industry and its money economics, and (4) Tolstoy's non-resistance. Much of course may be said for each and all these ideas, much indeed has been said; for each and all of them date essentially from the generation of 1830–1860. Their exponent has not expressed any ideas of later date, since none have appreciably impressed him.

Why then – as I often ask my countrymen in India- does he so alarm you, the powers that be? They cannot give the answer, though a simple one. For personal acquaintance with the mental outfit of the dominant British authorities in India at once reveals that their corresponding working set of ideas are those acquired at Oxford, etc, etc – from Burke's *Speeches on the French Revolution*, from Adam Smith's *Wealth of Nations*, and the like. Important ideas all but they are four generations back instead of only two, they naturally give Mr. Gandhi's an alarming air of novelty.

Here, then, is one of the historic viewpoints as yet too much unemployed in our contemporary social surveys. In a later article I shall exhibit the historic stratification of Edinburgh. Some of its social types date back a thousand years; yet none are as yet completely fossil. Their surviving representatives vary in number of course, but amount in all to an immense majority of its living population. This is of great interest to the social surveyor, thus to find in his city heirs of all the ages. But if he perchance dares to think of himself the while as in the foremost files of time, it is also well to realize that each of us is made up of many selves, dating from all periods, and certainly in various respects far from being up-to-date. Recalling our school days – {A Schoolboy's Bag and a City Pageant, February 1925}- we can now see that with our Euclid and our Grammar, we are still being 'kept in' at the University of Alexandria, sat three centuries B.C. the botanical systematist is proud of his continuity from Linnaeus in 1735, and with De Candolle and Robert Brown less than a century later; while the greater pride of the humanist is based on his far earlier loyalties. And since hardly any of us have mathematics enough really to follow Einstein, nor physics enough to feel at home in Madame Curie's laboratory or Professor Milliken's, it is manifest that, as regards the make-up and wording of the cosmic universe, we have not really got out of our earlier generation. At most we tolerate this succeeding one; at best congratulate it, on getting out of reach of our minds, arrested in our past, and too stiffened now to move on. Yet it is something for us to have acquired anything of such earlier heritage of science to which these later minds are now adding, and in their turn they are tolerant of us, though mainly helpful to their successors. This is no mere 'academic' discussion, but clear disclosure to ourselves of the intellectual conditions of internal progress, in any society. History is no mere keeping of annals, it is more than the general philosophy of history which historians have long sought, and sociologists go on seeking, and it is far more too than all such tracings of occupational origins as we have attempted in these pages.

Hence then the profound importance, – and for every science, every art – of its historic search and scrutiny. Such is that of Dr. George Sarton of Harvard Library, with his Isis – a still too little known review of the history of science; or again of the kindred work of Dr. Singer at Oxford and London, and of the other few workers scattered elsewhere. For thus to clear up 'the filiation of ideas', throughout the past, is laying bare the true foundations on which we have to build today; and this whether as researchers adding to knowledge or as students acquiring it,

> The new age stands as yet
> Half-built against the sky;
> Open to every threat
> Of storms that clamor by,
> Scaffolding veils the walls,
> And dim dust floats and falls,
> As moving to and fro, their tasks the masons ply.

Only in the measure in which we can come to understand and know our way in this city of thought which humanity has ever been building, can we attain to any measure of peace in it. Such true peace is then seen as of no mere rest and breathing space, amid its internecine wars; but as of renewing effort more effective, because more continuous and more cooperative than heretofore; and towards constructive peace.

III

It is thus by no mere coincidence that another task which interrupts – and yet encourages – the writing of these articles should be that of preparing a report towards the advancement of International Intellectual Relations, for M. Bergson's committee of that name, called into being by the League of Nations. Take its urgent problem of international scientific bibliographies. The profusion of present growths of the tree of knowledge can only be kept clear if we deal with them in historic spirit, i.e., in relation to those branches of previous growth-periods from which all this present leafage has arisen. The technical method of tracing this filiation of knowledge is after all very simple. Given any great initiator, of any order of ideas – be this Harvey with his circulation of the blood; or Linnaeus with his classification of plants and animals, his System of nature; or again Watt with his steam-engine, or whom you will – we may on the one hand enquire into his precursors, and on the other into his continuators. Mere critics, and mere expositors and commentators, naturally drop out of memory, and may be left so: but among the continuators there arise from time to time new initiators: as after Harvey soon Hales, with his 'circulation of the sap' thus founding vegetable physiology; as after Linnaeus, the founders of the Natural System, at any rate less artificial; or again from Watt, Stephenson and many more, on to our modern motor and aeroplane industry engineers.

(1) Precursors, (2) Initiators, (3) Continuators: here then is the elemental rhythm of progress; and in wave after wave of advance; though often there are dormant periods, sometimes even between individual continuators, let alone between initiative growth-waves. For seasons seem often unfavorable.

Recall now from our opening article – as helpful to this conception of the growth of the tree of knowledge – the main historic periods indicated by our survey of the contents of the boy's school-bag: - the Primitive, Matriarchal, Patriarchal; the Greco-Roman, Medieval, Renaissance, the modern Industrial, Imperial, Financial. We at once see that our tree – be it viewed as of knowledge or of social life – cannot end here; and if so, that the good people around us (including ourselves, of course, in our everyday moods) who think of our present civilization and its ways and ideas as to any great degree established and permanent, must be more or less sound asleep. Yet next, conversely, we see that those who suppose such ways and ideas can be suddenly transmuted, – as by any mere change of government, be this of revolution or of reaction, or by any other specific panacea – must be more or less dreaming in their unobservant sleep. So there is nothing for it but to go on with our surveys of our tree, branch by branch, even leaf by leaf by leaf at times, and again of all these seen together as far as may be. But thus we are started upon what is the very essence of all research; a matter to which, as we have seen, the very schoolboy can in principle be initiated. We thus cannot much longer keep it out of school and training college courses, and only expect it from our few candidates for the doctorate in the universities.

To any botanist, interested also in human affairs, it is a very curious experience that he finds that those who think their world fixed and practically settled – be this for good or ill matters not – are always surprised by the question 'Have you ever seen the foliage, flower, and even fruit, of next year?' Their answer is in the negative. But there on the nearest apple tree, plain before their eyes, are the buds of next year, 'foliage-buds' and 'fruit-buds', too. A peep at a section through the microscope shows next year's leaves already forming, crowded upon their axis, which will so swiftly stretch out as the long leafy shoot next spring. Nor do we find that he of the converse revolutionary spirit is likely to have seen this either, for all his talk of 'change' and 'progress'. Comte, Spencer, Ward, and many later sociologists have all insisted on the necessity of biology as a preparation for sociology: but we have left this proposition too much in the abstract; so nothing gets done; public education sticks too much as it was until we adjust such specific biological and social observations, and interpret them in harmonious groupings, we cannot hope for adequate popularisation of either science, still less for a fuller understanding of life simpler and life more evolved; and of these throughout their growths and phases.

Again notice the living twig of the tree before us; and see how each leaf, however the worse for tear and wear, is none the less mothering its bud for next year. Thence visualize the tree, the orchard, the forest, and these throughout the wide world; thereafter do we not feel more emancipated from both the current rival schools, of revolution and of reaction? Aye, even seen them as life-blind quarrelers in the dark? And though this be also the winter of our discontent, shall we not all the more take courage in assured hopefulness of the returning spring?

IV

Let us observe root as well as branch of our tree of knowledge, and visualize the leaf-molds of earlier cultures, from which our advancement of learning draws its sap. Herein we find the key to the paradox that our review of the sciences bespeaks not only a return to nature, but the indispensable renewal of education, as truly classic.

Our generation's task has been too much merely that of emancipating ourselves, or at least our children, from the dead verbiage of Latin, of Greek, of Hebrew, entombed in dull pseudo-logical grammars, in pedantic commentaries and ponderous lexicons. We have too long gone to school to outworn pedants of the decay of the Renaissance, with their centuries of formal composition and verse-making, not a line of which has lived, since so few deserved to. Conversely, the truer scholars have been busy in the re-excavation and recovery of classic cities, in the re-appreciation of their art, the re-translation of their drama. Above all, we are recovering their essential secrets. Thus Hellenism, with all its mythologies, was poetizing the life of man at its fullest and brightest, so that the Olympians were types of the phases of life, and the Muses the moods of its spirit. These were the true immortals, latent anew in every child. Here then is social heritage, as true as any organic 'heredity'; since in our own human possibilities, yet more in those of our children, who may thus more fully live out their lives. For though in heredity, our ancestors deeply determine us, as to heritage we choose our ancestors. That indeed is what libraries and universities are for helping us to do.

So too our sociology will not much longer be content with mere 'consciousness of kind', mere 'herd-instincts', 'mob-impulses' or other pallid abstractions of modern democracy, too often at its weakest and worst. We see that it is the region and its villages, its towns, above all its true cities, that yield the essential and substantial material of social science; so we have to survey and interpret all these. (Hence The Survey!)

On what lines of interpretation? The developmental of course, the evolutionary; brushing aside therefore the pre-evolutionary psychology and economics still lingering in so many of the universities, yet also in other 'dark places of the earth,' as are too much also its business cities. For the writer this emancipation in youth from such debased mythologies was not merely from upbringing in nature, nor from Emerson, Ruskin and Carlyle, and the poets; but notably also through having to write, now some forty years ago, the article Parasitism (Animal) for the Britannica. With all the known kinds of parasites, innumerable loathsome forms, marshalled and reviewed, and seen as all more or less degenerates from better stocks, their interpretation stood out clear. What was the evil spell under which so many forms of life had fallen, and are falling still? How is it that their young so often look at first like those of ungenerate kindred, and may for a time seem as full of life and energy? Why does the bright eye fade, even disintegrate and vanish, leaving its owner in darkness? Why do the keen sensitive feelers vanish, the brain-ganglion stop growing, and go back almost to nothingness? And yet active growth, multiplication even thousand or million fold, yet only to an inert bag when life is matured and complete? Why? Because the creature has adopted the utilitarian philosophy, the very economic doctrine which my own professor of that truly dismal science had so clearly expounded to me a few years before. For what such parasites aim at, and obtain in practical perfection, is exactly that ample and perfect nutrition, that successful and rapid increase of population, that escape from toil, and into general ease of living, that perfect security and safety – exactly that 'progress' we have all so long been taught to strive for! Progress indeed, but whitherward? Into degeneracy.

In short there are species by thousands, even tens of thousands, which have thus completely anticipated our hedonistic psychology and our utilitarian economics. So correspondingly, these psychologists and economists, with their politicians of course to match, have essentially been formulating for their own species in modern times like the process of degeneracy: so their indices and tests of progress, their all-essential doctrine of 'happiness', turn out to be of the wrong sort. Since as classifiers of species of all kinds, we have to find names for them, what better – in all their varieties (capitalistic or socialistic here mattering little) than one which adds a single letter, for precision, to their own – Futilitarians!

What then is the real path of progress throughout the organic world? Most briefly, that illuminated by 'the bright eyes of danger', that which climbs up Hill Difficulty, instead of evading it. for such paths involve the active use of all the organs and activities that the other choice leaves passive, and thus decay. Nor this merely as regards survival; but also, and yet more significantly, progress is through the evolution and cooperation of the sexes, and this towards the life and care of offspring. Self-interest has no program of education, nor even any economy of resources for its successors. It leaves its more degraded but more candid representatives to say outright – 'What has posterity done for us, that we should care for posterity?' Is not that, for evolutionary biology – not to speak of sociology or morals – the supreme blasphemy, of Life?

The very word 'happiness' has been so degraded and abused that we now need other terms, and fuller concepts, to express the psychologic urge, and organic drive of being, the élan of life. Observe this in the highest class of beings, the Mammalia, distinguished not – as Futilitarians, and their politicians, so constantly think – by their masculine vigor of predation or of war, but essentially by the degree and development of their special character – and name – of mothering. This comes of no mere passive happiness, of safety and secured wellbeing – goal of our middle-class retired business men or their politicians, and their moderately endowed professors. It comes first of all through the impassioned ecstasy of sex, which no fears, much less insecurities, can restrain, and which is ever rising above survival-considerations altogether. It culminates in the agony of birth, greatest in our own most developed species, and so far seeming-increasing as it advances. It further gathers head in an unprecedented and also assuredly increasing time and toil, towards care of offspring. On this prolonged nurturing – as all mankind has ever seen, yet left to John Fiske to especially develop its significance – has turned the superior and continued evolution of man.

V

When we find in old writings – even though these may have lost their formal authority for many of us – the conception of a contrast – between life on one side as a broad and easy way of safety, prosperity, security, and on the other side as a narrow path of difficulty and danger towards quite contrasted ideals, high and hard to reach – we shall not go far wrong in identifying the former as an ancient, yet truly classic, delineation of arrest, degeneracy and parasitism; and the latter as portrayal, in the vivid terms of an earlier epoch, of ascending evolution, in which life functions at higher and higher levels, and at cost whatever efforts and pains of higher adaptation.

Such past hostility of science toward religious teachings as there has been was essentially with the claims which used to be put forward for these as final authorities, thus limiting our scientific freedom of enquiry into the world of nature and the says of man. We have resisted these claims of such guardians, and still do so; but when we thus find that the literature they cherish, has long ago anticipated our modern studies of life, in its evolutionary forking of alternative roads, we are bound to acknowledge their priority.

Let me affirm then, from a long lifetime's experience of the toils and joys of botanical, zoological and anthropological studies, that there is no more fascinating or fruitful field for evolutionary study than that of religion.[27] From the present naturalistic approach, this becomes nothing less than the interpretation of human life, in terms of the highest ideals its founders have attained, and their highest exponents could express. It hence becomes for us a comparative study of previous theories of evolution – not especially of organic evolution, nor in a world made in six days, but of psychological, social and moral evolution, illuminating us at every turn.

So when my Indian students of sociology ask me what to read, I say, Do not forget your own sacred books; but read carefully also those of other peoples and faiths. Though, as you know, I am not in the least here as a missionary to convert you, I must say I know of nothing in the literature of sociology to compare with the Hebrew (and Christian) Scriptures. For here (whatever else) you have a comparatively simple society, of an unusually gifted people, in a

---

27. Papers of the Conference on Living Religions of the Empire, Sociological Society of London University, 1924.

small region, given over essentially to agriculture, yet with growing towns of their own, and one amazing culture-City. Moreover all this region and city was surrounded throughout its history by the successive Great Powers of the past. Hence a literature of many kinds, from early patriarchal times onwards, to kingly and imperial. And thus not only records of priceless value for the chequered history of civilization, but more, reflections upon life by man successive thinkers, and at all levels, from the homeliest folk-wisdom in proverbial aphorisms, to the most penetrating and outspoken criticisms ever penned of all these forms and states of society, throughout their ups and downs, their deteriorations and renewals. Of such society then we have a presentment surpassing those of any other civilization. And beyond this not only a wealth of great poetry, but an idealisation of individual conduct, of family and social life, and of region and city, in the main unsurpassed elsewhere in the historic world. Indeed thus, with science, Re-religion is in the making. So –

> Stand up to critic science,
> Good Christian, Moslem, Jew!
> The things you read in Sacred Books
> (Long since revealed to you)
> In solemn and archaic tone,
> – Respond to in a reverent moan,
> On Sunday – Friday – Sat. –
> Though seldom brought outside for use
> Are capable of that!
> Throughout the rest of week, they're – true!!!
> – Clear Social Science, that!

VI

Now let us return to that correlation between the simple occupational life and its high scientific achievement with which we began: recall the belated entrance of the scientist to the full professional status of the church and the law; and his kinship to the manual worker, whom indeed he experimentally continues. Hence the fact is, that science and its researches can no more be produced by city institutions apart from the nature-contacts from which they arose, and on which they depend for continued life, than can roses by grown in flower vases. A zoological station like Wood's Hole, on Cape Cod – a real fishery-place – is thus more productive than can be college departments without it, and this in the proportion of direct first-hand contacts with the life of the sea. Thus the modest station of Roscoff in Brittany was in my time far more really educative than the magnificent and better known institution at Naples. For at Roscoff we roughed it as comrades, and went out to sea and shore, with sailor-fishermen, themselves true naturalists.

Consider, for example, with the critical eye of common sense, a great national and central educational British institution like the Royal School of Mines and Museum of Practical Geology. Where in common sense should that be situated? In the heart of a mining-centre, one would naturally say: like that of Freiberg in Saxony, surely not where no mining is, was or can be; and where nothing of geology in nature can ever again be seen. But this is to forget that 'Royal' indicates metropolitan, that 'Practical' here means administrative, hence its situation must be within radiance of these atmospheres! Thus we find it not even in suburban London, where they at least mine clay for bricks; but at the centre – Piccadilly! Thus too the Imperial Institute of Technology is located in a region purer of contamination from such toil than any other that could be found upon this Kingdom's map – South Kensington! Similarly, the 'Ecole des Mines' (LePlay's!) of France lies in the Boul' Mich'. And even the Ecole d'Agriculture in the great city too! And in the corresponding college of our own city, I am told today of written examinations in bee-keeping with certificates for those who have never kept them nor even experienced the first real lesson of a sting!

Despite the profound self-deception of the would-be 'practical men', who put such institutions in such supremely wrong places, it is only fair to say that they have not been entirely without fruit. Thus Huxley was first at Piccadilly, and then Kensington. Breadwinning gave him no option but to accept his situation at the museums, and to work at such picked specimens as could be brought there; but he none the less had had a great voyage of youth behind him. LePlay was head of the Ecole des Mines, but constantly through life escaped to travel widely, knowing all about mines and miners, from English Midlands to the Ural. Distinguished names such as these are then of service, to justify, to their founders, and their shrine-worshipping public, such institutional misplacements; while their amazingly small productivity of successors to such men is blamed on the 'poverty of average intelligence'. But such average is produced artificially, and by 'the systematic blighting of buds' – as my gentle colleague Arthur Thomson, who never uses 'strong language', so accurately calls it. Stanley Hall's *Adolescence* is here the decisive classic, which no proper bureaucrat dare read; since once for all identifying young life with the varied potentialities of genius; although, like all young buds, only too easily examined and averaged away.

If we would educate for the physical sciences, we must above all keep in touch with their most characteristic natural phenomena, the most convenient centres for their study, and the corresponding workshops of their applications. So too for the sciences of nature. Darwin's inveterate truancy, at school, at Edinburgh and at Cambridge, prepared him for his Naturalist's Voyage, and his subsequent interpretations of it. The statue of Audubon's leading rival or successor in American ornithology (Wilson), stands today in his native town of Paisley; but with an inscription decently omitting the essential point of his history – that he left for America to escape transportation to Australia, as the most inveterate of local 'poachers' – a term which is our only correct legal verbiage for ramblers and explorers.

The two Geikie brothers, our best-known British geologists of the past generation, learned their science from boyhood in free rambling on our Edinburgh hills, and later in field surveying; but none of it at the University. Though successively professors of geology at Edinburgh, and with admirable teaching powers and resources, they turned out graduates indeed, but none to compare with themselves. The supreme work of Lyell, his Principles of Geology, owes no debt to his school or college education; it was derived from the observation and interpretation of his own familiar home-region and boyish haunts along Arbroath cliffs and caves; and later developed by travel. And thus it was that Lyell became above all Darwin's acknowledged teacher of evolution throughout nature.

This theme might be extended indefinitely; and indeed it needs to be, at a time when great educational institutions are rivaling each other in setting up schools and institutes apart from the natural realities they are intended to investigate, and from the activities they are devised to carry farther. For while the present association holds firm – throughout English-speaking Universities especially – between the 'practical' administrators and the old bookish and verbal communicators of knowledge, and while they 'stand together, and keep faithful to our great academic traditions' – (of verbalistic empaperment above all things), the pious donors' contributions will continue to be safeguarded – as in the parable of the napkin.

Meantime, let the science student, who 'means business', go to nature, and to her occupations, for himself. If it had been money or position that he wanted, he should have sought them outside, in their relevant occupations. Having selected science, let him not then lose its realities for academic gains or status – after all so insignificantly small in comparison with the rewards of active life and in active thought.

VII

If our study is not in nature, of rocks, or forces, but like Ruskin's in Venice, of the stones and human significance of cities, then shall we need to set our laboratory on their High Street; yet with scan of their plains to hills and sweep of the valley section of their civilization. So we shall come in the succeeding article more particularly to this Outlook Tower in Edinburgh. But before taking up its work of civic interpretation for city people, let me in my next paper bring what I have said of regional and occupational education to the touchstone of everyday lives – those of two Scotsmen here – my son and myself; since each is an outcome of it.

The Education of Two Boys[28]

LET ME BEGIN with mis-education: hence another illustration from life on the sea – but this time from its modern passengers – well-to-do people, highly fed, and mostly with nothing to occupy their long days. As I write this on board ship, two young fellows come round, asking each and all of us to take our share in the day's sweepstake, the usual form of betting on the ship's run. The acceptance is general; so much so that they are surprised at my 'No, thank you.' Some passengers no doubt consent from social timidity, lest they seem to be outsiders; but most are keen, many intensely so, running the numbers at auction up to high prices. Here then is a good sample of the modern popularity of gambling.

Some tell me 'it is just human nature.' And others that they hope and mean to 'put it down by law.' But what are these contrasted views, but the current and customary poles of (pre-sociological) thought and action? Let us try first to 'see the thing as it is' – that is, 'how it grows' and then ask – 'what can be done?'

I

Look again at the Valley-section from snows to seas we have looked at together from this (or other) Outlook Tower – the river-course, and life-river of nature-occupations, from which the modern city draws its historic and present vocations. The miner's life is of peculiar uncertainty, and especially where precious metals are concerned. So too the hunter's; even the most skilled may come home with empty bag. Likewise the fisher, the mariner, has obviously throughout life this same experience, and with more extra kinds of risks and uncertainties than any other. So, notoriously, it is these three occupations that have most practised gambling; and this from simplest working people to their sporting, warlike or piratic, mercantile or financial chiefs – the 'gentlemen' of history and of to-day, and thus the makers of example, the setters of fashion. Yet it is not in the nature of the peasant to gamble be he poor or rich. Despite uncertainties of weather and seasonal return, his essential grasp of his work-process – as rationally and causally related to its results – steadies him. Similarly it is not in the nature of any constructive art, simple or fine; nor yet of any science; any more than of any orderly religion or philosophy – to gamble, in the preceding or any other

---

28. Patrick Geddes, *The Education of Two Boys* (No. 6 in *Talks from my Outlook Tower*) in M. Stalley, *Patrick Geddes: Spokesman for Man & Environment*, Rutgers University Press, 1972) pp 365-380.

way. Do some of our modern artists show exception to this? Too often, but only since they lost the regular employment of the middle ages and the renaissance, and fell into the modern chance-world, where 'selling pictures is an art like angling,' as a dealer said to me. 'Yes,' said my sculptor companion angrily – 'angling for fools!' Not a gambler, he. Gamblers at Monte Carlo often have mathematical dreamings; but mathematicians and physicists know better the orderliness of all things even of 'probabilities'. Geologists have to know all about mines, and they go among miners, even of gold; naturalists have largely to be hunters, even to all kinds of 'small deer', but they don't gamble; nor do botanists bet on finding flowers. This is not at all from any conscious virtue; it is simply because Goddess Fortune with her wheel does not interest minds set towards the search of Order, and thus steadily working on in faith of discerning this.

Law has usually prohibited lotteries, and done well; since the dream of 'getting rich quick', without effort or labor, but merely by the lucky turn of Fortune's wheel, so obviously demoralizes production that no moderately sane community can afford to encourage it. Still is it not the essential matter so to educate the young – through real participation in the *orderly* work of the world – as to be steeped in its causal order and result? For thus – and only thus – can the chance element – mostly speculated on in hours of idleness – be overpowered by the skill element; that which increasingly dominates the difficulties of a situation, and which strengthens character to self-reliance and responsibility. Hence – despite a London mostly daft on Derby Day, and thus surprised, beyond measure, when the Shah of Persia declined to go to the great race, naively yet wisely giving as his reason – 'But it is already known to me that one horse can run faster than another horse!' – there is no reason to despair of such sanity again becoming less exceptional.

Do we not see in all this a renewal of the frequent dilemma – shall we repress evils by law from without? – or check their development, within the mind, by bettered education and conditions? We are now the better able to cope with its two horns. For our occupational studies show that it is of the very nature of occupational reality to be at once fundamental (1) to all kinds of really effective law, and (2) all kinds of real education as well. We see the great sport of hunting, and how it may mould men into correspondingly warlike communities; and conversely, that such war-minded communities should give to their sports of all kinds a character of as warlike a rivalry as may be; and this alike for competing sides and champions. Similarly, we may trace the interest in the precious metals, as a profound and spreading (miner-) obsession throughout the ages, ranging from simplest washers and diggers to goldsmiths, bankers and financiers, from moneymakers to misers in all lands; and thus often culminant in their economists and statesmen; even to the ruin of their country, as with old Spain. Yet mineralogists and geologists, metallurgists too, who have searched for and handled such objects of treasure most intimately and closely of all men, are immune to this obsession.

The like experience may be incorporated into education; as I happen to know and definitely, because experimentally, first from my own childhood, with its real wealth of mineral treasures, though of little money value, and then from handing these on to my own and other children; with their eager quests for more, their ardent collection and gloating possession. When this is gone through, the later life is immunized; the mind has been as it were vaccinated; the 'catharsis' is successful. But where these pretty things are kept from children, while gold and jewels are treasured by their elders, the opposite inoculation, of dreams and desires, is provided. Witness the immense – and fatuous – popular literature, cinema shows (and thence press-news), which revolve around treasures and jewels, crimes for them, and detections, yet which only too faithfully mirror one of the main obsessions of our contemporary city world.

I am well aware that such an educational proposition as the above is commonly received with incredulity; but this does not affect the experimentalism of science, which can merely reply – Wait, suspend judgement, till you also have given such experiments fair trial. Moreover, the general conditions we see about us in our modern cities – and their jewel-shops, money-shops, and their appropriate literature – may be interpreted as the result of the very converse experiment, so long in progress upon whole generations, that of starving childhood of one of the most fascinating kinds of natural beauty at the right age for appreciating it, and thus providing for all manner of its obsessions and perversions later, called boarding-schools (or more accurately standardizing shops) – lapse necessarily, and to a serious extent, from the mammalian level, and its intelligence accordingly, since thus acquired in nature and needing to be developed in civilization.

This is not of course the place for an extended discussion of educational philosophies, old or new. What I have been leading up to has been simply a more intimate consideration of those values of regional surveys and occupational education which have been advanced in these articles. I have taken my well-to-do fellow passengers, engaged in killing time aboard ship, as so many loose ends of civilization, and to illustrate something of its present fabric. Throughout life I have been active in these two causes of surveys and occupations, and have sought not only to practise these, but to bring them together as warp and woof of our fresh educational weave. In retrospect I can set down their values more concretely and clearly than our previous more general discussions have permitted. You will forbear with me, therefore, in putting my two theses more personally than heretofore.

II

With varied outdoor interest, naturalistic and humanistic by turns or together, and voracious reading from childhood onwards, and at an historic school not worse than others in Scotland, and in some respects, at least mathematically, better than most – I can see that my main good fortune lay before school days in a home modest enough in ordinary ways, but with a large garden – ample fruit-bushes, apples and great old wild cherry trees, with vegetables mainly cared for by my father, and a fair variety of flowers, to which my mother was devoted. I trotted by turns after both; and thus learned to help, as also to climb, to take the robins, to keep pets and so on. A great landscape too from our hillside windows, of which the range 'from Birnam Wood to Dunsinane' was but a quarter, and even that not the finest; a landscape that stretched over city and river, plain and minor hills, to noble Highland peaks, clear-cut against the evening sky. Behind came the fields, and a pool and ditch, rich in insect-life and wild flowers, a brook further away. Then a bit of moor with wild roses and golden gorse, and in this moor a large deep quarry in a basalt-dike. Then a nobly wooded hill, with fine old fir-masses and beech glades, and lovely birches here and there between. Soon, too, a really glorious hill-top which, though only some 700 feet above the Tay and its rich alluvial plain widening downwards, broke into a long range of noble precipice, finer than any along the Rhine, and with a fresh southward hill-panorama, complemental to the westerly and northern ones of home. In the quarry there were quartz crystal masses to be found; and along the precipice and its screes of broken rock one could hunt for agates. Thus I had all the joys of treasure-finding, with growing adventurousness of climbing too, for year by year the cliffs whispered more clearly – no fear, go anywhere and do anything! Ferns too, in variety, could be brought back for shady nooks and corners in the garden, and rockeries built for them with the beautiful stones of quarry and cliffs. Thus I made my first botanic garden!

By the time I was ten or twelve, I was fully in my naturalist's life, and even at my buildings too, indeed with finer materials than I have ever had since, larger though the scale now be. From the corner of the hill nearest the city you could look down upon it, lying beautiful between its north and south 'Inches'. These were two large old parks, each (as the Gaelic name means) islanded between river and mill-streams, ascribed to Roman origin. Perth is still something of 'the Fair City' its folk have long called it, and from the rock-ridge across the river you look down into it, almost as on a map, say rather a relief-model in perspective. Below our hill-side home the river-mist would sometimes lie over and conceal it, in a long grey-white lake, with only the spires rising through – a scene the father would call us all out to see. And in scanning these two aspects of my home-city again in memory, I realize that there were the best of preparations a town-planner could desire; at ordinary times the precise observation of the city in details; yet at others the discernment of its old ideals, emergent above the mist of nature and the smoke of its working life.

School lessons came easy; a varied home library was soon devoured, and the public one also soaked in. Games were enjoyed, especially the combative, from inter-scholastic snow-fights to football; but cricket seemed slow, and golf intolerably old and grownup. My wanderlust was encouraged from infancy by rambles with my father – whom I still think of gratefully as the best of my teachers, for though he had little beyond ordinary knowledge, in any field, he was open to nature and landscape interest, and full of human interests as well. This developed with each year of increasing strength, and to a habit of long Saturday rambles with comrades – from four and six miles to eight, then ten, twelve, even fourteen out, and as many back. These gradually covered the district, alike for nature-studies, landscapes and historic interests; and with such contemporary life and doings as one could understand. At times, too, longer excursions with my father, notably as a small boy a visit of a few days to Edinburgh, with its impression of never-forgotten beauty, deeply determinant for later life; and later a sixteen, a fortnight of long tramping through the Dee and Spey Highlands, our ancestral region.

Why here these reminiscences? Not merely from senescence, and its reviving memory; but partly in response to a positive and repeated mandate from an authority neither writer nor reader dare question (– no – not even the Editor!) – no less than my old and honored friend Stanley Hall – so to his account be it debited! Moreover, these are first as an exhibit of the thesis which the Freudians have so widely diffused (though they seem as yet to have limited it too narrowly within their special field), that of the fundamental significance of early experiences and impressions upon later life. The objection may be made that all children are not so fortunate; and that is only too true, especially for our dominant industrial age. Yet various answers are possible; first that vivid experiences, even brief ones, leave their definite impress and impulse; and further, that as such child-psychology is realized, more truly educational opportunities, of access to nature and regional experience, can be arranged for. Indeed that we are now at the beginning of this better period, the Boy Scouts and Girl Guides show; and in their turn they will develop such opportunities for their own children far more fully. Yet who need delay doing more than at present?

III

Despite these happy conditions, a curious perversion arose in me about fifteen. It took the form of an outbreak of impish practical joking. In this my demon made me a ringleader infectious to others. Not merely did we make appalling turnip-lantern ghosts, or range bells and run away; we tied people's bells along a terrace to their door-handles on Saturday night, so that the more they pulled to open their doors to go to church, the more they were exasperated by feeling them held fast against them, and as if by some one ringing furiously with the other hand. Kitchen chimneys were neatly closed with sods, houses were barricaded in; a small disused cottage, belonging to a farmer who had resented our depredations on his turnip fields, was pulled down by us altogether. In these and other ways we came obviously within the search of the police, but we were cunning enough to vary localities and methods, and thus remain unsuspected. When poorer boys do such things and are caught, their state-education, into criminals proper, used to begun, and indeed it still too largely does; though American juvenile courts have of late years been arising with their more understanding discipline, and reacting usefully on European ones.

Yet the attack ended, as suddenly as it had come on, some two or three months after, thanks to 'expulsive power of a new affection' as one of our good old Scots theologians calls conversion. In this case, our conversion was to the new and frightful joys of experimental chemistry; for which – after our burning holes in carpets, and blackening all brass and silver utensils in the house, and with odors unendurable – the wise father (who had in previous years shelved me a disused porch as a museum) had an outdoor lean-to shed erected as laboratory; and with carpenter's bench as well. Temptations to mischief, and even in these new forms, did, at rare times, appear, but were now resisted; and soon after came an experience which ended them altogether, and gave a new constructive purpose which has lasted through life – that of going to a real joiner's workshop in the mornings of a summer term, and to the art-school later in the day, with evening in the laboratory.

Here of course were the needed occupational outlets: the mischief-making was but symptom of starvation of activity of 'the thinking hand'; for between school-week and Saturday rambles, my former child-gardening habits had mostly died down save for a later botanic garden spurt; indeed they lay dormant till it was again time to make a real botanic garden; when my childish and boyish one returned to me. So here arises the question whether juvenile courts have as yet gone far enough; and if it be not to farms, workshops, laboratories, gardens and art-schools that our delinquent youngsters should most satisfactorily be committed? And of course the more we can do this before offences begin, the better. The pest of 'ragging' in England, of 'hazing' in America is also explained as above, and may be treated on similar lines.

IV

Enough of these memories; now seen as fundamental to a later life, which has been and still is essentially the continuation of such young interests and activities. Yet their cumulative value came later, when there were three children to educate. Thanks primarily to my life-companion, at once of kindred interests yet also of complemental ones (notably of music and song), it was possible for us to have our own home-school, in which an aunt of rare teaching initiative and aptitude joined us, with her bright young niece for additional pupil. Three teachers to four children – two girls and two younger boys: so no one was overworked.

Were this an educational paper, I might discourse upon our schemes and endeavors at length. We had real daily work, efficient according to ages, in household and gardening; and we had varied play, not only of ordinary kinds, but with more of music and song, and more of acting plays, than usual; more also of excursions and nature studies through the seasons, with their 'beauty-feasts', as the children called them. Similarly, also, children's arts and crafts went on, largely at their own constructive discretion; and with drawing happily stimulated by John Duncan, a predecessor and peer of Cizek himself, in his encouragement of young creative powers. From Scottish ballads to English and French ones, and thus to their further literature, was a natural and easy transition; by and by a little Latin too, and in its still living tradition from a young Benedictine; in short pretty much the range of projects now to be found in schools widely distributed, but in those days seldom in evidence. We counted among our best examples Colonel Parker's work and Professor Dewey's early experimental school at Chicago, which we visited in 1899 and 1900, and found of real encouragement and stimulus.

The main points of this little home-school story besides music, song and acting, drawing too, et., lay in two characteristics, more than yet usual of regional survey; and much more than yet usual for occupational education.

The former is now becoming adopted by progressive schools, so that it need not be enlarged upon, save to note that for our older boy especially, his surveys gradually extended not only to fairly wide roaming and camping in Scotland, England and Ireland, with bicycle and little tent; but also the like through Belgium, and a good part of France. The world-experience which made Elisée Reclus the supreme geographer of day grew out of his youthful long and adventurous tramps with his brother Elie (also later illustrious) in crossing yearly between their home at Montauban near the Western Pyrenees, and their school at Neuwied, well up the Rhine. This sort of touring, at its simplest, is now reviving among the youth of Germany, in its poverty, much as in the old days of wandering students and apprentices.

Coming now to occupational education, as a main feature of our scheme and practice, this began not only in our country garden, but through survey for our young folks from the Outlook Tower, with its wide prospect of the Forth Valley Section from snows to sea, and with each and all the typical nature-occupations around. To come to know and take part in as much as possible of all this, their essential world, and as type for the great world also, was thus readily understood as the fundamental idea, and increasingly as a working ambition.

Of course our more respectable professional and business friends were wont to say to us – 'Very interesting, no doubt, this varied education and experience you are giving your young folks; but what will become of them when it comes to the struggle for existence?' To which we could only reply, 'Never fear for them; we are educating them for the future and real work in it. Our anxiety is all for your children; since you go on having them instructed in the past, and thus towards little later; the present at most.'

Thus to begin with the sea; our summer home used yearly to be on the Firth of Tay, opposite Dundee. A good sailor and fisherman took them out in his boat as often as might be, and taught both girl and boy all their years and strength admitted of rowing, sailing and steering; while both of course also learned to swim. Later, at 15 or so, the lad was ready to be Professor Arthur Thomson's laboratory-boy at the Zoological Station of Millport on the West Coast of Scotland and the girl a student; he also got a few weeks job as boy-cook on board a herring-boat on the East Coast, and roughed it accordingly. Another vacation he was dredge-boy on the Fisheries Steamer in the North Sea. In another year or so he had passed the examination of the national Lifeboat Association, for steersman of the lifeboat at one of the most dangerous points of coast; and at eighteen he was invited to join one of Dr. W. S. Bruce's many arctic explorations, this time for mapping a little-known region of Spitzbergen; and as at once assistant and factotum to the director of the Ordnance Survey who took charge. Next he got the first invitation to join the Stefansson Polar Expedition via Northern Canada; but to our relief he declined, as this was to be a four-years' business. His substitute – another of my practical student-youths – never returned, as one of the ships was lost. When the War was upon us, a navy commission was naturally offered him, and this in its Air Force – but was soon exchanged for the Army Balloon Corps, of which, as the most life-trained of its observers and organizers, he soon became 'the ace', and next its youngest major. The French government in 1917 sent the Legion of Honor two British airmen, the aeroplanist who had destroyed most enemy machines, and the balloonist who had searched out most batteries for destruction. This latter honor came however, to my son only on time for his comrades to lay upon his grave, for the day before he had been killed in action: and through leaving his sell(cell?)-hole of safety for his men.

That this highly evolved efficiency was no accidental 'talent' or 'ability', but largely the result of lifelong repeated experiences on and off the sea, was plainly manifest. Similarly the organizing power which went with it, and which had also gradually been developed out of child-responsibilities, as in our annual migrations from town to country. At three years old he was charged with looking after his own pet kitten and next year with doves and hens; but gradually these responsibilities increased, until at twelve he could and did conduct the whole migration of the family and all its chattels. As a youth came the Cities and Town Planning Exhibition – gallery-ranges of a half mile of crowded pictures, to be hung, arranged and explained in one city, and then packed and rehung properly in the next – Ghent and Dublin, Madras and Bombay, the exhibition at the two latter being renewed, his best energies contributing, after the destruction of the former on in the War.

But neither maritime nor city interests, though thus actively developed, were his main interest; but the rural occupations. Without having either actually mined, or hunted, but being from childhood familiar with minerals, rocks and fossils, and with animals both of land and sea, he quite naturally graduated at Edinburgh with honors, winning his fellowship as the first among the graduates of three years in geology and zoology, as also in botany. This last came almost as a matter of course, since he had been laboratory-boy, and garden-boy too, of that college department, almost from childhood, and summer after summer before more regular university studies began. He had had experience too, in vacations, both of farm labor and of intensive gardening. As a forester he was at once scientific and practical enough to be offered the assistantship to its professor, as well as a choice of three botanical appointments. Three geographical assistantships, in different universities, were also offered him, two town-planning assistantships, and curiously enough, the librarianship of the new Science Library. On my surprised protest to the education officer that he could not know books sufficiently, having had a life far more practical than studious, I was answered, 'Yes, that is why I want him: he knows what the books are for.'

All these invitations were unsought, and came during the month after graduation, at twenty-three. it may seem therefore that this must have been either a very able or a very arduous life; but no; simply a good all-round character, and a fair, but not exceptional mental ability; but clearly possessed of (and by) the idea of being at home upon the Valley Section from snows to sea – and thus from ski-running and glacier crossing to ship or life-boat. To learn a fresh occupation, from ploughing or shepherding to carpentering or stone-hewing, or to drawing and modelling, was to him a fresh game of life, full of interest as well as of strenuousness, filling him with a new exhilaration and joy of life, radiant too to others. All this went with the songs of labour, in Scotch, in Gaelic, in French and more; and with their dances too; for he had danced from childhood, not only as Highlander and as sailor, but up to the standard teaching of the Paris Opera. Thus he had danced his way through our masques, from primitive man, and as Pan in hoofs and horns complete, onwards to courtly minuet; while folk-music on bagpipes, art-music with cello, were alternating joys. Nothing for him was painfully acquired – 'got up' as separate 'subjects': but all by turns were felt as fresh modes and moods of life worth trying and mastering, and thus genially entered into. So in social intercourse, he was easy and natural with all sorts and conditions of men, from fore-castle to quarter-deck, from laboratory-boys to students and to professors, from scientific men to artist and poet, and from laborer's firesides to court-functions; and thence back again.

V

Here, then, were some of the justifications of such education which he unconsciously offered to the anxiously critical friends I have mentioned. When at length reassured as to the results in his case (and also for the others I have not mentioned), they then asked: 'But how could he find time for so many and varied experiences, all the way from country labors to city accomplishments?' Again the answer was obvious. Simply by cutting out (all but one – tried experimentally) of the usual years of penal servitude, in schools of conventional respectable futility, and thus escaping the verbalistic empaperment upon which we have for so many centuries been specializing, and in too many ways worse now than ever; and instead of all this, by going on learning by living and working, drawing or modelling, playing, singing, and dancing through good days, from childhood onwards; and so from happy (and thus good) boy to joyous youth, yet already effective man – Dionysiac and Apollonian in one.

In more concrete terms, however, this education for the opening future, while having in it the incentive and encouragement of American example with its freer change of occupation than in the old world, was also an endeavor beyond this; since one free from premature thoughts of personal economic interest, and from aims of conventional success, prosperity or position. More clearly still, it expressed that elimination of customary middle-class standards which the after-War is now in so many European countries so sternly effecting. It applied, first of all, to the realities of the skilled laboring existence; and these practically along its main range, to various degrees of attainment, but always to some real attainment; and not infrequently to a developed skill. It omitted entirely the trading, percentaging and profiteering phases, indeed it was protected from all the mentally stimulating, morally paralyzing, conventional contacts with the price-economy, the financial interests and so on, on which the middle classes, and their economists, have so long been making moral shipwreck, now in Europe so widely becoming material also. It was in short a preparation, indeed in no small degree, a beginning, of the education of the truly directive classes; and this not merely through a good many departments of higher education, but in the actual organizing work of life. Both rural and urban directive experiences were thus part of its process;

from those of forest, farm and garden to regional planning, from organizing a civic exhibition and explaining it, to something of city-planning itself. So too on sea, and in air in war – up to its pitiable final loss of this young life, like so many more.

Ours then was a scheme and method of education more distinctly designed and adjusted than is yet customary towards several distinct aims and issues. Its aim was not simply one of individual development, although this was not forgotten. We had indeed traditions like that of my old Perth school, and University of St. Andrews as sharers in the education of 'the Admirable Crichton' – that paragon of the renaissance ideal of scholar and gentleman, at home alike in thought or action, and ready at once with book or sword. No, we by no means neglected this individual aim; nor – correspondingly for our own time – the usual specialistic training. Rather he was trained in more sciences and more arts than is usual, but these were linked together in life. There was inspiring this mode of training the definite social enquiry and experimentally treated problem – How far is it possible to give youth a full and true experience of the life and labor of the people, yet also thence to prepare the needed leadership, at once efficiently constructive, and fully sympathetic? Not merely the one *or* the other; like capitalism in its traditional practice on one hand, or labor aspirations on the other; or yet philanthropic endeavor between. It is hence – and from kindred cases – submitted, that such lines of education are practicable, and efficient. If so, the times are plainly such that we cannot too soon be organizing them, and far more fully than as yet.

VI

Yet again the almost converse question arose at times – especially from critical friends devoted to the English public school system (now also seriously deteriorative to Scotland and especially devastating Edinburgh), with its simple, combative vigor, for personal and group spirit alike – 'Very nice, your boy, so gently educated, by ladies, in great part, and with young ladies largely too, but how will he stand the rough experience of life which he will have to face later? – how will he learn the needful courage?' To this the reply: – Your schools aim at precocifying physical courage, through mere football and the like; and at developing this, with group-spirit and so on, through the 'public opinion' of your schools. That is, your young barbarians, with all their physical courage, get it largely at the expense of moral courage; since your boys avowedly fear the opinion of the others, and so grow up standardized, as the young gentlemen we know, unaccustomed and even afraid to think for themselves, much less to take an independent course against current opinion and fashion. Whereas I want the moral courage first. Let this be sheltered, mothered and sistered, for it takes time and encouragement to form character;

and rough handling at this stage does mischief, as your schools and their products so commonly show. Moreover, recall from history how the fighting castes of the middle ages, and indeed of the renaissance too, served only when grown youths as squires, but before that, through boyhood they were ladies' pages; and this is the very regime we are deliberately repeating for our boys, however you and your schools fear it, even despise it, for yours. Who then is right? Permit reference to the facts of life and sex, in their actual biology and psychology, matters kept quite outside your curriculum. By that mingling of indifference, neglect and false shame you permit, even provoke, the very sex-evils, and too often even the devilries, which you then feebly deplore; or at most seek to check by athletic over-exertion, often disastrous through later life. Whereas as naturalists, with our flowers blooming, fruiting and seeding before the children, and their pet rabbits, fowls and the rest breeding properly too, we see and teach sex from the lily's purity; that is, naked and not ashamed; so we don't get the sex-morbidities of your schools to trouble over, and thus we don't need these over-trained athletics which are your only remedy or safeguard. Furthermore, the natural history of courage is that it arises and develops normally with sex, for the youth, therefore, it grows with the down upon his lip; and then there is no fear of it. Still in boyhood even, the boat, the sea, the crags, the horse, the camping and travel, are all truer trainings in courage than school fields can provide.

So again, while organizing an education for peace for my boys, free from the sports that kill, and even with increasing substitutes for those that play at killing, I faced the possibilities of war, and far more clearly than did those others, with all their militaristic schools. For since awakened in boyhood by the Franco-German War of 1870–71, I had been much in both countries; and have always seen new war coming, and even before this schooling-time the great War, in which we might all have to take part. So even for that, I called their sort of education ridiculously inefficient, (as per Boer War, for choice) with all its boasted 'playing-fields of Eton,' where Waterloo was not won, save in comparison with class-rooms more futile still. For my young geographers and geotects were not kept between a barrack called a 'schoolhouse' and its desert exercise-yard called a 'playground': but preparing to go anywhere and do anything; and to know where they were, and how to make the best of it.

In summary then, this line of education – essentially in and from and among the nature-occupations – is clearly to be distinguished from mere 'vocational training' and 'technical instruction', though even these two mechanized endeavors are doubtless a notable advance upon the verbalistic empaperment of the conventionally 'classical' schools, and still too prevalent among would-be modern ones. For mere vocationism is but accepting our towns as they are, our social and cultural order (or rather disorder) as it is, with its existing division of labor, and trying to fit young lives into this or that heading of its alphabetical list. Whereas, we are concerned with education proper; and this primarily through opening the elemental range of activity to each young life, which thus grows more effective, more vital indeed, with each increasing and extending span of action on environment. Therein arise the opportunities, there even appear the evolutionary perspectives – of well nigh each and all the arts, the sciences, the ideals also, of our civilization, past, present and possible. We share its manifold heritage, and continue it. We realize also the burdens of evils which also accompany these heritages, and thus prepare our successors more intelligently to combat and abate them.

Here in truth are vital beginnings of the moral substitutes for war, leading thus towards veritable campaigns of constructive peace, thus far beyond our mere modern 'peace', which is too much still but breathing-space, and latent war. By return to the working world in its healthiest and sanest, and thus most truly useful forms, we escape the long spiritual desolation, and despotism, of the utilitarian political economy, revolving mechanically round the price-system, and towards the statistical intelligence of a cash-register. The modern conflict between the capitalistic and the socialistic schools of thought is thus seen as too much but a quarrel round a money-box, and over the distribution of its contents: while the work opening before each young life appears as a fresh career in the real world outside, which is practically unknown to such mechanists and mammonists, – a world of regions and cities more worthy of their best past, and again advancing towards their bettered future.

I have outlined here the aims and methods of this little home school (indeed here for the first time, at any rate, so fully) because of its definite and purposive experimental endeavors; and this during years when not only Dewey, Stanley Hall, and other educational reformers were busy, but also when Thompson Seton with his 'Seton Indians', and Baden Powell with his 'Boy Scouts', were in their earlier phases of active initiative. It was thus encouraging to find ourselves so much in sympathy with them, and working on parallel lines. Although the experiment was but on the small scale of a single family, and thus naturally came to a close, it opened perspectives more clearly and socially defined than as yet by these larger educational organizations. So, after the War, and in our present breathing-space, I venture to recall them; and now leave them to such consideration as they may win.

The Notation of Life[29]

The Notation of Life (see diagram below) at first sight looks complex enough, with its 36 squares, but we can easily produce it by folding an ordinary sheet of double note-paper.

TAKE THIS DOUBLE SHEET of paper for our ledger of life; the left side is for the more passive aspects, or man shaped by place and his work, while the right side is for action; man guiding his daily life and remaking place. Now fold this ledger in half horizontally; we thus get four quarters, one for each of the main chambers of human life; the out-world both active and passive, and the in-world both passive and active. In each of these quarters belongs a nine-squared thinking machine, but before introducing them let us make clear the general structure and relationships of the chart. Here it is:

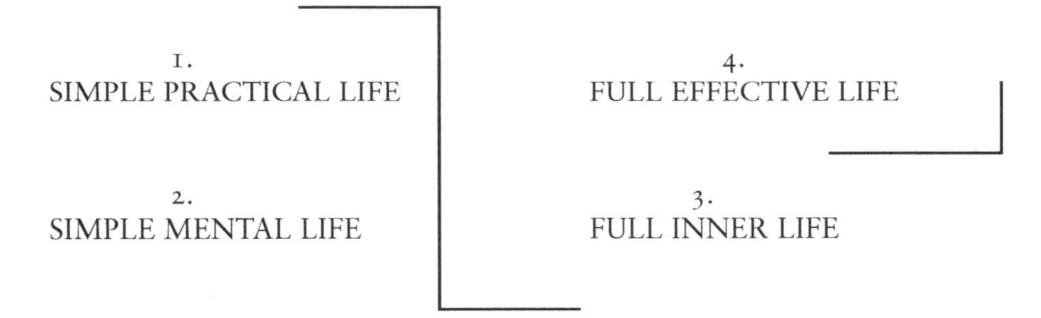

1. SIMPLE PRACTICAL LIFE	4. FULL EFFECTIVE LIFE
2. SIMPLE MENTAL LIFE	3. FULL INNER LIFE

The movement from one quarter to another corresponds to facts easily verifiable, for everyone in some degree goes through these four steps of life. How full and rich each step might be and ought to be will become apparent as we fill in the subdivisions of the main squares. But one further general observation. Where does the fourth quarter lead? To the first again, or a fifth if you prefer. That is, the world as remade by effective men of action becomes in turn the environment that shapes other men, stimulates their mental life, which in turn leads them on to change the world still further. Thus we may diagram the whole process of history, the succession of human generations by means of lines symbolising this unending interplay of the four parts of life. Thus also is it vividly shown how history both ever and never repeats itself.

---

29. *Edinburgh Review*, Patrick Geddes Special Issue, No. 88, Summer 1992, pp. 42-47

1. *Now let us start with the passive objective life of the upper left hand group of nine squares.*

Here the study of Place grows into Geography; that of Work into Economics; that of Folk into Anthropology. But these are commonly studies apart, or in separate squares, touching only at a point. Witness the separate Chairs and Institutes and Learned Societies of each name. But here we have to bring them into a living unison. Place studies without Work of Folk is a matter of atlases and maps. Folk without Place and Work are dead – hence anthropological collections and books contain too much of mere skulls and weapons. So too for economics, the study of Work, when apart from definite Place and definite Folk, comes down to mere abstractions.

But what do these side squares mean? Below our maps of Place we can now add pictures of the human Work-places, i.e., of field or factory; next of Folk-places of all kinds, from farmhouse or cottage in the country to homes or slums in the modern manufacturing town. Our geography is now fuller and our town planning of better Work-places, better Folk-places, can begin.

So again for Folk, Place-folk are natives or neighbours; and Work-folk are too familiar at all levels to need explanation. Our anthropology thus becomes living and humanised and surveys the living town.

Work too becomes clearer. For Place-work is a name for the 'natural advantages' which determine work of each kind at the right place for it; and Folk-work is our occupation, often tending to accumulate into a caste, not only in India.

Our geography, economics and anthropology are thus not simply enlarged and vivified; they are now united into a compact outline of Sociology.

From these three separate notes of life we thus get a central unified Chord of Life, with its minor chords as well.

We so far understand the simple village, the modern working town. But thus to unify geography, economics and anthropology is not enough. Social life has its mental side; so we must here call in the psychologist.

2. *Let us turn to the lower subjective group of squares.*
Sense, Experience, Feeling. Can we not relate these to Place, Work and Folk? Plainly enough. It is with our Senses that we come to know our environment, perceiving it and observing it. Our Feelings are obviously developed from our folk in earliest infancy by our mother's love and care. And our Experiences are primarily from our activities, of which our work is the predominant one.

Thus to the chord of Elemental and Objective Life in village and town, there now also exactly corresponds the elemental Chord of Subjective Life, and with this chord we must evidently play the same game of making nine squares as before.

THE NOTATION OF LIFE

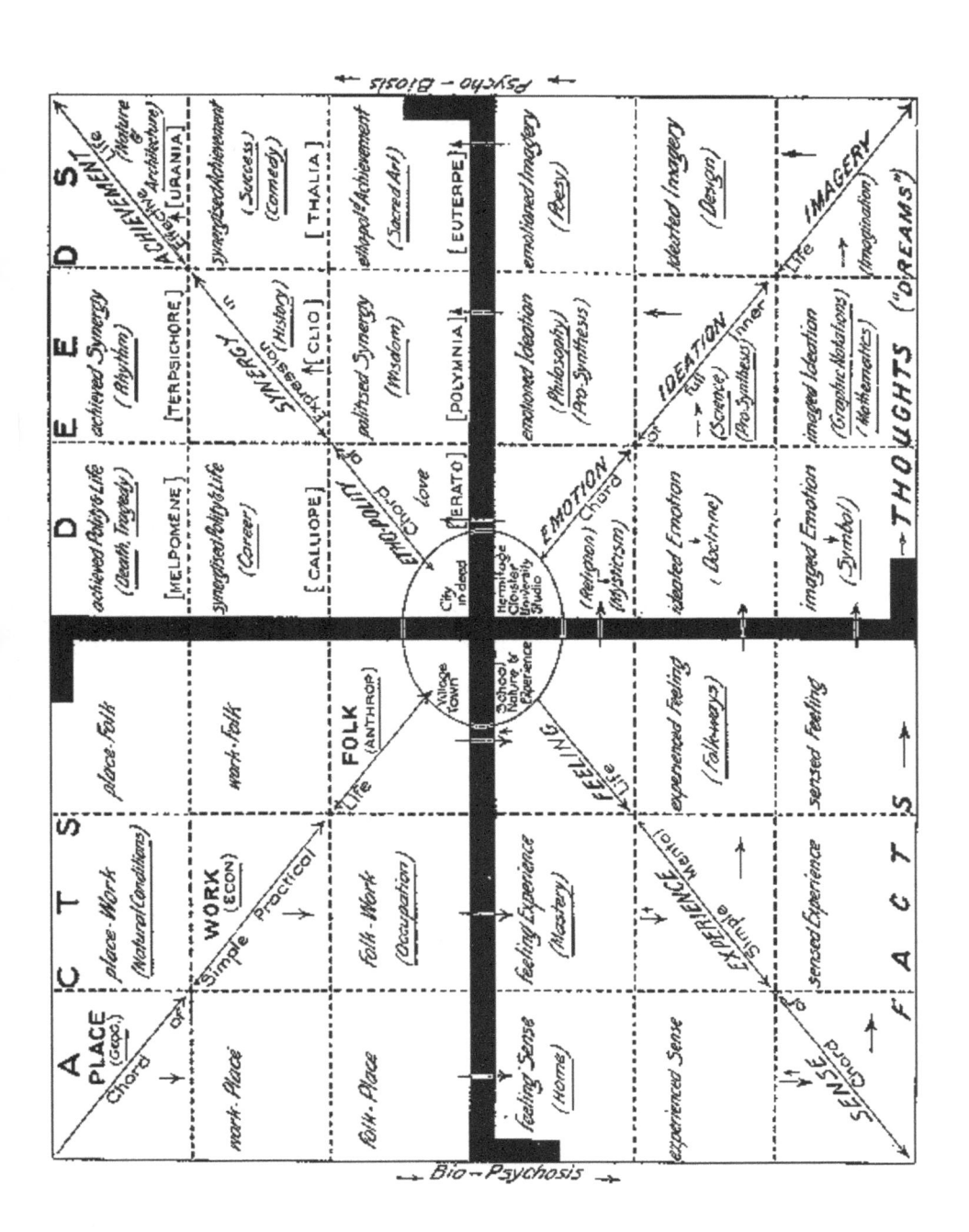

how can we go further? Can we penetrate into the world of imagination in which the simple natural sense impressions and activities, which all observers can agree on, are transmuted in each separate mind into its own imagining?

3. *Let us turn to the lower group of squares on the right hand side.*
How indeed has it come as it so often has done, through individual (and even social) history, to seek for the transcendent and divine, to reach all manner of mystic ecstasy? Without asking why, or even here considering exactly how, we must agree that all these three transmutations are desirable. From the present viewpoint, let us call them the three conversions, or, in more recent phrase, three sublimations: Emotion, Ideation, Imagination the essential Chord of the Inner Life.

Ideation of Emotion thought applied to the mystic ecstasy, to the deepest and the most fully human emotions from that process comes the Doctrine of each Faith, its Theology, its Idealism. But Ideation calls for Imagery, and this in every science, from geometry onwards, Mathematics, Physics, Chemistry have long had these notations and the historian condenses his annals into graphic 'rivers of time'. Thought of all kinds was first written in pictorial hieroglyphics, and it is from these that have come even the printed letters of this modern page.

So far then this cloister of thought with its ninefold quadrangles; and here for many, indeed most who enter it, the possibilities of human life seem to end. Yet from this varied cloister there are further doors; and these open out once more into the objective world though not back into the too simple everyday town-life we have long left. For though we have outlived these everyday Acts and Facts, and shaped our lives according to our highest Dreams, there comes at times the impulse to realise them in the world anew, as Deeds.

4. *So we turn to the last upper group of squares.*
Not every thought takes a form in action; but the psychologist is ever more assured that it at least points thither. With increasing clearness and interests, with increasing syntheses with other thoughts, ideas become emotionalised towards action. Synthesis in thought thus tends to collective action – to Synergy in deed: and Imagination concentrates itself to prefigure, for this Etho-Polity in Synergy, the corresponding Achievement which it may realise.

Here then is a new Chord of Life – that in which the subjective creates its objective counterpart. We thus leave the cloister. We are now out to re-shape the world anew, more near the heart's desire. Here then is the supreme Chord of Life and its resultant in Deed that is in fullest Life.

This is no small conclusion; that from the simplest chord of the Acts of everyday life, from the Facts of its ordinary experience, there may develop not only the deep chord of the inward life and Thought, but that also of life in Deed. And is it not now a strange – indeed a wholly unsought for but now evident – coincidence that, in this continuously reasoned presentment of life in everyday, modern scientific terms; first as geographic, economic, anthropological, next as psychological, elemental and developed; there should emerge this unexpected conclusion – that the Greeks of old knew all this before, and had thought it out to these same conclusions, albeit in their own nobler, more intuitive way. For our diagram next turns out to be that of Parnassus, the home of the nine Muses; and their very name and their symbolisms will be found to answer to the nine squares above, and to connect them with those below, and this more and more precisely as the scheme is studied. Not indeed that there are not one or two difficulties at first sight, but these can easily be cleared away by a little psychological and social reflection.[30]

---

30. Condensed from a paper written by Geddes when in India and quoted in *The Interpreter: Geddes,* by A. Defries, Routledge, 1927.

Scottish University Needs And Aims.[31]

THE OCCASIONS ON which a Professor has any opportunity of speaking to a wider public than that of his classroom are so rare, that I must be pardoned if, instead of endeavouring to make the sort of after-dinner speech which 'might best suit the present festal occasion', I deliver myself of some more serious thoughts which have long been in my mind. Moreover, the important change through our union with St. Andrews, which gives this the full position of a University seat, makes the present occasion one peculiarly suitable for the consideration of our Scottish university needs and aims.

Unpleasant Truths

Here again I am going to say some unpleasant truths such as people too rarely hear. But let me first urge in extenuation that I am not a candidate for political honours from the other side of the Tweed that I should repeat the usual cheap flatteries about our being the best educated and the most advanced people in the world, from whose country his own benighted land has still everything to learn; and then, like him, go home to London or Oxford laughing in my sleeve at people who can believe such things. On the contrary, I claim to be no less enthusiastic a Scotsman than any here, and with that patriotism too, which a man never feels so fully as when he has lived some thousand miles from home, but which does not shrink from honestly comparing the strong and weak sides of one's own people with those others. Historical studies do not as yet exist in Scotland. Hence we are divided between two exaggerations – one that of a legendary superiority in almost every conceivable respect to almost all conceivable people; the other of excessive self-depreciation, as if we had no nationality worth the name. But when we get down to the actual facts of the case we find one set of facts which do indeed gratify the national pride and even explain it; another set which no less deeply humbles that pride again.

Scotland Before the Age

The first set of facts, of which we are naturally proud, is afforded by the extraordinary number of marked and historic individualities whom for centuries we have sent forth in most (though not in all) departments of thought and action. Think of the Scottish missionaries at the very dawn of civilisation; the Scottish thinkers, whose names are still echoing down to us from the middle ages; think of the faithful and valiant allies of France, of

---

31. 'Scottish University Needs and Aims' University College, Dundee, Closing Address for 1889–90 and Scots Magazine Aug 1890 pp 3-15.

the soldiers of Gustavus Adolphus, or in later days of the conquerors and administrators of India. Or, taking the golden age of Scottish culture and influence, the last quarter of last century and the beginning of this, we see in Glasgow and Edinburgh the growing up of world-influences such as had never radiated from Scotland before. In Glasgow we see James Watt and Adam Smith, the initiators of that industrial movement which has transformed the world. In Edinburgh we see Hume, and Reid, and Stewart, philosophers towering in an age of giants; or Scott the enchanter not only awakening the past, but shaping half that has since been greatest in European Literature. We see our countrymen excelling in all forms of literature, from the lyric song of Burns to the burning prophecies of Carlyle. Nor in our own day are we without kinsmen in the foremost ranks of thought and action. So much, then, in justice to our national pride. We must not ignore, however, the historical facts which I said exist to humble it.

Scotland Behind the Age
Remember that history is a matter of great movements as well as of great men. Watch these movements of civilisation as they have flowed over the map of Europe. In the great Hebrew and Greek times it will, I trust, be freely admitted that we were practically nowhere; although so deep and ancient is our national vanity, that many a Highland name still bears witness how widespread was once the flattering tradition that our forebears were the Trojans. That Rome and civilisation touched us least and latest, and left us first is also unquestionable; that Christianity, too, despite the efforts of the Irish saints of Iona, was slow of coming, is also undenied. See how slowly civilisation penetrated to the Court of Dunfermline, Perth, or even Edinburgh; much less to the provincial townlets, to the great feudal baronies. The foundation of even the cathedrals, of the universities came slowly and late; so, too, did the introduction of printing. The learning of the Renaissance seems to have reached us slowly. Notoriously, too, our Scottish Reformation, however proud we may be of it, was a full generation behind that of England, as England in turn was behind Germany.

There are indeed few more continuous tragedies than this history of ours – the noblest of our ancestors in each century dying manfully for a dead cause, that of the ideas of the century before. At Flodden they fell for the faith their orphan sons were soon to forsake, at Dunbar for their false king, and at Culloden for a race of worn-out tyrants who had absconded nearly 60 years before. Or when, after all these lost battles, the modern age begins, culture and prosperity alike find their way but slowly over the border. Even with the largest discount for Johnson's obvious limitations and prejudices, it is hopeless to deny that general inferiority to England did exist upon which he so tiresomely harped. Our industrial prosperity, too, in almost every great town is one or two or even three whole generations newer and cruder; and our justly-boasted leadership in agriculture has been gained within the memory of living men. And when we have done something we go to sleep again. Witness the Edinburgh advocate living upon the literary and social glories of his guild two generations back; while from the city, which not so long ago was both the Weimar and the Leipzig of the English speaking peoples, the last great writer has long vanished, and the last publisher will doubtless soon have fled.

The general fact of history then is, that along with the strength and intensity of our individual types, of which we are so proud, we must also recognise the fact that all the great world-movements have reached us slowly. In short, our history may be summed up in this one sentence – that while the Scotsman has often led the age, Scotland has no less often lagged in it. All the great waves that echo round the world do indeed reach Ultima Thule[32] sooner or later, but generally later and sometimes weakened also.

Scotland and Germany

'But what has this to do with Scottish University needs and aims?' you ask me. Well, let us first fairly face the facts. The present University reform which we are all discussing is just a ripple of that wave of academic progress which began in Germany in 1809; and which out of a jumble of small, sleepy, hidebound, so-called Universities, essentially mere secondary schools, made the vast thought centres from which the world has ever since been learning. This new renaissance has followed the same laws as the old one. It took, indeed, forty years to reach England, and here is coming into sight after fourscore. Is it indeed fully in sight? We are to have some widening of curricula and even some modest standard of preparation for profiting by them; yet not so much as the Germans got three generations ago. We are going to have, perhaps, nearly half as many teachers – at least in the best equipped subjects; we are even to have (such is the liberality of Oxford politicians and Cambridge treasury-clerks) a possible increase of twenty per cent. in the funds which have hitherto been doled out from our taxation (so vastly increased since the Union) for the support of all this! Let us imagine all this has come to pass. Surely our institutions, however late, shall then have got ahead of the civilised world?

Shall I compare any of our University centres with a great Continental one? Shall I take Strasbourg, where the conquerors twenty years ago, to arise the former French University on a level with the best German ones existing, spent three-quarters of a million on buildings, and gave an annual revenue of more than all our four Universities together are to divide among them,

---

32. Ultima Thule (far north) denotes any place beyond the borders of the known world in old maps.

which means an endowment of a million and a quarter. But you say this was done for political reasons, and we don't care for these. Not entirely. The same thing is done elsewhere. The little State of Baden, with half the population of Scotland and with two Universities, has lately spent a million. But even if it were essentially political, that only shows that the Germans understood, and have understood all along ever since 1809, that the Universities have a profound political importance. Every German schoolboy knows that it is the Universities which have made modern Germany, politically as well as intellectually; aye, and that keep it standing. It is true, I do not know any politician whether labelled Conservative or Liberal, Home Ruler or Imperialist, who thinks of our University policy as of any political importance at all. But the simple principle I have been insisting on helps us to understand this. The idea is on its way, and will reach him (or his grand-son) in due time. In Edinburgh, at least, it is sometimes realised that education is, at anyrate, a great and profitable industry – which is always something.

It is needless to quote figures how not only the great but the small countries – Sweden or Switzerland, Belgium or Holland – have long been ahead of our largest hopes at the present. I should only be called unpractical if I asked for the like. So I shall merely refer to the facts and figures of Sir Lyon Playfair's Presidential Address to the British Association at Aberdeen five years ago. Whoever wishes to feel what University reform really is like, when a nation is in earnest about it, cannot indeed go back to live in Germany at the beginning of this century. But he may go to France to-day, a country, which I must be permitted to say, people so commonly think of as the France of the Empire, and therefore totally misunderstand and misjudge.

French Provincial Universities

A mighty national revival in wellnigh every department of thought and action is being made by the men who were young enough to be in the terrible year of 1870, and to be deepened and moralised for life by its sorrows and disasters; and who are working as men have seldom worked before, with but one ambition – *il faut refaire la patrie*. Higher education is now on the first plane of their internal politics, just as the organisation of the Exposition was a couple of years ago, or primary education before that, or the fortifications before all. But what has France done? The provincial University centres practically were defunct. Their full renaissance has begun. The University budget of the last ten years has a total of four millions (pounds, of course – not francs). Lille and Nancy are growing up to rival Strasbourg as intellectual citadels, no less than material ones. The Faculties of Marseilles have laid their foundation stones, and those of Bordeaux are housed in palaces. But the phenomenal success, specially interesting to us in Dundee, is that of the entirely new academic centre of the great manufacturing town of Lyons. Here the Municipality has spent £400,000 in the last decade upon its University, of which the larger part (not one tithe of what we shall venture to ask for the same purpose) in medical and science buildings – a vast edifice with six quadrangles, while the ground is already cleared for housing the Faculties of Letters and of Law. Better than all this, these buildings are already full. The teaching staff is already larger than that of Edinburgh, and in seven years has gathered 1200 students. The quality of the medical studies is the highest in France; while the productivity of the professoriate is such that it needs yearly a fair-sized volume to index and summarise its publications. Or let us pass from the new University of Lyons to the ancient one of Montpellier. The six-centenary fêtes just concluded have inaugurated the replacement of this old and famous, but also sadly decayed, University upon the rank and effectiveness of a German one; first, in the indispensable material resources and appliances, and also in educational energy. As evidence of this I may say for my assistant, Mr. Herbertson, and myself, that we have both found this newly-revived University on the whole better, so far as our personal work is concerned, than any other British or Continental one we know of; and that the other two members of the botanical staff (with, I trust, one or two other young Scottish botanists) will be working there next winter, since no other place offers such a combination of advantages.

Paris

Let us pass to Paris, which has been reviving steadily during these twenty years. As to the number of students, to equal this we need to put not only our four Scottish universities, but Oxford and Cambridge or Berlin as well, all into the Latin quarter. Nor would teachers be much fewer, in some respects even more numerous. The student may choose, for instance, between six or seven different Institutes of Botany; between seven or eight of Chemistry, and so on – most of these, too, equipped with German completeness. Or consider the study of history. Among our Scottish Universities we have a portion of the time of one Professor; and at least some of our Senates are modestly asking for a lectureship on Ancient and Modern History – practically a chair of double or quadruple work, with a half to quarter pay. In a small country like Belgium there are from three to six historical courses in each of the four Universities, in Berlin there are twenty or so, in Paris there are about sixty. The idea is growing up of making Paris once more the central University of Europe, just as she was in the middle ages; and the number of men is rapidly increasing to whom this idea is just as definite as was the analogous one which brought about the unique and unapproachable splendour of last year's Exposition. The task is a more difficult one assuredly, and it is too soon to discuss the probabilities of its success. No one will deny that good to France and all the world must come from trying.

Position of Scotland

Returning to our Scottish Universities, let us note what position they have in the eyes of the people whom we pass on the homeward way. The French and Germans, impressed as they have been by our individual men of genius, and by such brief personal visits as to the Edinburgh Tercentenary five years ago, and helped, too, by the enchantment of distance, and a sound upbringing upon Sir Walter Scott, are disposed to give us credit for Universities of fully modern type; may indeed credit Edinburgh with a general superiority to Oxford and Cambridge themselves, which I always feel sorry my respect for veracity makes me unable to confirm in every particular. In England, on the other hand, our national pride is very hardly treated. We often hear our ancient and venerable institutions put into line merely with the new University Colleges, sometimes, must I confess, even with the larger public schools, and not with the great Universities at all. Which of these positions are we to accept as final? The next few years will have decided, and we should only have to go on as we have been doing to fix ourselves at one or the other of the lower ones. That medical teaching has been till lately neglected by the English Universities, and that we have taken it up and do it fairly and profitably, has too long blinded us to all else. There is no use in making mere jeremiads over our present low standing among the Universities of Europe, but it is worth while reflecting on the meanings of such a fact as this, that the majority of our professoriate (almost every man of us here) have got their education, at anyrate their essential education, outside Scotland altogether. Even our best men are constantly beaten for such appointments as they may be fully ready for, until in despair they go away to Oxford and Cambridge, and begin all over again. And thus, despite all we hear of the cheapness of Scottish Universities, it is little wonder that so many Scotsmen are finding it cheaper and quicker not to study there at all. Do not suppose that I would seek to advance Scottish culture by interfering with either these imports of Professors or exports of students, much as the Americans protect themselves against good pictures; but the balance, should not be so great against us – the garden which cannot rear most of its own stock and have some to plant afield is in a bad way.

University Residence in Scotland

What are we to do? Cry to Jove and the Commissioners? Go round and beg for money? Certainly, and the louder the better. But we must also recognise that our University needs lie deeper, that our aims must rise higher; that we have to modify the spirit of the Universities themselves. And this needs changes over and above those of mere curriculum and staff, which the Commissioners are doing their best to give us. Let me suggest two of these; and first, some rational adaptation of that College life which gives the English University man his superior geniality and breadth, his greater readiness to enter upon the best work of the world. Three years' experience of our rising University Hall in Edinburgh enables me to say – and I appeal to old residents and actual ones to confirm it – that all that is best in such collective student life is as readily realised here in Scotland as anywhere, that its apparent loss of time connected with such social life is in the long run a gain, its apparent sacrifices the most real of educational benefits. St. Andrews, with its noble city and associations, its traditions of genial student life, has in it all the makings of a Northern Oxford, and if Dundee be naturally less attractive as an academic city, there is all the more need for our helping to enlarge and deepen its student life and culture in this most excellent of ways.

Foreign Travel

The second and last point of which I wish to speak is that of the organisation of foreign travel, primarily, of course, to Germany and France. I want our Universities not only each to have its University Hall for undergraduates in Scotland, but to send its best graduates, helped by scholarships if need be, for a year or two of foreign work and travel. Many men do this already, of course, to the help of all professions, but I appeal to them whether they would not have been better of some precise and friendly direction whey they left this side, and of friendly reception and counsel when they arrived bewildered at the other. Just as the inexperienced traveller needs his Cook's ticket, his Baedeker's Guide, if he is not to waste time and money, if he is to save blundering and disappointment, – so must it be with the student. We should be able to say to him explicitly go to so and so for this subject, go somewhere else for that. He needs a better greeting than the railway porter's when he arrives at his destination; friends and a home, studies and expenses, all must be provided for in advance. Nor is such an organisation hard to arrange; indeed, it almost exists already. At Paris, at Montpellier or Lyons, for instance, at Geneva, at Jena or Freiburg, I can positively promise a student far more than is yet arranged for him, outside University Hall at anyrate, in any Scottish University. We can give him full particulars of studies, expenses, and what not; he will be received when he arrives, introduced to some of the best among his fellow-students and to the cultured society of the town; he will be looked after in sickness, his studies will be arranged for and directed, his work and regularity faithfully certified to his University. Such a reception – I can appeal to some here who have already enjoyed – it is often a veritable escape from the Slough of Despond to the Interpreter's House; nay, it may be from the dungeon of Giant Despair, and even graver perils, to within sight of the Delectable Mountains.

The Scots College in Paris

Such a widespread organisation, soon, I trust, to be a fully cosmopolitan one, besides its centre of information in Scotland, would need a main centre upon the Continent. For this purpose no scheme is so practical as that of the revival of our ancient Scots College in Paris. need I tell its story: I fear I must. The very schools of Paris were, they say, founded by two wandering Scots – Clement and Aleuin – one, I suspect, an Irishman from Iona, the other a Northumbrian of Lindisfarne, but genuine Scotch professors all the same; and what confirms this is, that whenever they were brought to Charlemagne, and he asked their business, they said, 'If any man in your dominions seeketh knowledge, here are we – to sell it.' Whereupon the kindly monarch, himself no common man of business, gave them a lecture-room in his palace forthwith. In 1325 we have the Scots College, built by the good Bishop of Moray upon its present site behind the Pantheon. In 1680 it was rebuilt as it now stands, a dignified old pile, of which the little chapel with its monuments is still worth the passers' while to see. The Scots College did good service until broken up by the Revolution and the wars of the present century, and (whether we recover the mere building or not, being mainly a matter of sentiment) it soon will again. A modest inquiry as to how its possible reorganisation would be received in Paris has brought a reply cordial and generous beyond anticipation. From the highest circles of thought and statesmanship, from the great schools of learning and of fine art, from the most distinguished private citizens, a Committee, which includes many of the greatest names in the present intellectual renaissance of France, has offered us its services. The list begins with the very head of the Education Department himself, and his colleague the Directeur des Beaux Arts. It includes not only the Rector and Deans of every Faculty of the University, with some of the most illustrious and also most genial of their colleagues, but representatives of all the other great institutions, such as M. Milne Edwards for the Museum, M. Pasteur for the Ecole Normale, or M. Berthelot (who, to avoid alarming Scottish susceptibilities, has taken the place of M. Renan) for the College de France. Such a Committee, offering what I have outlined above, will, I doubt not, soon find its Scottish counterpart, and this historic adjunct of our University culture will thus be reorganised, I trust even in time for next winter session. Our young artists, who will also be welcomed, are already returning to Scotland with deepened training and renewed aspirations, to work for their own local schools. Witness how the Glasgow men have suddenly leaped into the foremost rank among British schools; and the same process is already becoming visible in all professions. Such beginnings of more definite organisation as these will, I doubt not, recommend themselves to all thoughtful men, whatever their profession or their politics, for they indeed reconcile the advantages most claimed by the Home Ruler and the Imperialist alike. Yet in bringing the claims of these two beginnings before the students and teachers of all our four Universities – and, let me add, before the five academic cities which are their home – I feel that we are only at the outset of new perspectives, new possibilities, new duties; so vast are our Scottish University needs, and also aims.

Note – To avoid misconceptions, it should perhaps be explained that the proposed Scots College is not a teaching institution, which is quite unnecessary, nor even, like University Hall, a complete boarding-house, which would have the disadvantage of isolating the residents from the student life around them. It is, in the first place, an agency for enabling the student to find studies and friends; in the second, it offers suitable lodgings. Students who think of residing in Paris or elsewhere on the Continent are invited to communicate with the writer, or with the Resident Secretary for the Scots College next winter, Mr A Herbertson, University Hall, Mound Place, Edinburgh.

Rabindranath Tagore on the Environment

Rabindranath Tagore in Santiniketan

Brikshoropana (Tree Plantation Festival) in Santiniketan

The Religion of the Forest (1922)[33]

I

WE STAND BEFORE this great world. The truth of our life depends upon our attitude of mind towards it – an attitude which is formed by our habit of dealing with it according to the special circumstance of our surroundings and our temperaments. It guides our attempts to establish relations with the universe either by conquest or by union, either through the cultivation of power or through that of sympathy. And thus, in our realization of the truth of existence, we put our emphasis either upon the principle of dualism or upon the principle of unity.

The Indian sages have held in the Upanishads that the emancipation of our soul lies in its realizing the ultimate truth of unity. They said:

> *Isha-va-syam idam sarvam yat kinch jagatya-m jagat.*
> *Yéna tyakténa bhunjitha- ma- gridha kayasvit dhanam.*
> (Know all that moves in this moving world as enveloped by God;
>   and find
> enjoyment through renunciation, not through greed of possession.)

The meaning of this is, that, when we know the multiplicity of things as the final truth, we try to augment ourselves by the external possession of them; but, when we know the Infinite Soul as the final truth, then through our union with it we realize the joy of our soul. Therefore it has been said of those who have attained their fulfilment, – '*sarvam evá vishanti*' (they enter into all things). Their perfect relation with this world is the relation of the union.

This ideal of perfection preached by the forest-dwellers of ancient India runs through the heart of our classical literature and still dominates our mind. The legends related in our epics cluster under the forest shade bearing all through their narrative the message of the forest-dwellers. Our two greatest classical dramas find their background in scenes of the forest hermitage, which are permeated by the association of these sages.

The history of the Northmen of Europe is resonant with the music of the sea. That sea is not merely topographical in its significance, but represents certain ideals of life which still guide the history and inspire the creations of that race. In the sea, nature presented herself to those men in her aspect of a danger, a barrier which seemed to be at constant war with the land and its

---

33. In Das, vol 2, pp. 511-519. First published in *Creative Unity*, (New York: Macmillan, 1922).

children. The sea was the challenge of untamed nature to the indomitable human soul. And man did not flinch; he fought and won, and the spirit of fight continued in him. This fight he still maintains; it is the fight against disease and poverty, tyranny of matter and of man.

This refers to a people who live by the sea, and ride on it as on a wild, champing horse, catching it by its mane and making it render service from shore to shore. They find delight in turning by force the antagonism of circumstances into obedience. Truth appears to them in her aspect of dualism, the perpetual conflict of good and evil, which has no reconciliation, which can only end in victory or defeat.

But in the level tracts of Northern India men found no barrier between their lives and the grand life that permeates the universe. The forest entered into a close living relationship with their work and leisure, with their daily necessities and contemplations. They could not think of other surroundings as separate or inimical. So the view of the truth, which these men found, did not make manifest the difference, but rather the unity of all things. They uttered their faith in these words: *Yadidam kinch sarvam prâna éjati nihsratam* (All that is, vibrates with life, having come out from life). When we know this world as alien to us, then its mechanical aspect takes prominence in our mind; and then we set up our machines and our methods to deal with it and make as much profit as our knowledge of its mechanism allows us to do. This view of things does not play us false, for the machine has its place in this world. And not only this material universe, but human beings also, may be used as machines and made to yield powerful results. This aspect of truth cannot be ignored; it has to be known and mastered. Europe has done so and has reaped a rich harvest.

The view of this world which India has taken is summed up in one compound Sanskrit word, *Sacchidânanda*. The meaning is that Reality, which is essentially one, has three phases. The first is *sat*; it is the simple fact that things are, the fact which relates us to all things through the relationship of common existence. The second is *chit*; it is the fact that we know, which relates us to all things through the relationship of knowledge. Third is *ânanda*: it is the fact that we enjoy, which unites us with all things through the relationship of love.

According to the true Indian view, our consciousness of the world, merely as the sum total of things that exist, and as governed by laws, is imperfect. But it is perfect when our consciousness realizes all things as spiritually one with it, and therefore capable of giving us joy. For us the highest purpose of this world is not merely living in it, knowing it and making use of it, but realizing our own selves in it through expansion of sympathy; not alienating ourselves from it and dominating it, but comprehending and uniting it with ourselves in perfect union.

II

When Vikramaditya became king, Ujjayini a great capital, and Kâlidâsa its poet, the age of India's forest retreats had passed. Then we had taken our stand in the midst of the great concourse of humanity. The Chinese and the Hun, the Scythian and the Persian, the Greek and the Roman, had crowded round us. But, even in that age of pomp and prosperity, the love and reverence with which its poet sang about the hermitage shows what was the dominant ideal that occupied the mind of India; what was the one current of memory that continually flowed through her life.

In Kâlidâsa's drama, *Shakuntalâ*, the hermitage, which dominates the play, overshadowing the king's palace, has the same idea running through it – the recognition of the kinship of man with conscious and unconscious creation alike.

A poet of a later age, while describing a hermitage in his *Kâdambari*, tells us of the posture of salutation in the flowering lianas as they bow to the wind; of the sacrifice offered by the trees scattering their blossoms; of the grove resounding with the lessons chanted by the neophytes, and the verses repeated by the parrots, learnt by constantly hearing them; of the wild-fowl enjoying *vaishva-deva-bali-pinda* (the food offered to the divinity which is in all creatures); of the ducks coming up from the lake for their portion of the grass seed spread in the cottage yards to dry; and of the deer caressing with their tongues the young hermit boys. It is again the same story. The hermitage shines out, in all our ancient literature, as the place where the chasm between man and the rest of creation has been bridged.

In the Western dramas, human characters drown our attention in the vortex of their passions. Nature occasionally peeps out, but she is almost always a trespasser, who has to offer excuses, or bow apologetically and depart. But in all our dramas which still retain their fame, such as *Mrit-Shakatikâ, Shakuntalâ, Uttara-râmacharita*, Nature stands on her own right, proving that she has her great function, to impart the peace of the eternal to human emotions.

The fury of passion in two of Shakespeare's youthful poems is exhibited in conspicuous isolation. It is snatched away, naked, from the context of the All; it has not the green earth or the blue sky around it; it is there ready to bring to our view the raging fever which is in man's desires, and not the balm of health and repose which encircles it in the universe.

Ritusamhâra is clearly a work of Kâlidâsa's immaturity. The youthful love-song in it does not reach the sublime reticence which is in *Shakuntalâ* and *Kumâra-Sambhava*. But the tune of these voluptuous outbreaks is set to the varied harmony of Nature's symphony. The moonbeams of the summer evening, resonant with the flow of fountains, acknowledge it as a part of its own melody. In its rhythm sways the Kadamba forest, glistening in the first cool rain of the season; and the south breezes, carrying the scent of the mango blossoms, temper it with their murmur.

In the third canto of *Kumâra-Sambhava,* Madana, the God Eros, enters the forest sanctuary to set free a sudden flood of desire amid the serenity of the ascetics' meditation. But the boisterous outbreak of passion so caused was shown against a background of universal life. The divine love-thrills of Sati and Shiva found their response in the world-wide immensity of youth, in which animals and trees have their life-throbs.

Not only its third canto but the whole of the *Kumâra-Sambhava* poem is painted upon a limitless canvas. It tells of the eternal wedding of love, its wooing and sacrifice, and its fulfilment, for which the gods wait in suspense. Its inner idea is deep and of all time. It answers the one question that humanity asks through all its endeavours: 'How is the birth of the hero to be brought about, the brave one who can defy and vanquish the evil demon laying waste heaven's own kingdom?'

It becomes evident that such a problem had become acute in Kâlidâsa's time, when the old simplicity of Hindu life had broken up. The Hindu kings, forgetful of their duties, had become self-seeking epicureans, and India was being repeatedly devastated by the Scythians. What answer, then, does the poem give to the question it raises? Its message is that the cause of weakness lies in the inner life of the soul. It is in some break of harmony with the Good, some dissociation from the True. In the commencement of the poem we find that the God Shiva, the Good, had remained for long lost in the self-centred solitude of his asceticism, detached from the world of reality. And then paradise was lost. But *Kumâra-Sambhava* is the poem of paradise Regained. How was it regained? When Sati, the Spirit of Reality, through humiliation, suffering, and penance, won the Heart of Shiva, the Spirit of Goodness. And thus, from the union of the freedom of the real with the restraint of the Good, was born the heroism that released Paradise from the demon of Lawlessness.

Viewed from without, India, in the time of Kâlidâsa, appeared to have reached the zenith of civilization excelling as she did in luxury, literature and the arts. But from the poems of Kâlidâsa it is evident that this magnificence of wealth and enjoyment worked against the ideal that sprang and flowed forth from the sacred solitude of the forest. These poems contain the voice of warnings against the gorgeous unreality of that age, which, like a Himalayan avalanche, was slowly gliding down to an abyss of catastrophe. And from his seat beside all the glories of Vikramaditya's throne the poet's heart yearns for the purity and simplicity of India's past age of spiritual striving. And it was this yearning which impelled him to go back to the annals of the ancient

Kings of Raghu's line for the narrative poem, in which he traced the history of the rise and fall of the ideal that should guide the rulers of men.

King Dilipa, with the Queen of Sudakshinâ, has entered upon the life of the forest. The great monarch is busy tending the cattle of the hermitage. Thus the poem opens, amid scenes of simplicity and self-denial. But it ends in the palace of magnificence, in the extravagance of self-enjoyment. With a calm restraint of language the poet tells us of the kingly glory crowned with purity. He begins his poem as the day begins, in the serenity of sunrise. But lavish are the colours in which he describes the end, as of the evening, eloquent for a time with the sumptuous splendour of sunset, but overtaken at last by the devouring darkness which sweeps away all its brilliance into night.

In this beginning and this ending of his poem there lies hidden that message of the forest which found its voice in the poet's words. There runs through the narrative the idea that the future glowed gloriously ahead only when there was in the atmosphere the calm of self-control, of purity and renunciation. When downfall had become imminent, the hungry fires of desire, aflame at a hundred different points, dazzled the eyes of all beholders.

Kâlidâsa in almost all his works represented the unbounded impetuousness of kingly splendour on the one side and the serene strength of regulated desires on the other. Even in the minor drama of *Mâlavikâgnimitra* we find the same thing in a different manner. It must never be thought that, in this play, the poet's deliberate object was to pander to his royal patron by inviting him to a literary orgy of lust and passion. The very introductory verse indicates the object towards which this play is directed. The poet begins the drama with the prayer, *Sanmârgâlókayan vyapanayatu sa nastâmasi vritimishah* (Let God, to illumine for us the path of truth, sweep away our passions, bred of darkness). This is the God Shiva, in whose nature Parvati, the eternal Woman, is ever commingled in an ascetic purity of love. The unified being of Shiva and Parvati is the perfect symbol of the eternal in the wedded love of man and woman. When the poet opens his drama with an invocation of this Spirit of the Divine Union it is evident that it contains in it the message with which he greets his kingly audience. The whole drama goes to show the ugliness of the treachery and cruelty inherent in unchecked self-indulgence. In the play the conflict of ideals is between the King and the Queen, between Agnimitra and Dhârini, and the significance of the contrast lies hidden in the very names of the hero and the heroine. Though the name Agnimitra is historical, yet it symbolizes in the poet's mind the destructive force of uncontrolled desire – just as did the name Agnivarna in *Raghuvamsha*, Agnimitra, 'the friend of the fire,' the reckless person who in his love-making is playing with fire, not knowing that all the time it is scorching him black. And what a great name is Dhârini, signifying the fortitude and forbearance that comes from majesty of soul! What an association it carries of the infinite dignity of love, purified by a self-abnegation that rises far above all insult and baseness of betrayal!

In *Shakuntalâ* this conflict of ideals has been shown, all through the drama, by the contrast of the pompous heartlessness of the king's court and the natural purity of the forest hermitage. The drama opens with a hunting scene, where the king is in pursuit of an antelope. The cruelty of the chase appears like a menace symbolizing the spirit of the king's life clashing against the spirit of the forest retreat, which is *sharanyam sarva-bhûtânâm* (where all creatures find their protection of love). And the pleading of the forest-dwellers with the king to spare the life of the deer, helplessly innocent and beautiful, is the pleading that rises from the heart of the whole drama. 'Never, oh, never is the arrow meant to pierce the tender body of a deer, even as the fire is not for the burning of flowers.'

In the *Râmâyana*, Rama and his companions, in their banishment, had to traverse forest after forest; they had to live in leaf-thatched huts, to sleep on the bare ground. But as their hearts felt their kinship with woodland, hill, and stream, they were not in exile amidst these. Poets, brought up in an atmosphere of different ideals, would have taken this opportunity of depicting in dismal colours the hardship of the forest-life in order to bring out the martyrdom of Râmachandra with all the emphasis of a strong contrast. But, in the *Râmâyana*, we are led to realise the greatness of the hero, not in a fierce struggle with Nature, but in sympathy with it, Sitâ, the daughter-in-law of a great kingly house, goes along the forest paths. We read:

'She asks Râma about the flowering trees, and shrubs and creepers which she has not seen before. At her request Lakshmana gathers and brings her plants of all kinds, exuberant with flowers, and it delights her heart to see the forest rivers, variegated with their streams and sandy banks, resounding with the call of heron and duck.

'When Râma first took his abode in the Chitrakuta peak, that delightful Chitrakuta, by the Mâlyavati river, with its easy slopes for landing, he forgot all the pain of leaving his home in the capital at the sight of those woodlands, alive with beast and bird.'

Having lived on that hill for long, Râma, who was *giri-vana-priya* (lover of the mountain and the forest), said one day to Sitâ:

'When I look upon the beauties of this hill, the loss of my kingdom troubles me no longer, nor does the separation from my friends cause me any pang.'

Thus passed Râmachandra's exile, now in woodland, now in hermitage. The love which Râma and Sitâ bore to each other united them, not only to each other, but to the universe of life. That is why, when Sitâ was taken away, the loss seemed to be so great to the forest itself.

III

Strangely enough, in Shakespeare's dramas, like those of Kâlidâsa, we find a secret vein of complaint against the artificial life of the king's court – the life of ungrateful treachery and falsehood. And almost everywhere, in his dramas, foreign scenes have been introduced in connection with some working of the life of unscrupulous ambition. It is perfectly obvious in *Timon of Athens* – but there nature offers no message or balm to the injured soul of man. In *Cymbeline* the mountainous forest and the cave appear in their aspect of obstruction to life's opportunities. These only seem tolerable in comparison with the vicissitudes of fortune in the artificial court life. In *As You Like It* the forest of Arden is didactic in its lessons. It does not bring peace, but preaches, when it says:

> Hath not old custom made this life more sweet
> Than that of painted pomp? Are not these woods
> more free from peril than the envious court?

In the *Tempest*, through Prospero's treatment of Ariel and Caliban we realize man's struggle with nature and his longing to sever connection with her. In *Macbeth*, as a prelude to a bloody crime of treachery and treason, we are introduced to a scene of barren heath where the three witches appear as personifications of Nature's malignant forces; and in *King Lear* it is the fury of a father's love turned into curses by the ingratitude born of the unnatural life of the court that finds its symbol in the storm on the heath. The tragic intensity of *Hamlet* and *Othello* is unrelieved by any touch of Nature's eternity. Except in a passing glimpse of a moonlight night in the love scene in the *Merchant of Venice*, Nature has not been allowed in other dramas of this series, including *Romeo and Juliet* and *Antony and Cleopatra*, to contribute her own music to the music of man's love. In *The Winter's Tale* the cruelty of a king's suspicion stands bare in its relentlessness, and nature cowers before it, offering no consolation.

I hope it is needless for me to say that these observations are not intended to minimize Shakespeare's great power as a dramatic poet, but to show in his works the gulf between nature and human nature owing to the tradition of his race and time. It cannot be said that beauty of nature is ignored in his writings; only he fails to recognize in them the truth of the interpenetration of human life with the cosmic life of the world. We observe a completely different attitude of mind in the later English poets like Wordsworth and Shelley, which can be attributed in the main to the great mental change in Europe, at that particular period, through the influence of the newly discovered philosophy of India which stirred the soul of Germany and aroused the attention of other Western countries.

In Milton's *Paradise Lost*, the very subject – Man dwelling in the garden of Paradise – seems to afford a special opportunity for bringing out the true greatness of man's relationship with Nature. But though the poet has described to us the beauties of the garden, though he has shown to us the animals living there in amity and peace among themselves, there is no reality of kinship between them and man. They were created for man's enjoyment; man was their lord and master. We find no trace of the love between the first man and woman gradually surpassing themselves and overflowing the rest of creation, such as we find in the love scenes in *Kumâra-Sambhava* and *Shakuntalâ*. In the seclusion of the bower, where the first man and woman rested in the garden of Paradise –

> Bird, beast, insect or worm
> Durst enter none, such was their awe of man.

Not that India denied the superiority of man, but the test of that superiority lay, according to her, in the comprehensiveness of sympathy, not in the aloofness of absolute distinction.

IV

India holds sacred, and counts as places of pilgrimage, all spots which display a special beauty or splendour of nature. These had no original attraction on account of any special fitness for cultivation or settlement. Here, man is free, not to look upon Nature as a source of supply of his necessities, but to realise his soul beyond himself. The Himalayas of India are sacred and the Vindhya Hills. Her majestic rivers are sacred. Lake Mânasa and the confluence of the Ganges and the Jamuna are sacred. India has saturated with her love and worship the great Naturewith which her children are surrounded, whose light fills their eyes with gladness, and whose water cleanses them, whose food gives them life, and from whose majestic mystery comes forth the constant revelation of the infinite in music, scent, and colour, which brings its awakening to the soul of man. India gains the world through worship, through spiritual communion; and the idea of freedom to which she aspired was based upon the realization of her spiritual unity.

When, in my recent voyage to Europe, our ship left Aden and sailed along the sea which lay between the two continents, we passed by the red and barren rocks of Arabia on our right side and the gleaming sands of Egypt on our left. They seemed to me like two giant brothers exchanging with each other burning glances of hatred, kept apart by the tearful entreaty of the sea from whose womb they had their birth.

There was an immense stretch of silence on the left shore as well as on the right, but the two shores spoke to me of the two different historical dramas enacted. The civilization which found its growth in Egypt was continued across long centuries, elaborately rich with sentiments and expressions of life, with pictures, sculptures, temples, and ceremonials. This was a country whose guardian-spirit was a noble river, which spread the festivities of life on its banks across the heart of the land. There man never raised the barrier of alienation between himself and the rest of the world.

On the opposite shore of the Red Sea the civilization which grew up in the inhospitable soil of Arabia had a contrary character to that of Egypt. There man felt himself isolated in his hostile and bare surroundings. His idea of God became that of a jealous God. His mind naturally dwelt upon the principle of separateness. It roused in him the spirit of fight, and this spirit was a force that drove him far and wide. These two civilizations represented two fundamental divisions of human nature. The one contained in it the spirit of conquest and the other the spirit of harmony. And both of these have their truth and purpose in human existence.

The characters of two eminent sages have been described in our mythology. One was Vashishtha and another Vishvâmitra. Both of them were great, but they represented two different types of wisdom; and there was conflict between them. Vishvâmitra sought to achieve power and was proud of it; Vashishtha was rudely smitten by that power. But his hurt and his loss could not touch the illumination of his soul; for he rose above them and could forgive. Râmachandra, the great hero of our epic, had his initiation to the spiritual life from Vashishtha, the life of inner peace and perfection. But he had his initiation to war from Vishvâmitra, who called him to kill the demons and gave him weapons that were Irresistible.

Those two sages symbolize in themselves the two guiding spirits of civilization. Can it be true that they shall never be reconciled? If so, can ever the age of peace and co-operation dawn upon the human world? Creation is the harmony of contrary forces — the forces of attraction and repulsion. When they join hands, all the fire and fight are changed into the smile of flowers and the songs of birds. When there is only one of them triumphant and the other defeated, then either there is the death of cold rigidity or that of suicidal explosion.

Humanity, for ages, has been busy with the one great creation of spiritual life. Its best wisdom, its discipline, its literature and art, all the teachings and self-sacrifice of its noblest teachers, have been for this. But the harmony of contrary forces, which give their rhythm to all creation, has not yet been perfected by man in his civilization, and the Creator in him is baffled over and over again. He comes back to his work, however, and makes himself busy, building his world in the midst of desolation and ruins. His history is the history of his aspiration interrupted and renewed. And one truth of which he must be reminded, therefore, is that the power which accomplishes the miracle of creation, by bringing conflicting forces into the harmony of the One, is no passion, but a love which accepts the bonds of self-control from the joy of its own immensity — a love whose sacrifice is the manifestation of its endless wealth within itself.

Can Science Be Humanized? (1933)[34]

THERE IS NO MEANING in such words as spiritualising the machine; we can spiritualise our own being, which makes use of the machine, just as there is nothing good or bad in our bodily organs, but the moral qualities that are in our mind. When the temptation is small our moral nature easily overcomes it, but when the bribe that is offered to our soul is too big we do not even realize that its dignity is offended. Today the profit that the machine brings to our door is too big and we do not hesitate to scramble for it even at the cost of our humanity. The shrinking of the man in us is concealed by the augmentation of things outside and we lack the time to grieve over the loss. We can only hope that science herself will help us to bring back sanity to the human world by lessening the opportunity to gamble with our fortune. The means that science has produced through which to gain access into Nature's storehouse is tremendously complex which only proves her own immaturity just as simplicity is wanting in the movements of a swimmer who is inexpert. It is this cumbersome complexity in the machinery which makes it not only unavailable to the majority of mankind but also compels us to centralise it in monster factories, uprooting the workers' life from its natural soil creating unhappiness. I do not see any other way to extricate us from these tangled evils except to wait for science to simplify our means of production and thus lessen the enormity of individual greed.

I believe that the social unrest prevalent today all over the world is owing to the anarchy of spirit in the modern civilization. What is called progress is the progress in the mechanical contrivances; it is in fact an indefinite extension of our physical limbs and organs which, owing to the enormous material advantage that it brings to us has tempted the modern man away from his inner realm of spiritual value and thus the balance is lost. The attainment of perfection in human relationship through the help of religion and cultivation of our social qualities occupied the most important place in our civilization up until now. But today our homes have dissolved into hotels, community life is stifled in the dense and dusty atmosphere of the office, man and woman are afraid of love, people clamour for their rights and forget their obligations and they value comfort more than happiness and spirit of display more than that of beauty.

Great civilizations in the East as well as in the West have flourished in the past because they produced food for the spirit of man for all time; they

---

34. Das, vol 3, pp. 665-666.

tried to build their life upon their faith in ideals, the faith that is creative. These great civilizations were at last run to death by men of the type of our precocious schoolboys of modern times, smart and superficially critical, worshippers of self, shrewd bargainers in the market of profit and power, efficient in their handling of the ephemeral who presume to buy human souls with their money and throw them into their dustbins when they have been sucked dry, and who, eventually, driven by suicidal forces of passion, set their neighbours' houses on fire and are themselves enveloped by the flame.

It is some great ideal which creates great societies of men; it is some blind passion which breaks them to pieces. They thrive so long as they produce food for life; they perish when they burn up life in insatiate self gratification. We have been taught by our sages that it is Truth and not things which saves man from annihilation.

The reward of truth is peace, the reward of truth is happiness. People suffer from the upsetting of equilibrium when power is there and no inner truth to which it is related, like a motor car in motion whose driver is absent.

The Relation of the Individual to the Universe (1913)[35]

THE CIVILIZATION OF ancient Greece was nurtured within city walls. In fact, all the modern civilizations have their cradles of brick and mortar.

These walls leave their mark deep in the minds of men. They set up a principle of 'divide and rule' in our mental outlook, which begets in us a habit of securing all our conquests by fortifying them and separating them from one another. We divide nation and nation, knowledge and knowledge, man and nature. It breeds in us a strong suspicion of whatever is beyond the barriers we have built, and everything has to fight hard for its entrance into our recognition.

When the first Aryan invaders appeared in India it was a vast land of forests, and the new-comers rapidly took advantage of them. These forests afforded them shelter from the fierce heat of the sun and the ravages of tropical storms, pastures for cattle, fuel for sacrificial fire, and materials for building cottages. And the different Aryan clans with their patriarchal heads settled in the different forest tracts which had some special advantage of natural protection, and food and water in plenty.

Thus in India it was in the forests that our civilization had its birth, and it took a distinct character from this origin and environment. It was surrounded by the vast life of nature, was fed and clothed by her, and had the closest and most constant intercourse with her varying aspects.

Such a life, it may be thought, tends to have the effect of dulling human intelligence and dwarfing the incentives to progress by lowering the standards of existence. But in ancient India we find that the circumstances of forest life did not overcome man's mind, and did not enfeeble the current of his energies, but only gave to it a particular direction. Having been in constant contact with the living growth of nature, his mind was free from the desire to extend his dominion by erecting boundary walls around his acquisitions. His aim was not to acquire but to realize, to enlarge his consciousness by growing with and growing into his surroundings. He felt that truth is all-comprehensive, that there is no such thing as absolute isolation in existence, and the only way of attaining truth is through the interpenetration of our being into all objects. To realize this great harmony between man's spirit and the spirit of the world was the endeavour of the forest-dwelling sages of ancient India.

---

35. In Das Vol 2 p281-289. Footnotes in Sanskrit have been dropped. Originally published in *Sadhana/The Realization of Life*, (London: Macmillan, October 1913).

In later days there came a time when these primeval forests gave way to cultivated fields, and wealthy cities sprang up on all sides. Mighty kingdoms were established, which had communications with all the great powers of the world. But even in the heyday of its material prosperity the heart of India ever looked back with adoration upon the early ideal of self-realization, and the dignity of the simple life of the forest hermitage, and drew its best inspiration from the wisdom stored there.

The west seems to take a pride in thinking that it is subduing nature; as if we are living in a hostile world where we have to wrest everything we want from an unwilling and alien arrangement of things. For in the city life man naturally directs the concentrated light of his mental vision upon his own life and works, and this creates an artificial dissociation between himself and the Universal Nature within whose bosom he lies.

But in India the point of view was different; it included the world with the man as one great truth. India put all her emphasis on the harmony that exists between the individual and the universal. She felt we could have no communication whatever with our surroundings if they were absolutely foreign to us. Man's complaint against nature is that he has to acquire most of his necessaries by his own efforts. Yes, but his efforts are not in vain; he is reaping success every day, and that shows there is a rational connection between him and nature, for we never can make anything our own except that which is truly related to us.

We can look upon a road from two different points of view. One regards it as dividing us from the object of our desire; in that case we count every step of our journey over it as something attained by force in the face of obstruction. The other sees it as the road which leads us to our destination; and as such it is part of our goal. It is already the beginning of our attainment, and by journeying over it we can only gain that which in itself it offers to us. This last point of view is that of India with regard to nature. For her, the great fact is that we are in harmony with nature; that man can think because his thoughts are in harmony with things; that he can use the forces of nature for his own purpose only because his power is in harmony with the power which is universal, and that in the long run his purpose never can knock against the purpose which works through nature.

In the west the prevalent feeling is that nature belongs exclusively to inanimate things and to beasts, that there is a sudden unaccountable break where human-nature begins. According to it, everything that is low in the scale of beings is merely nature, and whatever has the stamp of perfection on it, intellectual or moral, is human-nature. It is like dividing the bud and the blossom into separate categories, and putting their grace to the credit of two different and antithetical principles. But the Indian mind never has any hesitation in acknowledging its kinship with nature, its unbroken relation with all.

The fundamental unity of creation was not simply a philosophical speculation for India; it was her life-object to realize this great harmony in feeling and in action. With meditation and service, with a regulation of her life, she cultivated her consciousness in such a way that everything had a spiritual meaning to her. The earth, water and light, fruits and flowers, to her were not merely physical phenomena to be turned to use and then left aside. They were necessary to her in the attainment of her ideal of perfection, as every note is necessary to the completeness of the symphony. India intuitively felt that the essential fact of this world has a vital meaning for us; we have to be fully alive to it and establish a conscious relation with it, not merely impelled by scientific curiosity or greed of material advantage, but realising it in the spirit of sympathy, with a large feeling of joy and peace.

The man of science knows, in one aspect, that the world is not merely what it appears to be to our senses; he knows that earth and water are really the play of forces that manifest themselves to us as earth and water – how, we can but partially apprehend. Likewise the man who has his spiritual eyes open knows that the ultimate truth about earth and water lies in our apprehension of the eternal will which works in time and takes shape in the forces we realize under those aspects. This is not mere knowledge, as science is, but it is a perception of the soul by the soul. This does not lead us to power, as knowledge does, but it gives us joy, which is the product of the union of kindred things. The man whose acquaintance with the world does not lead him deeper than science leads him, will never understand what it is that the man with the spiritual vision finds in these natural phenomena. The water does not merely cleanse his limbs, but it purifies his heart; for it touches his soul. The earth does not merely hold his body, but it gladdens his mind; for its contact is more than a physical contact – it is a living presence. When a man does not realize his kinship with the world, he lives in a prison-house whose walls are alien to him. When he meets the eternal spirit in all objects, then is he emancipated for then he discovers the fullest significance of the world into which he is born; then he finds himself in perfect truth, and his harmony with the all is established. In India men are enjoined to be fully awake to the fact that they are in the closest relation to things around them, body and soul, and that they are to hail the morning sun, the flowing water, the fruitful earth, as the manifestation of the same living truth which holds them in its embrace. Thus the text of our everyday meditation is the Gayatri, a verse which is considered to be the epitome of all the Vedas. By its help we try to realize the essential unity of the world with the conscious soul of man; we learn to perceive the unity held together by the one Eternal Spirit, whose power creates the earth, the sky, and the stars, and at the same time irradiates our minds with the light of a consciousness that moves and exists in unbroken continuity with the outer world.

It is not true that India has tried to ignore differences of value in different things, for she knows that would make life impossible. The sense of the superiority of man in the scale of creation has not been absent from her mind. But she has had her own idea as to that in which his superiority really consists. It is not in the power of possession but in the power of union. Therefore India chose her places of pilgrimage wherever there in nature some special grandeur or beauty, so that her mind could come out of its world of narrow necessities and realize its place in the infinite. This was the reason why in India a whole people who once were meat-eaters gave up taking animal food to cultivate the sentiment of universal sympathy for life, an event unique in the history of mankind.

India knew that when by physical and mental barriers we violently detach ourselves from the inexhaustible life of nature; when we become merely man, not man-in-the-universe, we create bewildering problems, and having shut off the source of their solution, we try all kinds of artificial methods each of which brings its own crop of interminable difficulties. When man leaves his resting-place in universal nature, when he walks on the single rope of humanity, it means either a dance or a fall for him, he has ceaselessly to strain every nerve and muscle to keep his balance at each step, and then, in the intervals of his weariness, he fulminates against Providence and feels a secret pride and satisfaction in thinking that he has been unfairly dealt with by the whole scheme of things.

But this cannot go on for ever. Man must realize the wholeness of his existence, his place in the infinite; he must know that hard as he may strive he can never create his honey within the cells of his hive, for the perennial supply of his life food is outside their walls. He must know that when man shuts himself out from the vitalising and purifying touch of the infinite, and falls back upon himself for his sustenance and his healing, then he goads himself into madness, tears himself into shreds, and eats his own substance. Deprived of the background of the whole, his poverty loses its one great quality, which is simplicity, and becomes squalid and shamefaced. His wealth is no longer magnanimous; it grows merely extravagant. His appetites do not minister to his life, keeping to the limits of their purpose; they become an end in themselves and set fire to his life and play the fiddle in the lurid light of the conflagration. Then it is that in our self-expression we try to startle and not to attract; in art we strive for originality and lose sight of truth which is old and yet ever new; in literature we miss the complete view of man which is simple and yet great. Man appears instead as a psychological problem, or as the embodiment of a passion that is intense because abnormal, being exhibited in the glare of a fiercely emphatic artificial light. When man's consciousness is restricted only to the immediate vicinity of his human self, the deeper roots of his nature do not find their permanent soil, his spirit is ever on the brink of starvation, and in the place of healthful strength he substitutes rounds of stimulation. Then it is that man misses his inner perspective and measures his greatness by its bulk and not by its vital link with the infinite, judges his activity by its movement and not by the repose of perfection – the repose which is in the starry heavens, in the ever-flowing rhythmic dance of creation.

The first invasion of India has its exact parallel in the invasion of America by the European settlers. They also were confronted with primeval forests and a fierce struggle with the aboriginal races. But this struggle between man and man, and man and nature lasted till the very end; they never came to any terms. In India the forests which were the habitation of barbarians became the sanctuary of sages, but in America these great living cathedrals of nature had no deeper significance to man. They brought wealth and power to him, and perhaps at times they ministered to his enjoyment of beauty, and inspired a solitary poet. They never acquired a sacred association in the hearts of men as the site of some great spiritual reconcilement where man's soul had its meeting-place with the soul of the world.

I do not for a moment wish to suggest that things should have been otherwise. It would be an utter waste of opportunities if history were to repeat itself exactly in the same manner in every place. It is best for the commerce of the spirit that people differently situated should bring their different products into the market of humanity, each of which is complementary and necessary to the others. All that I wish to say is that India at the outset of her career met with a special combination of circumstances which was not lost upon her. She had, according to her opportunities, thought and pondered, striven and suffered, dived into the depths of existence, and achieved something which surely cannot be without its value to people whose evolution in history took a different way altogether. Man for his perfect growth requires all the living elements that constitute his complex life; that is why his food has to be cultivated in different fields and brought from different sources.

Civilization is a kind of mould that each nation is busy making for itself to shape its men and women according to its best ideal. All its institutions, its legislature, its standard of approbation and condemnation, its conscious and unconscious teachings tend toward that object. The modern civilization of the west, by all its organised efforts, is trying to turn out men perfect in physical, intellectual, and moral efficiency. There the vast energies of the nations are employed in extending man's power over his surroundings, and people are combining and straining every faculty to possess and to turn to account all that they can lay their hands upon, to overcome every obstacle on their path of conquest. They are ever disciplining themselves to fight nature and other races; their armaments are getting more and more stupendous every day; their machines, their appliances, their organisations go on multiplying at an amazing rate. This is a splendid achievement, no doubt, and a wonderful manifestation of man's masterfulness, which knows no obstacle and has for its object the supremacy of himself over everything else.

The ancient civilization of India had its own ideal of perfection towards which its efforts were directed. Its aim was not attaining power, and it neglected to cultivate to the utmost its capacities, and to organize men for defensive and offensive purposes, for co-operation in the acquisition of wealth and for military and political ascendancy. The ideal that India tried to realize led her best men to the isolation of a contemplative life, and the treasures that she gained for mankind by penetrating into the mysteries of reality cost her dear in the sphere of worldly success. Yet, this also was a sublime achievement–it was a supreme manifestation of that human aspiration which knows no limit, and which has for its object nothing less than the realization of the Infinite.

There were the virtuous, the wise, the courageous; there were the statesmen, kings and emperors of India; but whom amongst all these classes did she look up to and choose to be the representative of men?

They were the rishis. What were the rishis?

> They who having attained the supreme soul in knowledge were filled with wisdom, and having found him in union with the soul were in perfect harmony with the inner self; they having realized him in the heart were free from all selfish desires, and having experienced him in all the activities of the world, had attained calmness. The rishis were they who having reached the supreme God from all sides had found abiding peace, had become united with all, had entered into the life of the Universe.

Thus the state of realising our relationship with all, of entering into everything through union with God, was considered in India to be the ultimate end and fulfilment of humanity.

Man can destroy and plunder, earn and accumulate, invent and discover, but he is great because his soul comprehends all. It is dire destruction for him when he envelopes his soul in a dead shell of callous habits, and when a blind fury of works whirls round him like an eddying dust storm, shutting out the horizon. That indeed kills the very spirit of his being, which is the spirit of comprehension. Essentially man is not a slave either of himself or of the world; but he is a lover. His freedom and fulfilment is in love, which is another name for perfect comprehension. By this power of comprehension, this permeation of his being, he is united with the all-pervading Spirit, who is also the breath of his soul. Where a man tries to raise himself to eminence by pushing and jostling all others, to achieve a distinction by which he prides himself to be more than everybody else, there he is alienated from that Spirit. This is why the Upanishads describe those who have attained the goal of human life as *'peaceful'* and as *'at-one-with-God'*, meaning that they are in perfect harmony with man and nature, and therefore in undisturbed union with God.

We have a glimpse of the same truth in the teachings of Jesus when he says, 'It is easier for a camel to pass through the eye of a needle than for a rich man to enter the kingdom of Heaven' – which implies that whatever we treasure for ourselves separates us from others; our possessions are our limitations. He who is bent upon accumulating riches is unable, with his ego continually bulging, to pass through the gates of comprehension of the spiritual world, which is the world of perfect harmony; he is shut up within the narrow walls of his limited acquisitions.

Hence the spirit of the teachings of the Upanishads is: In order to find him you must embrace all. In the pursuit of wealth you really give up everything to gain a few things, and that is not the way to attain him who is completeness.

Some modern philosophers of Europe, who are directly or indirectly indebted to the Upanishads, far from realising their debt, maintain that the Brahma of India is a mere abstraction, a negation of all that is in the world. In a word, that the infinite Being is to be found nowhere except in metaphysics. It may be, that such a doctrine has been and still is prevalent with a section of our countrymen. But this is certainly not in accord with the pervading spirit of the Indian mind. Instead, it is the practice of realising and affirming the presence of the infinite in all things which has been its constant inspiration.

We are enjoined to see *whatever there is in the world as being enveloped by God.*

I bow to God over and over again who is in fire and in water, who permeates the whole world, who is in the annual crops as well as in the perennial trees.

Can this be God abstracted from the world? Instead, it signifies not merely seeing him in all things, but saluting him, in all the objects of the world. The attitude of the God-conscious man of the Upanishad towards the universe is one of a deep feeling of adoration. His object of worship, is present everywhere. It is the one living truth that makes all realities true. This truth is not only of knowledge but of devotion. '*Namonamah*,' – we bow to him everywhere, and over and over again. It is recognized in the outburst of the Rishi, who addresses the whole world in a sudden ecstasy of joy: *Listen to me, ye sons of the immortal spirit, ye who live in the heavenly abode, I have known the Supreme Person whose light shines forth from beyond* the *darkness.* Do we not find the overwhelming delight of a direct and positive experience where there is not the least trace of vagueness or passivity?

Buddha, who developed the practical side of the teaching of the Upanishads, preached the same message when he said,

> With everything, whether it is above or below, remote or near, visible or invisible, thou shalt preserve a relation of unlimited love without any animosity or without a desire to kill. To live in such a consciousness while standing or walking, sitting or lying down till you are asleep, is Brahma vihâra, or, in other words, is living and moving and having your joy in the spirit of Brahma.

What is that spirit? The Upanishad says, *The being who is in his essence the light and life of all, who is world-conscious, is Brahma.* To feel all, to be conscious of everything, is his spirit. We are immersed in his consciousness body and soul. It is through his consciousness that the sun attracts the earth; it is through his consciousness that the light-waves are being transmitted from planet to planet.

Not only in space, but *this light and life, this all-feeling being is in our souls.* He is all-conscious in space, or the world of extension; and he is all-conscious in soul, or the world of intension.

Thus to attain our world-consciousness, we have to unite our feeling with this all-pervasive infinite feeling. In fact, the only true human progress is coincident with this widening of the range of feeling. All our poetry, philosophy, science, art, and religion are serving to extend the scope of our consciousness towards higher and larger spheres. Man does not acquire rights through occupation of larger space, nor through external conduct, but his rights extend only so far as he is real, and his reality is measured by the scope of his consciousness.

We have, however, to pay a price for this attainment of the freedom of consciousness. What is the price? It is to give one's self away. Our soul can realize itself truly only by denying itself. The Upanishad says, *Thou shalt gain by giving away. Thou shalt not covet.*

In the Gita we are advised to work disinterestedly, abandoning all lust for the result. Many outsiders conclude from this teaching that the conception of the world as something unreal lies at the root of the so-called disinterestedness preached in India. But the reverse is the truth.

The man who aims at his own aggrandizement underrates everything else. Compared with himself the rest of the world is unreal. Thus in order to be fully conscious of the reality of all, man has to be free himself from the bonds of personal desires. This discipline we have to go through to prepare ourselves for our social duties – for sharing the burdens of our fellow-beings. Every endeavour to attain a larger life requires of man 'to gain by giving away, and not to be greedy'. And thus to expand gradually the consciousness of one's unity with all is the striving of humanity.

The Infinite in India was not a thin nonentity, void of all content. The Rishis of India asserted emphatically, 'To know him in this life is to be true; not to know him in this life is the desolation of death.' How to know him then? 'By realising him in each and all.' Not only in nature, but in the family, in society, and in the state, the more we realize the World-conscious in all, the better for us. Failing to realize this, we turn our faces to destruction.

It fills me with great joy and a high hope for the future of humanity when I realize that there was a time in the remote past when our poet-prophets stood under the lavish sunshine of an Indian sky and greeted the world with the glad recognition of kindred. It was not an anthropomorphic hallucination. It was not seeing man reflected everywhere in grotesquely exaggerated images, and witnessing the human drama acted on a gigantic scale in nature's arena of flitting lights and shadows. On the contrary, it meant crossing the limiting barriers of the individual, to become more than man, to become one with the All. It was not a mere play of the imagination, but it was the liberation of consciousness from all the mystifications and exaggerations of the self. These ancient seers felt in the serene depth of their mind that the same energy, which vibrates and passes into the endless forms of the world, manifests itself in our inner being as consciousness; and there is no break in unity. For these seers there was no gap in their luminous vision of perfection. They never acknowledged even death itself as creating a chasm in the field of reality. They said, *His reflection is death as well as immortality*. They did not recognize any essential opposition between life and death, and they said with absolute assurance, 'It is life that is death.' They saluted with the same serenity of gladness 'life in its aspect of appearing and in its aspect of departure' – *That which is past is hidden life, and that which is to come*. They knew that mere appearance and disappearance are on the surface like waves on the sea, but life which is permanent knows no decay or diminution.

Everything has sprung from immortal life and is vibrating with life, for life is immense.

This is the noble heritage from our forefathers waiting to be claimed by us as our own, this ideal of the supreme freedom of consciousness. It is not merely intellectual or emotional, it has an ethical basis, and it must be translated into action. In the Upanishad it is said, *The supreme being is all-pervading, therefore he is the innate good in all.* To be truly united in knowledge, love, and service with all beings, and thus to realize one's self in the all-pervading God is the essence of goodness, and this is the keynote of the teachings of the Upanishads: *Life is immense.*

'Introduction' to Elmhirst's address, 'The Robbery of the Soil'[36]

THE STANDARD OF living in modern civilization has been raised far higher than the average level of our necessity. The strain which this entails serves at the outset to increase our physical and mental alertness. The claim upon our energy accelerates growth. This in its turn produces activity that expresses itself by raising life's standard still higher.

When this standard attains a degree that is a great deal above the normal it encourages the passion of greed. The temptation of an inordinately high level of living, which was once confined only to a small section of the community, becomes widespread. The burden is sure to prove fatal to the civilization which puts no restraint upon the emulation of self-indulgence.

In the geography of our economic world the ups and downs produced by inequalities of fortune are healthy only within a moderate range. In a country divided by the constant interruption of steep mountains no great civilization is possible because in such places the natural flow of communication is always difficult. Like mountains, large fortunes and the enjoyment of luxury are also high walls of segregation; they produce worse divisions in society than any physical barriers.

Where life is simple wealth does not become too exclusive and owners of individual property find no great difficulty in acknowledging their communal responsibility. In fact wealth can even become the best channel for social communication. In former days in India public opinion levied heavy taxes upon wealth and most of the public works of the country were voluntarily contributed by the rich. The water supply, medical help, education and amusement were naturally maintained by men of property through a spontaneous sense of mutual obligation. This was made possible because the limits set to the individual right of self-indulgence were narrow and surplus wealth easily followed the channel of social responsibility. In such a society civilization was supported by strong pillars of property, and wealth gave opportunity to the fortunate for self-sacrifice.

But, with the rise of the standard of living, property changes its aspect. It shuts the gate of hospitality which is the best means of social communication. Its owners display their wealth in an extravagance which is self-centred. This

---

36. In Leonard Elmhirst, *The Poet and the Plowman*, (Calcutta: Visva-Bharati, 1975) also Das Vol 3 pp. 866-871.

creates envy and irreconcilable class division. In other words property becomes anti-social.

Because property itself, with what is called material progress, has become intensely individualistic, the method of gaining it has become a matter of science and not of social ethics. Property and its acquisition break social bonds and drain the life sap of the community. The unscrupulousness involved plays havoc the world over and generates a force that can coax or coerce peoples to deeds of injustice and of wholesale horror.

The forest fire feeds upon the living world from which it springs till it exhausts itself completely along with its fuel. When a passion like greed breaks loose from the fence of social control it acts like that fire, feeding upon the life of society. The end is annihilation. It has ever been the object of the spiritual training of man to fight those passions that are anti-social and to keep them chained. But lately abnormal temptation has set them free and they are fiercely devouring all that is affording them fuel.

There are always insects in our harvest field which, in spite of their robbery, tend to leave a sufficient surplus for the tillers of the soil, so that it does not pay us to try to exterminate them altogether. But when some pest, that has an enormous power of self multiplication, attacks our total food crop we must consider this a great calamity. In human society, in normal circumstances, there are many causes that make for wastage, yet it does not cost us much to ignore them. But today the blight that has fallen upon our social life and its resources is disastrous because it is not restricted within reasonable limits. This is an epidemic of voracity that has infected the total area of civilization. We all claim our right, and freedom, to be extravagant in our enjoyment if we can afford it. Not to be able to waste as much upon myself as my rich neighbour does merely prove a poverty in myself of which I am ashamed, and against which my women folk, and other parasites, naturally cherish their own grievance. Ours is a society in which, through its tyrannical standard of respectability, all the members are goading each other to spoil themselves to the utmost limit of their capacity. There is a continual screwing up of the ideal level of convenience and comfort, the increase in which is proportionately less than the energy it consumes. The very shriek of advertisement itself, which constantly accompanies the progress of unlimited production, involves the squandering of an immense quantity of material and of life force which merely helps to swell the sweepings of time. Civilization today caters for a whole population of gluttons. An intemperance, which could safely have been tolerated in a few, has spread its contagion to the multitude. This universal greed, which now infects us all, is the cause of every kind of meanness, of cruelty and of lies in politics and commerce, and vitiates the whole human atmosphere. A civilization, which has attained such an unnatural appetite, must, for its continuing existence, depend upon numberless victims. These are being sought in those parts of the world where human flesh is cheap. In Asia and Africa a bartering goes on through which the future hope and happiness of entire peoples is sold for the sake of providing some fastidious fashion with an endless supply of respectable rubbish.

The consequence of such a material and moral drain is made evident when one studies the condition manifested in the grossness of our cities and the physical and mental anaemia of the villages almost everywhere in the world. For cities inevitably have become important. The city represents energy and materials concentrated for the satisfaction of an exaggerate appetite, and this concentration is considered to be a symptom of civilization. The devouring process of such an abnormality cannot be carried on unless certain parts of the social body conspire and organize to feed upon the whole. This is suicidal; but, before a gradual degeneracy ends in death, the disproportionate enlargement of the particular portion looks formidably great. It conceals the starved pallor of the entire body. The illusion of wealth becomes evident because certain portions grow large on their robbery of the whole.

A living relationship, in a physical or in a social body, depends upon sympathetic collaboration and helpfulness between the various individual organs or members. When a perfect balance of interchange begins to operate, a consciousness of unity develops that is no longer easy to obstruct. The resulting health or wealth are both secondary to this sense of unity which is the ultimate end and aim, and a creation in its own right. Whenever some sectarian ambition for power establishes a dominating position in life's republic, the sense of unity, which can only be generated and maintained by a perfect rhythm of reciprocity between the parts is bound to be disturbed. In a society where the greed of an individual or of a group is allowed to grow uncontrolled, and is encouraged or even applauded by the populace, democracy, as it is termed in the West, cannot be truly realized. In such an atmosphere a constant struggle goes on among individuals to capture public organizations for the satisfaction of their own personal ambition. Thus democracy becomes like an elephant whose one purpose in life is to give joy rides to the clever and to the rich. The organs of information and expression, through which opinions are manufactured, and the machinery of administration, are openly or secretly manipulated by the prosperous few, by those who have been compared to the camel which can never pass through the needle's eye, that narrow gate that leads to the kingdom of ideals. Such a society necessarily becomes inhospitable, suspicious, and callous towards those who preach their faith in ideals, in spiritual freedom. In such a society people become intoxicated by the constant stimulation of what they are told is progress, like the man for whom wine has a greater attraction than food.

Villages are like woman. In their keep is the cradle of the race. They are nearer to nature than the towns and are therefore in closer touch with the fountain of life. They have the atmosphere which possesses a natural power of healing. Like woman they provide people with their elemental needs, with food and joy, with the simple poetry of life and with those ceremonies of beauty which the village spontaneously produces and in which she finds delight. But when constant strain is put upon her through the extortionate claims of ambition, when her resources are exploited through the excessive stimulus of temptation, then she becomes poor in life. Her mind becomes dull and uncreative; and, from her time-honoured position as the wedded partner of the city, she is degraded to that of maid servant. The city, in its intense egotism and pride, remains blissfully unconscious of the devastation it is continuously spreading within the village, the source and origin of its own life, health and joy.

True happiness is not at all expensive. It depends upon that natural spring of beauty and of life, harmony of relationship. Ambition pursues its own path of self-seeking by breaking this bond of harmony, digging gaps, creating dissension. Selfish ambition feels no hesitation in trampling underfoot the whole harvest field, which is for all, in order to snatch away in haste that portion which it craves. Being wasteful it remains disruptive of social life and the greatest enemy of civilization.

In India we had a family system of our own, large and complex, each family a miniature society in itself. I do not wish to discuss the question of its desirability, but its rapid decay in the present day clearly points out the nature and process of the principle of destruction which is at work in modern civilization. When life was simple, needs normal, when selfish passions were under control, such a domestic life was perfectly natural and truly productive of happiness. The family resources were sufficient for all. Claims from one or more individuals of that family were never excessive. But such a group can never survive if the personal ambition of a single member begins separately to clamour for a great deal more than is absolutely necessary for him. When the determination to augment private possession, and to enjoy exclusive advantage, runs ahead of the common good and of general happiness, the bond of harmony, which is the bond of creation, must give way and brothers must separate nay even become enemies.

This passion of greed that rages in the heart of our present civilization, like a volcanic flame of fire, is constantly struggling to erupt in individual bloatedness. Such eruptions must disturb man's creative mind. The flow of production which gushes from the cracks rent in society gives the impression of a hugely indefinite gain. We forget that the spirit of creation can only evolve out of our own inner abundance and so add to our true wealth. A sudden increase in the flow of production of things tends to consume our resources and requires us to build new storehouses. Our needs, therefore, which stimulate this increasing flow, must begin to observe the limitation of normal demand. If we go on stoking our demands into bigger and bigger flames the conflagration that results will no doubt, dazzle our sight, but its splendour will leave on the debit side only a black heap of charred remains. When our wants are moderate, the rations we each claim do not exhaust the common store of nature and the pace of their restoration does not fall hopelessly behind that of our consumption. This moderation leaves us leisure to cultivate happiness, that happiness which is the artist soul of the human world, and which can create beauty of form and rhythm of life. But man today forgets that the divinity within him is revealed by the halo of this happiness. The Germany of the period of Goethe was considered to be poverty stricken by the Germany of the period of Bismarck. Possibly the standard of civilization, illuminated by the mind of Plato or by the life of the Emperor Asoka, is underrated by the proud children of modern times who compare former days with the present age of progress, an age dominated by millionaires, diplomats and war lords. Many things that are of common use today were absolutely lacking in those days. But are the people that lived then to be pitied by the young of our day who enjoy so much more from the printing press but so much less from the mind?

I often imagine that the moon, being smaller in size than the earth, produced the condition for life to be born on her soil earlier than was possible on the soil of her companion. Once she too perhaps had her constant festival of colour, of music and of movement; her store-house was perpetually replenished with food for her children. Then in course of time some race was born to her that was gifted with a furious energy of intelligence, and that began greedily to devour its own surroundings. It produced beings who, because of the excess of their animal spirit, coupled with intellect and imagination, failed to realize that the mere process of addition did not create fulfilment; that mere size of acquisition did not produce happiness; that greater velocity of movement did not necessarily constitute progress and that change could only have meaning in relation to some clear ideal of completeness. Through machinery of tremendous power this race made such an addition to their natural capacity for gathering and holding, that their career of plunder entirely outstripped nature's power for recuperation. Their profit makers dug big holes in the stored capital of the planet. They created wants which were unnatural and provision for these wants was forcibly extracted from nature. When they had reduced the limited store of material in their immediate surroundings they proceeded to wage furious wars among their different sections, each wanting his own special allotment of the lion's share. In their scramble for the right of self-indulgence they laughed at moral law and took it to be a sign of superiority to be ruthless in the satisfaction each of his own desire. They exhausted the water, cut down the trees, reduced the surface of the planet to a desert, riddled with enormous pits, and made its interior a rifled pocket, emptied of its valuables. At last one day the moon, like a fruit whose pulp had been completely eaten by the insects which it had sheltered, became a hollow shell, a universal grave for the voracious creatures who insisted upon consuming the world into which they had been born. In other words, they behaved exactly in the way human beings of today are behaving upon this earth, fast exhausting their store of sustenance, not because they must live their normal life, but because they wish to live at a pitch of monstrous excess. Mother Earth has enough for the healthy appetite of her children and something extra for rare cases of abnormality. But she has not nearly sufficient for the sudden growth of a whole world of spoiled and pampered children.

Man has been digging holes into the very foundations not only of his livelihood but of his life. He is now feeding upon his own body. The reckless waste of humanity which ambition produces is best seen in the villages where the light of life is gradually being dimmed, the joy of existence dulled, and the natural bonds of social communion are being snapped every day. It should be our mission to restore the full circulation of life's blood into these martyred limbs of society; to bring to the villagers health and knowledge; a wealth of space in which to live, a wealth of time in which to work, to rest and enjoy mutual respect which will give them dignity; sympathy which will make them realize their kinship with the world of men and not merely their position of subservience.

Streams, lakes and oceans are there on this earth. They exist not for the hoarding of water exclusively each within its own area. They send up the vapour which forms into clouds and helps in a wide distribution of water. Cities have a special function in maintaining wealth and knowledge in concentrated forms of opulence, but this should not be for their own exclusive sake; they should not magnify themselves, but should enrich the entire society. They should be like the lamp post, for the light it supports must transcend its own limits. Such a relationship of mutual benefit between the city and the village remains strong only so long as the spirit of co-operation and self-sacrifice is a living ideal in society as a whole. When some universal temptation overcomes this ideal when some selfish passion finds ascendancy then a gap is formed and widened between them. The mutual relationship between city and village becomes that of exploiter and victim. This is a form of perversity in which the body becomes its own enemy. The termination is death.

We have started in India, in connection with Visva-Bharati, a kind of village work the mission of which is to retard this process of race suicide. If I try to give you details of the work the effort will look small. But we are not afraid of this appearance of smallness, for we have confidence in life. We know that if, as a seed, smallness represents the truth that is in us, it will overcome opposition and conquer space and time. According to us the poverty problem is not so important. It is the problem of unhappiness that is the great problem. The search for wealth which is the synonym for the production and collection of things can make use of men ruthlessly and can crush life out of the earth and for a time can flourish. Happiness may not compete with wealth in its list of needed materials, but it is final, it is creative therefore it has its own source of riches within itself. Our object is to try to flood the choked bed of village life with streams of happiness. For this the scholars, the poets, the musicians, the artists as well as the scientists have to collaborate have to offer their contribution. Otherwise they live like parasites, sucking life from the country people, and giving nothing back to them. Such exploitation gradually exhausts the soil of life, the soil which needs constant replenishing by the return of life to it through the completion of the cycle of receiving and giving back.

The writer of the following paper, who was in charge of the rural work in Visva-Bharati, forcibly drew our attention to this subject and made it clear to us that the civilization which allows its one part to exploit the rest without making any return is merely cheating itself into bankruptcy. It is like the foolish young man, who suddenly inheriting his father's business, steals his own capital and spends it in a magnificent display of extravagance. He dazzles the imagination of the onlookers, he gains applause from his associates in his dissipation, he becomes the most envied man in his neighbourhood till the morning when he wakes up, in surprise, to a state of complete indigence. Most of us who try to deal with the poverty problem think of nothing else but of a greater intensive effort of production, forgetting that this only means a greater exhaustion of materials as well as of humanity, and this means giving a still better opportunity for profit to the few at the cost of the many. But it is food which nourishes and not money. It is fullness of life which makes us happy and not fullness of purse. Multiplying materials intensifies the inequality between those who have and those who have not. This is the worst wound from which the social body can suffer. It is a wound through which the body is bled to death!

1922

Patrick Geddes on the Environment

Cities, and the Soils They Grow from[37]

WHETHER YOU LOOK out with me from my Outlook Tower in Edinburgh – or from the Eiffel Tower in Paris or the old dome of St. Paul's in London, the city we scan is set in the matrix of a vastly and minutely complex and heterogeneous world.

It is the same if we view Chicago's lake-front from the high office building which (financially speaking) your Mr. Wrigley built out of chewing gum or overlook New York's skyscrapers from the topmost story of the loftiest and most impressive of them that owes its steel girders and graceful pinnacles alike to the profits from the five and ten cent counters which Mr. Woolworth set up in a hundred American Main Streets. It is as true of provincial towns as of national capitals, as true for yesterday and tomorrow as for today. What encompasses us if we climb the Washington Monument, with its stone from every state in the Union, would have held a hundred years ago had we perched ourselves on the Liberty Pole that marked the centre of the typical American village.

Where then, as town dwellers, yet also general inquirers, shall we get our bearings in the world about us. We must find our beginnings somewhere. Conveniently for us of the Western world, our Occidental traditions are distinguishable from those of Oriental cultures: enough so that we can concentrate upon that comparatively small peninsula of Asia which is called Europe; and in this we must focus first upon the eastern Mediterranean region. From thence has arisen most of our present common civilization, thanks largely to what it acquired from Asia and from Egypt.

I

We are thus brought face to face with the enormous and laborious studies of histories, literatures, origins, to which Van Loon or Wells give excellent introductory primers. Take first however, from among older books a single volume, helpful for our quest: Marsh's story *of The Earth and Man*. I hail its author as one of the greatest of geographers, and even of historians, since he did for geography what no predecessor had adequately done; and likewise for history, what no other successor of our greatest historian has been able to do; he outranged Gibbon. As American minister to Italy, and interested in old Rome as every cultivated visitor must be, he became dissatisfied with

---

37. Patrick Geddes, 'Cities, and the soils they grow from', No.2 in *'Talks from my Outlook Tower, 1925'* (in ed. Stalley, M.,) pp.309-320.

Gibbon's *Decline and Fall* as an historic and social narrative (albeit the very greatest), and came to see this retrogression of City and Empire, afresh, as deeply a geographical matter.

Below, behind, beyond this great history of Rome, he got down to bedrock; down to the primitive, matriarchal, and persistent, fact, that women are in the way of feeding men, provided their men will bring them the stuff to cook, and the fuel to cook it with.

This elementary human division of labor, whereby the man brings the game or cultivates the crop, and the woman cooks, provided there be also provision of fuel, is basic to Mediterranean civilization, as to every other since fire was discovered and men left off eating all things raw. 'Fir tree' is really 'Fire tree'; and down it comes. Advancing civilization also clears the forests for its crops; it needs more and more wood, lumber for dwellings and for ships, for implements and weapons; but beyond all else for fuel. The forest seems for a long time limitless, and no one thinks of replanting; so man is even now deforesting the earth. This great region of the Mediterranean has longest been steadily desolated of its woods, from end to end, from Spain to Palestine.

Now the rain in these lands falls often in torrents. Where trees bind and hold up the soil, the waters are absorbed into its sponge, and sink into and saturate the rocks below; the mountain range is thus a great reservoir also. But where the trees are cleared, their roots no longer hold and bind. Irregularities catch and retain some of the soil, but we often find regular slopes which have been washed well nigh as clear as our roofs. The mountains are denuded, their vast reservoirs of moisture dry up, and the humus is carried down to the plains below. Thus lately in planning the town of Haifa on the northward coast of Palestine, I learned the soil was no less than fifty feet deep on the plain below Mount Carmel – a useless depth for any purpose – while the hill-sides above were correspondingly bared. The shallowed port too has the same explanation; and this process alone accounts for many a city's decline.

Under such conditions large rivers – especially those like the Rhone, and the Durance – in their spring floods bring down not only earth and sand, but gravel, and even boulders, and thus fertile estuary plains have been made stony deserts. Note also that though of old there must have been river floods, these came from forested hills, bringing but light washings of their surface soil, and thus of the best agricultural and manurial value, like those which the Nile deposits upon Egypt to this day. When the trees are gone, the torrent is of briefer duration, but far stronger and swifter while it lasts, since there is no longer the forest humus to retain it. Hence light soil is now carried impetuously out to sea, shallowing and spoiling the old ports though our age would need them at their deepest; while up-stream stones, formerly well embedded, are now loosened, and whirled down upon the plain, henceforward irregular and uneven, here dry and barren, there marshy and malarious. Again, the washed-down soil, on reaching the sea, may be carried along the coast by currents and tides, and make shallow lagoons useless and unfavorable for supping, but harbors for pestiferous mosquitoes. The disasters of deforesting are thus manifold.

As I revise this manuscript, our ship is running along the east coast of Sicily, between Messina and Catania – a noble landscape, with Etna towering behind the minor mountain-masses which rise from near the shore. Fine valleys separate them; but down through each there runs a long swathe of desert, so amazingly broad that most passengers can hardly believe it to be a stream-bed, until they have passed round the binoculars. These have now been embanked by modern engineers, at great expense, to prevent further mischief. But along these thirty miles or so there seems enough bed-space for all the rivers of the British Isles – so great is the loss of what was formerly the very best area for agriculture.

Worst of all, the uneven deposit of detritus upon the plain in flood-time leaves lakelets or useless marshes, throughout all seasons. The larger pools dry up gradually into smaller ones, which none the less are rimmed with a greater aggregate length of shallow edges. In all these the mosquito finds the growing water weeds or the rotting grasses, often a mixture of both, which afford it nutrition for its larval life and protection from being devoured by the smaller fishes. To mature her eggs the female mosquito must have at least one meal of blood; and hence not only cattle are bitten, but man, with his thin smooth skin, is tormented yet more, until he is driven to shut out air, as far as may be, from his dwelling at night; and in the open to sleep with head so deeply wrapped up that air of our most crowded slums may be fresh in comparison.

II

The modern interpretation of the spread of malaria as a 'germ' alternating between the mosquito and man, and with a complicated life cycle in each, is well set forth in every natural history museum, and so needs no explanation here. But 'the pestilence walketh in darkness'; and hence comes the old dread of 'night air,' which I remember often hearing in my Scottish childhood. It may be found today persisting in New York, for example, especially among Italians and other Mediterraneans. The main point for us, however, as regards the secret of malaria, is its significance in classic history. for it has become increasingly clear that we have here a further contribution to the story of the decline and fall of Rome – of Athens too, of Greece, and indeed of much of the whole Mediterranean littoral; an interpretation underlying that of

Marsh, as his underlay that of Gibbon; and thus giving us the long tragedy as a more continuously intelligible whole – in which man not only destroys his fellow-man, but Nature; and she avenges herself, not only in the fall of man's age-long rich cultivation, to poverty, but even by his disease and death.

This last point has been worked out with considerable thoroughness, by Jones and others, beginning with the age when philosophy was culminating in Plato, but when the ruin and decadence of Greece was also setting in. Some of Plato's word-painting of types of men he noticed, is now identified by the medical reader as a good diagnosis, alike of the bodily and mental effects of malaria. These again he reads into the characters and doings of some of the worst Roman emperors and kindred decadents – so strangely akin to attributes at which we shudder in the story of the slave-trade – yet now with a touch of medical compassion for the deeds of emperor and slaver alike, as stirred to madness of crime by fever. The corresponding swing-back to indifference and apathy is a yet more characteristic (and fortunately more general) expression of the malarious taint. This is the usual symptom – that of the depression of life, mental as well as bodily. Its ruinous effect upon working powers, and thence easily upon habits, even after recovery, throws further light upon the widespread Mediterranean decline. And, of course, also upon our understanding of many 'backward' places, and their people, to this day.

The Campagna of Rome – once a fertile and populous farmland, important for its food supplies to the great city, thus fell into a de-populated and pestiferous region through the middle ages. Only now, with our modern knowledge of how to combat the mosquito, is it becoming reclaimed. The historic shrinkings of the population of Rome are thus largely explained by fever-infection, aggravated by diminished food supplies: and though the city itself stands high enough above its plain to afford comparatively few breeding-places, the mosquito can do with small puddles. The many aqueducts which were the glory of ancient Rome, and brought a supply of water per head than that of any modern city, must also have contributed not a little to its decline, as they fell into disrepair.

In such ways then the city could not but decline; and thus lose heart. Yet so great a center could not disappear altogether; the more since its fallen temporal power was replaced by a spiritual one, in its way yet more potent and more enduring. Curiously enough too, the malarious Campagna proved more defensive to the Holy City than its surviving towers and ramparts could have been. Again and again, beleaguering armies, encamped here, melted down to retreating remnants. In the absence of the modern explanation, what more obvious than that of divine protection of the sacred city, and displeasure with its enemies?

Here then is the long and tragic panorama, as modern science draws it, of the decline and fall of this great Mediterranean region – yesterday the garden of the world and the mother of its western civilizations – today a region of poverty, mostly waiting to be redeemed; though happily now in renewing progress at many points, and, by and by, at all.

III

What then was the old state of Nature? Let us again visualize it, and as clearly as we can. A vast region of forested mountain slopes, at best with narrow plains, and these in forest too. Very much like the land to which the Pilgrim Fathers came; all waiting to be cleared; and needing axe to do it, often helped – swiftly, but wastefully – by fire, and this especially on the mountain slopes. But mountains are not merely rocky: think of them rather as water-sponges, soaked and filled with long-accumulated rainfall, and thus an unfailing source which enables their trees to survive dry seasons and keep the plain of the subsoil moist. A tree is not a static object: think of it as Ruskin truly called it, a living fountain, pouring out through its leaves, into the air, enormous quantities of water-vapor daily; and see too how the fall of leaves makes deep, rich soil, which the roots, and the undergrowth, hold firm. But when the trees are cut from the hill-side, down goes the soil as mud with every rainfall, soon exposing the bare rocks to the sun. The 'water-plane', normally so near the surface, thus sinks down; and that that is the falling tide of Mediterranean history. Our surviving natural terraces hence become decreasingly watered, their soil becomes exhausted; and dry seasons soon ruin the cultivators. Barren marshes and pools form upon the plain with its irregular deposits; malaria arises and spreads; cities and empires fall. This is our modern reading of history, deeper than Gibbon's, yet profoundly illuminating it with Marsh's aid, and essentially explaining it, with that of the malariologist's.

Still, the world is always beginning anew, though too often on a far poorer level. Nowhere can one see today a more strenuous and encouraging agricultural endeavor than for example on the Italian and French Riviera. On a steep rock slope, well nigh as bare and free of soil as a house-roof, I have watched an enterprising young couple, who had built themselves a little cottage, building up their land as well. The man not only gathered stones, but broke up rocks, to build his terrace wall. His wife trotted down to the brook and filled her basket with earth, then came uphill slowly with it upon her head, and tilted the contents behind his new wall. So they were gradually making a narrow range of soil; deep behind the wall and shallowing upwards to where a new terrace would begin. Last year's terrace had not only vines, but two or three young olives, with vegetables below. They were not only building up a modest but real prosperity for their later life, but pioneering for their country's renewing up their country's renewing future, as truly as any American settlers yesterday, or Canadian today; indeed in some ways yet more significantly.

In such ways, throughout the ancient and unhistoric past, far more truly progressive than the later historic age, which has seen so much of tragedies and deteriorations, these all-essential terraces were built, higher and higher up the hills, often to the very tops. Hence their survivals, their traces at least, through all Mediterranean lands from Spain to Syria, and beyond, through Persia, along the Himalayan valleys, and on to those of China. Indeed northward too, as in the bronze age on Arthur's Seat, and even here in Old Edinburgh; where our 'Outlook Tower Gardens' but restore a terrace cultivation lost for centuries unnumbered.

You still get the impression of wealth in visiting Barcelona, Marseilles and Genoa, Rome and Naples, Athens and other great cities. Yet nothing is more certain, no economic statement can be more clear and sound, than that the ancient Mediterranean past, with its ranges of terraces from Spain to Syria, was enormously richer – in well-invested capital and in actual return – than are these regions now, with all their modern wealth, of manufacturing, shipping, railways and what not. This old world was immeasurably richer, and correspondingly more deeply and truly civilized. Why then did it decline? By the continual destruction, for all uses, of the remaining timber above the terraces without replanting. That foresight was lacking; and indeed it is only beginning to dawn upon us. Thus, even the daily need of women, who must have fuel before they can cook, involved first the steady ruin of the forests; and to the day even of the shrubs and brushwood, the clearing of which for faggots prevents natural regeneration, and makes artificial planting always more difficult and slow.

Only since the later decades of the 19th century have France, Italy and even Spain in some measure awakened to re-foresting. Thanks to foresters like Pinchot, and to energists like Roosevelt, America is now also on the move. Yet in all lands still far too insufficiently. The decisive modern object-lesson may thus be that of the Zionists, where in Palestine they are gradually re-building their hillside terraces made thousands of years ago, and broken down for ages; and where we may see before long the vast electric power of the Jordan Valley applied to carrying up earth for the cultivation of its terraces, and the renewal of the forests above. That would be a regenerated Holy Land; for in this 'building up the old waste places' lies the concrete future of Zionism. Here in fact is the essential, fundamental and rational view of their problem – one underlying all other modern social, political and cultural considerations. These indeed at present too much obscure this fundamental task, though they should be grounded upon it.

IV

Do I seem to be undervaluing such higher considerations? By no means, but preparing for them. Take a salient example. Every orator in every country uses 'the olive branch' as symbol of peace, but how few can tell why that stock phrase stands for it? Since earliest Athens, the olive tree of Pallas has stood for wisdom too, Academic orators constantly so refer to it; but how often do they really know why? Yet it is very simple.

Suppose as young men we start building our terraces; growing meanwhile what little corn and vegetables we can in strips along them. The vines we plant against the terrace walls are bearing profitably in four years. But with our olives, we have to wait fifteen years before we have a paying crop of fruit. Thus, even starting in our early twenties, we get to middle life before our olive trees really pay. That is a far longer and stiffer discipline than had the colonists of America; for, hard through their work was of clearing the land, their plowing thereafter brought quick return, and with no waiting for half a generation. Our olives, however, go on improving till they are sixty, and then they last, no one yet knows how long, but assuredly for many centuries. A few thick gnarled old survivors in Palestine are known as 'Romans'; and though this popular name may be challenged, it is not impossible it may be right. With such slow but steady investment then, for our main fortune, is it not manifest that we are on the side of peace? For we have the very strongest desire not to have our olive trees cut down for boiling the pots of even friendly armies, let alone hostile ones. We see that, either way, war comes to much the same thing.

In Palestine this inevitable destruction, by both combatants, of too many of the few remaining olives, along with the last oak forests, was one of the inconspicuous but genuine tragedies of the world war. Again, nothing was more aggravating to the French on the western front than the cutting down of their fruit trees by the Germans in retreat. Such an ordinary fruit tree takes a vigorous man a few blows with an axe, and down it goes. But no soldiers, after a day's march, will attack the tough proposition of an olive-trunk if they can possibly help it. Only hunger, only the need of fuel for food, compels this task. Still, down they went, and with them the last resource of prosperity of a region. Yet it must be added, that now in peace-time fuel has become frightfully dear, so that the needy peasant, who has a few old olive trees left, has often to cut them down to sell for firewood in Jerusalem, and so aggravate his ruin.

In short, then, nothing can more clearly protest against war, and plead for peace, than an olive region, since its destruction, of all cultures, is the most lamentably hard and long to repair.

What now of the olive as tree of wisdom? This tree was traditionally given to Athens by the Wisdom-Goddess, Pallas Athena, who thus won from the Olympian Gods the reward of giving to the city its immortal name. Why? After toil of planting our trees and waiting for their crop, we come to have its return with comparative leisure; leisure after all fairly early in middle life; and leisure (*'schola'*) from the first for the younger generation; hence their 'school'. The intensive culture of fruit trees is one of care and skill, but not excessive toil. It is a pleasant and fairly easy occupation, which gives long periods of leisure; yet keeps up foresight and attentive skill; and so maintains character. Our area of cultivation needed for moderate prosperity is small: we are near our neighbors, and so we form a congenial community; yet, as the olive tree usually bears well only every second year, we have a permanent education in thrift as well. And so we might go on with the cultural aspects of fruit-growing, in all lands and times, and this alike upon political and pacific levels, on intellectual levels also – scientific, philosophic and artistic – as at Athens; on spiritual levels – as at Jerusalem.

Jerusalem and Athens – each in its own way the supreme culture-city of humanity – were both of them founded on, and associate with, the olive tree. Each – above all in its supreme influences – is best understood, and remembered, as a 'Mount of Olives'.

V

The much-talked of 'economic interpretation of history' is thus no mere formula of modern schools of doctrine; as from Montesquieu, Buckle and more to Karl Marx. It has to be traced throughout the whole life and labor of man, and thence onwards, into its highest outcomes. The school of Marx is too easily satisfied with its modern industrial rendering of the story; but the earlier and later schools of Le Play, as yet so little known in English or German, have long been working out the wider and deeper method I have touched upon. But why this current neglect of the Le Play method and teaching by our scholarly world? – indeed even more by the religious? Because here is science 'shaking the very foundations of (conventional) belief,' by proving that the venerable stories of Athens, which our elder scholars have thought 'mythology,' and those of Jerusalem which our religious teachers have too much thought of as 'sacred poetry,' are really, both of them, solid matter-of-fact prose as well; and all this not only in the past, but for the future also. For here in fruit-culture, best of all cultures, and with olive-growing first among them, we have not only a main clue towards the interpretation of these ancient civilizations, but towards their renewal upon our modern spiral. For this culture we now see sweeping from Palestine, with its Zionist ambition to build second to none among the world's universities; and along the Mediterranean; and thence again across the world, to fruit-growing California, with its manifold cultural developments, its yet vaster and nascent ambitions, to become a new and greater Hellas for the American continent, if not for all the wide Pacific.

VI

As specific illustration of the need for regional planning – and wellnigh world-planning – what greater field for geotechnics than Afforestation? We need not here recapitulate the many endeavors in progress – in various parts of Europe, the ruined Mediterranean especially, yet also from Scotland to India, and back again, and similarly in the United States, from great schemes for the too largely desolated Appalachians to the admirable educational lessons of Arbor Day. Assuming these as known, they are all admittedly insufficient to cope with a situation so manifold.

Capital, and on a great scale, is needed for such task; and this has to be sunk, at first with no return, and then with small, say for ten years with even the quicker-growing trees, and for fifteen, twenty, thirty years and more, for slower ones. Under these circumstances, old men see no return. Young men need all they have for their start in life, and by maturity they have their funds fully involved in their concerns, and in ways of more speedy promise. Hence many cry to the state to intervene, and this now and then it does, but with measures in most countries, indeed all, quite inadequate. Yet a government has no magic purse, and under growing democratic conditions, too often but a hand-to-mouth existence. Let us therefore face the situation – that no ordinary funds are available! On closer examination, there comes into view one fund, and that not inconsiderable, of annual savings by an ever-increasing proportion of the public, which are not invested in any highly remunerative returns, though appreciably cumulative within a lifetime. I refer, of course, to our regularly paid premiums of life-insurance. But what dare our companies do with these, save invest them upon the best security they can find; and therefore at comparatively low interest? One of the most frequent forms of this investment, in fact the predominant one, must needs be in mortgages upon land; for they thus avoid the uncertainties, even risks, of its cultivation.

Yet is not this task of afforestation one – even the very one – which may thus be undertaken? Suppose we form a Foresting Insurance Company, and so put our premiums into trees? They grow slowly, yet at compound interest, while we are sleeping and they are ready to be cut down and realized – at normally increasing values also, as timber and fuel prospects indicate – in time for our own life-cutting by the inexorable shears.

True, there are forest fires, and blights and disasters of many kinds, but existing forest owners already insure against these; and so must we.

The technique of forestry is well known: skilled direction and labor can readily be had; and on very reasonable terms, so attractive is such life. And this also of peculiarly high character; for the forester, of all occupations, with his long foresight, best learns the wisdom of his craft, with all its varied seasonal labors, from planting to felling, and then replanting; and with patient and thrifty vigilance meanwhile. And if so, is not all this an invaluable element of insurance?

Many years before the famous 'rubber-boom', I had been preaching as botanist and tree-lover, yet something of rural economist too, the coming need of rubber, and the desirability of planting accordingly. But to deaf ears; for 'the practical man' was not practical enough: and when in this case he did come to act, it was in haste of speedy returns.

Our forestry, then, as insurance, begins with family finance, at one end; yet it is also regional development at the other. As such, it is in principle a substantial economic interest, to be regulated and guarded by governments. But if so, here is another social element of security: so with all this why should not its policies be esteemed and come into demand as have those of older companies, on their existing business basis? Ordinary insurance reports are after all not very interesting reading; but ours would have cheering photo-blocks of its forests in growth; and it might even encourage its shareholders to come and see, and camp, in their own property, of pines, oranges or oil-palms, as their travel might allow. Surely these are forms of advertising more interesting than can be mere ordinary print; and calculated to make new agents, interested in the propaganda, and not solely in their commissions?

So far we have been outlining this scheme towards afforestation as a new and separate undertaking; but may we not also incite the existing insurance companies to look into the matter, and begin experimenting for themselves?

Enough however of this illustration; for this is not a prospectus, but an example of the thesis of these papers; that of the coming in of survey and service, of geography and geotechnics along lines of constructive individual and social action, and towards turning declines and falls into renewing rise.

The Valley Plan of Civilisation[38]

WARS ARE NOT fundamental to human history. But, it is often asked, what is history but a perpetual tale of wars? Between three and four thousand wars have been recorded on paper or stone within its span of but a few thousand years, yet war is not that permanent state and outcome of 'human nature' which these have led so many of us to believe. Indeed we now know wars to be of fairly recent origins; for they were substantially preceded by a long age – a comparatively Golden Age – in which men were quietly cultivating the plants and domesticating the animals, and thus were themselves being cultivated by their plants, and domesticated by their animals. Here in truth is the explanation of the lateness of the appearance of History. Quiet, decent, constructive, agricultural and village civilisation is comparatively uneventful, and thus, in the conventional sense, it is non-historic. Hence the poverty of Indian history, the comparative monotony of Chinese history; yet so far also to the credit of these steady old peoples. Historians have too much always been like the press of our own period, which mainly records unusual and tragic incidents; and which (after all not quite unfairly) asks – what else can we do? – is not one man who throws his chair out of the window of more curious interest to our readers than all the millions who use their chairs in the ordinary way?

The unravelling of war-origins however, we must postpone to our (Illustration of The Valley Plan of Civilization... appears here in the text)

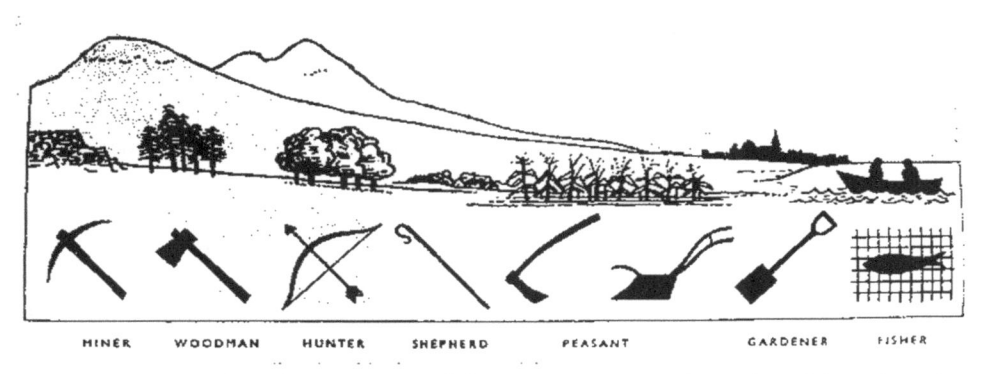

The Valley Plan of Civilization, From Philip Mairet, Pioneer of Sociology: The Life and Letters of Patrick Geddes (London: Lund Humphries, 1957), Courtesy of the New York Public Library.

---

38. Patrick Geddes, Valley plan of civilization (No. 3 in *'Talks from my Outlook Tower, 1925'*, in ed. Stalley, M. pp. 321-333.

next article; for in the social sciences, as with biological and evolutionary studies, the essential is to have as clear an understanding as we may of normal life-processes before we come to pathological interruptions.

So before coming (or going to War), let us learn more of the ways of Peace.

I

Take a simple agricultural interpretation; that of the fundamental staff of life – corn of various kinds for the West, and rice for the East. On the significance of wheat-corn we have the enormous volumes of Frazer's *Golden Bough*, now happily condensed into one, in which his striking treatment of comparative religions stands out clear. But let us look at cereal culture for ourselves, and in a plainer way; of which Frazer says little, even for his wheat; while rice seems never to have occurred to him as of social significance at all. Let us think of our forefathers in the old days of colonization in America, or from past till now in Europe. Each drives his own plow upon his own field; and without cooperation. Each can whistle the old tune,

I care for nobody, no not I,
And nobody cares for me.

Each in short, 'minds his own business', and let others alone. That is the civilization of corn growing. The land is plowed and sowed, and the crop is cut, by each farmer himself, the women and children are but mere accessory helpers at harvesting, until at length their parts in the work are invented away. Here then, in the cereal cultivation of the West, from old Rome to modern America, we have the basic factor of our fundamental Western concept of individuality and independence; and we may trace it at leisure, from Roman origins to current law, politics and more.

But if we are Easterners, cultivating rice, this makes us quite a different proposition. We can have no adequate cultivation of rice in any district until we all form ourselves into one big water-committee; for we have to deal with the water supply of our valley, and to adjust its flow, so that everybody gets as his share enough to cover and maintain his rice-fields. Here, now, is necessity for community action; and its reward. And here again is a further element; that while corn needs the strong man to drive the plow, and to do the later operations, not only the women but the little children, and the old grandparents, in fact everybody, can put the tiny plant of rice into the soft mud and press it in with the foot. So too at harvest every one can take a handful and cut it, another handful and shear that, and so on. Thus men have no such great superiority over women, children and old folks: all members of the family are united in a small cooperative group, as the neighborhood, the village, into a comprehensive one.

Hence, in contrast to the deeply corn-based individualism of the West, we have the deeply rice-based 'community family' and village of the East, with its widely different institutions. We have dug below the too simple views of New York or London, whether those of the market – the merchant and his conventional economist, interested only in how the year's crops are selling at various and oscillating pecuniary values; or again those of the household, and if need be its dietetic physician, with their wheaten-bread and rice-pudding, and their respectively physiological values and limitations. We have now got deeper down than our current economics and our dietetics reach, for we have been reaching the *Civilization-Values* of wheat and rice, as respectively individualistic and communitary. We have thus got on the level of sociology proper, which conventional studies too rarely reach: though excellent preliminaries when we do not stop there.

A curious verification of this contrast came after rice was introduced into Lombardy, along the valley of the River Po. After half a generation or so, the peasants petitioned for specific changes of the laws of inheritance and so on. The rest of the Lombard and Italian public, and their representatives, naturally did not see much sense in that. But a member of the Italian parliament, who had been in China, looking over this petition, cried out 'Why, these people are petitioning for Chinese institutions!' of course, they were, since they were cultivating rice.

We might work in such ways very many other specific and definite civilization-values. The kind of place, and the kind of work done in it, deeply determine the ways and institutions of history; economists, not only the classical but even the socialistic (despite all their talk of 'the economic interpretation of history'), the Sociological Society in London has its abode in Le Play House, so-called after the founder of this doctrine, and summed in his formula – Lieu, Travail, Famille: Place, Work, Folk, as we say.

II

Pass now to general geography – and let us try to make clear its essential scenes for the drama of civilization. Here the atlas, with its flat maps, though indispensable, is far from being enough. It is thus well here to recall that the greatest of descriptive geographers – Elisée Reclus, with his rightly-named Géographie Universelle, was of all men also the most active exponent of the need for advancing beyond maps to relief-models, and thus even to his Great Globe – still to be realized in its full relief, a scheme which will make the first city adequately to produce and use it the capital of the geographic sciences, and with them the economic and social. To realize any country, any region or any city, we have always first to think in terms of its relief, and this whether our task be the fullest understanding of its history, or the simplest details of its development, present or possible. For the city-planner, his success, or his wasteful failures, fundamentally depend upon his realization, or omission of relief and contours – as there is no lack of American (and also Canadian) instances to show.

For our present purpose, an outline of such relief as a 'Valley Section', may be simply drawn (see the diagram at the head of this article), of that general slope from mountains to sea which we find everywhere in the world. This we can readily adapt to any scale, and to any proportions, of our particular and characteristic range, of hills and slopes and plain. Thus viewed as looking northward, I have here not simply my particular home-view, from our Edinburgh Outlook Tower, from snows down to sea, and back again, from Lowlands west to Highlands; but in principle also a section across Wales and England; across Ireland; across Norway and Sweden; even across mountainous Europe and the Siberian plain: - or again, across North America or Canada with the Rockies, across South America with the Andes. Broadly speaking, this way the world is built.

First of all, then, this Valley Section, as we commonly call it, makes vivid to us the range of climate, with its corresponding vegetation and animal life. Not only snows on the mountains may here be realized; but their geologic nature and structure also. Then too the forests, the pastoral slopes, the minor hills, the plains, their uniting rivers; all things are here. This is no longer our mere school-book, with its images of a 'country' as a colored space on a flat map, with only 'boundaries' and 'capital', and so on; it is first of all the essential sectional outline of a geographer's 'region', ready to be studied. Next then it is an anthropologist's, and thence also an evolutionary economist's; in time we shall even work down to the modern urban view of the conventional economist, of the politician and more. But first of all we must proceed in natural order.

We can grasp something of the help which geography brings to the modern renewal of historic studies, if we go over any old historical atlas; especially therefore of the Mediterranean, and compare it with climatic and vegetation maps of recent date. At a glance we see how closely the colonization range of Greek civilization was at once invited by the olive-regions, and limited to them. Hence it did not spread northward from southern Italy, though this became 'Magna Graecia'; nor yet did it get far into Gaul, or Spain. Similarly the course of Roman expansion was essentially into that of the vine climate of Gaul, and its northward limit broadly agrees with the limits of modern vine-growing in Germany and Austria. Wheat no doubt tempted them further, as into Britain; but they initiated vine-growing even there: though it died out, partly through the old wars with France, largely too with the Reformation, but above all from that growing competition of the cheaper and heavier beer of the north with the lighter and brighter wine of the south. This competition has entered even into our patriotisms: thus deeply into that of England, however unavowed, witness that of 'the beerage', who have been so mighty a factor in our houses of parliament, and thus for foreign policy no less than at home.

Consider now, upon the general outline of our Valley Section, the soil. And this first of all with its natural forests, at least on the uplands, the coniferous above the deciduous; hence we see that in these the natural occupation can but be that of the hunter, until the coming of the woodman. Next we come to spaces of pasturage, with flocks and shepherds. Below these, but still on comparatively high, thin and poor soils, we find the struggling peasant, the 'crofter' as we call him in Scotland, with his share of hill-pasture from old times, but mainly dependent on hard and strenuous tillage; and this is only of the poorer grains, oats or rye, and in modern times of potatoes, but not wheat. Wheat can only flourish on the deeper and richer land below; so there at length we have the farmer proper, the normally rich peasant; i.e. him of white bread, not ryebread or oatcake. So far the cool temperate lands. But our section may next be enriched for warmer temperate climates also; where to the wheat-growing peasant is added the vine grower upon his terrace-slopes. Follow southwards, towards the more sheltered Mediterranean coastlands, and we reach the warm-temperate at its best: the land of the olive. Wheat, wine and oil: at length we have agriculture at its richest and best, and with highest civilization-record accordingly. Still, as we have already seen, this Mediterranean region is sadly ruined: so that it is now with the farmer to northward, with his wheat-land, that prosperity has more generally maintained itself; though alas, too unstably everywhere.

III

More closely examined, our valley section diagram finds place for all the nature-occupations, since the full theater of their range of activities. Reading it from left to right, we may conveniently start with one not yet mentioned, yet essential from the first – the Miner, of course not yet of coal, but first of the flints with which civilization so essentially began. For a long time he dug and worked the rude flints, whence his 'Paleolithic' implements, into whose stages we need not here enter, socially significant through they have proved. In later times, he finely shaped and polished those 'Neolithic' implements, which as we have come to learn, indicate no mere far-away 'barbarians of the stone age', but the essential founders of most of the main elements of our present civilization. Comparatively lately, as the vast periods of archaeology now show, came the age of copper, and thence of bronze; with war thus becoming much more prominent; as again far more so, with the comparatively recent introduction of iron, and its terrible sword of steel, with whose doings history is soon full. Flints, coarse and fine; bronze, iron and steel: here are now the marks of historic ages – the chronology of the miner, as at length the metallurgist. And is he not in these times anew significant – with new alloys, with aluminium, even with radium?

But the Woodman may next make his claim to an essential leadership of civilization. Far beyond his mere gathering of brushwood and branches for the fire, his stone or bronze axe hewed out the clearing; and then at length, with steel, he cut the modern highways of the western world. Thus, for salient instance, the old bronze-age land-route from the Mediterranean through Gaul to Britain (for its copper and tin) kept to the southwest, through Languedoc over the Loire and by Brittany to Cornwall. It was the later steel axe that first cleared the route up the Rhone valley, and thence to west and north, by Dijon and Paris, the predominant way for and since Roman times, as every traveler or history-student knows.

The woodman too has been the treat initiative house-builder, the furniture-maker; and the boat builder, of course, too: moreover with his palisade, the fortifier as well. Beyond all this, we owe to him the mechanical powers, the lever, the wedge, the wheel and axle, the pulley; and the inclined plane, if not the screw. He is thus the primal engineer. In this conception it is worth remembering that the father and educator of James Watt, was one of the last old wood-workers who were complete 'wrights', ready to build either a house or a ship to demand; surely here a perfect linking of the old industrial order with the new; and illustration of the later origin in metal from him of wood-work, as wheel-wright, and so on.

Next the Hunter, tracking and killing his game. Here plainly we have not merely a rude survivor of primitive society, but a type of permanent and increasing significance in history. Though in the old hunting societies, from arctic Eskimos to southmost Australians, in various ways truly and even deeply civilized and thus essentially peaceful, we of the west have learned to think of the hunter, and only too justly, as readily becoming hunter of his fellow-man, and thence increasingly, far beyond all other occupations, he has been the maker and the leader of war. It has not been for nothing that hunters became nobles and that kings and rulers have ever remained hunters, even to our own day and its great war. Nor has it been for nothing that 'sport', and games mostly in principle of the hunters' spirit, have been, and remain more than ever, a main technical education, of the youth of all other origins and occupations; and this towards war-service, whether it be thus recognized or no.

IV

But the Shepherd, what of him? A widely contrasted type, trained by the gentle tending of life instead of the stern arts of taking it. See too his normally long life, producing patriarchal supremacy accordingly, and hence the temperament as well; in utter contrast to the short-lived hunter whose best years pass with early manhood. Here then is the contrast of patience with impatience, diplomacy with war. Thus of old Abraham and Lot separated when their young men quarrelled, and again in recent times Kruger delayed, while Chamberlain and Rhodes pressed on for the Boer War. But this occupation has higher associations, typical for three great religions – Jewish, Christian and also Buddhist – so that their teachers, widely variant though they be, are still 'pastors' at their best. While the hunter ever becomes 'warlord', and claims all temporal power, the patriarchal shepherd-tradition accumulates too the often far higher spiritual power; witness its historic names, as Holy Father, as Pastor Pastorum. And the like for other faiths. Our modern image of 'The Good Shepherd' is plainly derived, as the Pope's own archaeologists of the Catacombs have shown, from Apollo the shepherd, even to the lamb or kid upon his shoulder. There are statues and pictures of the Buddha older than these, yet in essential the same. And has not this good shepherd of the Far East had peace among his peoples far more than have we of the ever-warring West?

But returning to the practical life of the shepherd peoples, we must not forget Father Jacob, sending down his sons to Egypt to buy corn. The shepherds became caravaneers, and hence they are the makers of land commerce with its market junctions. They were thus the makers and the maintainers of communications, and thus at their best, they became also the spreaders of peace and order, and well-being. The route often wellnigh creates the social type, as Desmoulins has so strongly claimed. Another of his school has interpreted – and ably and suggestively, if not yet convincingly – old Father Odin himself was the great primal caravaneer, between Babylon and Odensee on the Baltic; and hence that the later Norsemen's sea-rovings were inspired by their search for this great-walled Garth of Asia. This, he argues, was their 'quest of Asgard', when the Mongoloid migrations involved by the desiccation of Central Asia had cut their old land-route – albeit in a different direction, curiously analogous to that of Columbus in later days, when the old Red Sea route to the Indies had been closed by the Turkish conquest of Constantinople.

With these daring theories before us, it is not far to link the old caravan kings to their modern successors, the railway kings. I well remember an old countryman, of pastoral origins, and first trained in trade in Aberdeen, who soon went roving over to the Hudson's Bay Company as fur-trader, and by and by, with a comrade of the very same origin, laying the Trans-Canadian Railway. Seldom can there have been a more adventurous or further-ranging caravan lord than this old Strathcona, effectively ruling the modern Canada he had thus so largely helped to build; and whom I remember, as imperious and terrible as Father Odin, up to the patriarchal age of ninety – if not beyond.

Yet the pastoral life can produce still higher types – the spiritualized caravaneers, who once and again stand out as supreme forces in history. Note first one Saul of Tarsus, a native by 'the Cilician Gates', that great pass for all caravans between Europe and Asia Minor on the one hand, and Mesopotamia, Syria and Egypt on the other. Significantly a tentmaker's son, and learning his father's trade, he cannot but have imbibed the 'Wanderlust' from the caravaneers he worked for. Tarsus had had its mystic priest-king, like the high priest of Jerusalem, yet it had become a Greek university city, as we may fairly call it; and next it had come under the rule of Rome. So here and as nowhere else in the wide world so fully could there have been combined, into one young man's life-training, those fourfold elements – of the traveler's spirit, of Jewish idealism and learning, of Greek philosophy and subtlety, yet also of Roman citizenship – which prepared Saul first for high influence among the Pharisees, and thence – as Paul – to his primacy in extending throughout the Roman Empire the then but germinating Christian faith; and this in the individually developed form he gave it.

Again what essentially is Islam? What but the discipline of the caravan, strengthened and moralized in its own way for the journey across the desert: and with the good time at the journey's end fully idealized for its encouragement. That its prophet should have been, and until maturity, a caravan-leader, is thus the essential, since fundamental, evolutionary explanation for his whole system; and this alike in its spiritual idealism and intensity, and in its expansion; albeit also, and in various ways, the explanation of its limitations, and of its decline.

V

But it is time to pass on to the next type of our valley-section, the poor peasant, the crofter as we call him, not yet the fully developed farmer proper. He has had a hard time, for when we leave the green and flowery pastures, with their milk and honey, and eat the alluring but sour-sweet apple of knowledge which grows up to that boundary, we come down to toil and sweat on poor and stony soils, better fitted for thorns and thistles than for our upland corn. In short here is a sad coming down in the world, a 'fall' indeed. Labour strenuous beyond all other is now needed, and this well-nigh continuous throughout the season; moreover, economies are of the very essence of survival. We must store for the winter's food, and for seed, and us both with frugal care.

The verse in the Psalms of 'one that goeth forth weeping, bearing precious seed, but returneth rejoicing bringing his sheaves with', is plain enough in its second clause, for all men rejoice at harvest home. But in our literate modern world, one may ask learned Jew or Christian alike to explain why the sower should be described as 'weeping'; and we get only metaphorical guesses for answer, whereas here in the first clause of our text is compressed the vividly pathetic reality of the early history of the poor peasant. By spring-time his harvest-store is all but eaten; yet now he cannot but take away the few precious grains that remain, albeit from children crying for food, from starving mother sobbing over them. And so he strides out past them to the field with stern-set face. Once out of doors and away, he too breaks down, and weeps for those he has left behind, and with what misgivings for the future crop, above all for food meanwhile! Lent with its long weeks of scanty fare is thus of the nature of things agricultural and far older than any spiritualizing of it; from its poverty comes its essence – a moral discipline, which has become fundamental in the strength of peasant character. Has not this discipline been the very backbone of many regions – of which New England or old Scotland are but near examples, and this despite their abandonment of Catholic traditions, their forgetfulness of the origins of these? It is more easy for a modern reader to see in the life economy of the poor peasant the origins of the bank and the insurance company.

Pass now to the rich peasant, upon the deep and fertile ploughlands of the plain, once prairie; see him with his tall heavy-headed wheat, his good white bread accordingly to eat, his ample surplus of grain to sell. Hence population thrives and increases, so that instead of the poor peasant isolated, or at most in hamlet, we can have the goodly village, and by and by even the town. In old societies indeed, the need for defence from hungry hunter, and at times too from cornless shepherd, could not but have compelled such grouping: and these dangers soon led to the walling in of the farm-town with its substantial gates. The old story of Cain and Abel is thus plainly pastoral, the Hebrew version of the immemorial and world-wide tension between peasant and shepherd. With all the spirituality of the pastoral culture, its caravans have not always paid fully in wool what they took in grain. Where else but in peaceful England, and her daughter America, after the period of Indian wars, has the farmer been able to live upon his land in the detached way which there to both has become a matter of course? The long distances which we see daily tramped from village to fields in pretty nearly every valley from France to India, and which thus so largely impoverish all concerned, register the far more widespread history of the old agricultural life beset with invading dangers.

To city development we shall come later; but here may be briefly noted that of all occupations it is the farmer's with his yearly harvest, that most needs binding bargains and definite records, as for land-tenure and crop-sales; for taxation too, and more. It is thus he naturally who develops one of his sons as recorder, by and by lawyer, who inscribes his records on calf's or lamb's skin (parchment or vellum) accordingly.

Again, it is his occupation that yields the main beverages, wine in the south, beer in the north; and thus the wine-shop and the ale-house. As caste and wealth develop, each readily becomes exclusive; and thus the club. Talk of affairs in congenial company is thus with loosened tongues and freer range; in such symposia the concrete farming viewpoint and the more abstract legal one interact: discussions thus reach political levels, and so ere long the glories of parliamentary oratory foam from the mug and sparkle from the glass. (What may become of 'politics' for a country (or a sex) without these traditional incentives to eloquence, is a question only lately being raised!)

VI

Into the elaborations of agriculture, to gardening and intensive culture, whether in the old tradition of China, or as nowadays with increasing progress in the west, we need not here enter; but rather pass to the last of our main occupations, that of the sea. Anthropologists tell how woman initiated fishing in streams and rivers, and invented nets, but that when it came to seafaring, the man took over her work with his boat, while she largely took over the man's work on land, the distribution of the fish, and thus increasingly his predominance. Hence her strengthened individuality and self-reliance in these parts. This not only old tales or current observation of fisher life fully confirm, as also does a survey of the modern feminist movements, for it is by no mere coincidence that such initiatives have essentially been along the maritime fringes of the northern seas, spreading thence more slowly inland. Indeed it is thus by no mere accident, but also from deep-rooted tradition that my old and honored friend, the veteran president of the International Council of Women should bear the title of Marchioness of (the old fishing-port) of Aberdeen.

The North Sea fisherman is naturally tempted out from salmon river and fiord to sea-fishing, for herring and cod. He grows richer and more adventurous. With his larger boat and crew he soon becomes more authoritatively organized, since thus more efficient in a hard environment, which calls for prompt decision and instant obedience and gives no time and safety for discussion. Moreover, what the caravan does on land, that the fisher can do at sea, he thus becomes merchant-adventurer, passenger-carrier. In time he is readily also emigrant, even settler; and thus the far-reaching Northman and Norman conqueror, whose spreading sails the British sailor-folk have but carried further in their time. For since, like the hunter, the fisher's calling is of the taking of life, not the tending of it, and since endless opportunities of quarrel arise between fisher and fisher, and yet more between seafarer and landsman, he soon goes armed. Hence the gradual admixture of seafaring with buccaneering and piracy, yet also their disentanglement and ordering, into navies, both mercantile and combative, as history tells. Enough here for the present if we see all together, as the story of the fisher, throughout his varied evolution.

VII

So, back to our valley diagram which called up for us the main make-up of the great world.

Hunter and shepherd, poor peasant and rich: these are our most familiar occupational types, and manifestly successive as we descend in altitude, and also come down the course of social history. Hence it was long the bookish habit to speak of them not only as main types in civilization (which they do broadly represent) but as if each had succeeded the other in successive 'stages,' and for good and all. And these too as but 'phases' before the present predominance of the industrial and commercial urban order, since which, to many of whose writers they have seemed henceforth insignificant, if not practically negligible. But all these fundamental occupations we have always with us. And as our urban studies progress, we shall find them, even in every city; and there not simply with their produce in the open market-place, or in the resulting shop rows which are its modern development; but also as evolved into correspondingly developed urban vocations. Against the background of our valley section we shall understand them better than has the economist or lawyer, the politician or the historian.

v: Ways to the Neotechnic City[39]

IN CHAPTER II we viewed our immense coalfield city-groups, our conurbations, as in the process of indefinite growth; while in the next chapter we presented the threatening arrest of the lower industry and cheaper life of our own and kindred lands, not only by internal exhaustion of coalfields, or by competition upon lower levels, but rather by competition upon a higher one – that of the neotechnic order, now so plainly arising in other lands – Norway being but the best example, as having no paleotechnic development to speak of.

Yet, as already indicated, and as the reader must once and again have felt – this neotechnic order is open to us also; we have had no small part in initiating it. Where better may this advance than in a land, one of the best situated of any, still of cheap and abundant coal, of easy communications, of ample and industrious population? not to speak of resources still only opening, like water-courses and peat-bogs, or of those yet untouched, like winds and tides. Each inventor is busy with his part of this complex task; and the integration of such progresses is one main aspect of the civic movement.

Since cities are thus in transition, is a defence needed of this two-fold presentment, this sharply marked forking of the path of evolution – industrial, social, civic? Our general view of the paleotechnic city has been anything but a roseate one; yet the half has not been said. Its evils – as per its' reporters' columns, its realistic novels, its problem plays – are here viewed as congruent with its industrial (image ' A children's garden in Old Edinburgh ...) and commercial level, and thus normal to it, not removable while it persists, whether by statesmen or by philanthropists, who, alike too much, but poultice symptoms. A view surely pessimistic enough! Yet this pessimism is but apparent, its faith in the order of Nature, and thus, in lowered functions, in diseased conditions, does give us disease. But, as we improve conditions, and with them vitalise functions, Nature gives us, must give us, health and beauty anew – renewing, it may be surpassing, the best records of old.

The paleotechnic order should, then, be faced and shown at its very worst, as dissipating resources and energies, as depressing life, under the rule of machine and mammon, and as working out accordingly its specific results, in unemployment and misemployment, in disease and folly, in vice and apathy, in indolence and crime. All these are not separately to be treated, as our too specialised treatments of them assume, but are logically connected, inseparably connected, like the symptoms of a disease, they are worked out,

---

39. Patrick Geddes *Cities in Evolution*, 1915 ch. 5, in ed. Stalley, M. pp. 155-166.

in sequent moves, upon the chessboard of life. They even tend to become localised upon the chequers of a town plan, and thus become manifest to all as its veritable Inferno. Yet, with the contrasted development of the normal life, no less continuous moves of ascent appear, no less clear and definite city-development also. Our town plans are thus not merely maps but also symbols, a notation of thought which may concretely aid us towards bettering the towns of the present, and thus preparing for the nobler cities of a not necessarily distant future.

It may, again, be said, each of these cities is a logical dream: the city is not so bad as your Inferno, nor is it ever likely to be as good as your Utopia. So far admitted. Every science works with ideal concepts, like the mathematician's zero and infinity, like the geographer's directions – north, south, east, and west – and can do nothing without these. True, the mathematician's progress towards infinity never gets him there, nor do the geographer's journeyings, the astronomer's search attain the ultimate poles. Still, without these unattainable directions, these cardinal ideals, who could move from where he stands, save to sink down into a hole? So far, then, from losing ourselves, either in the gloom of the paleotechnic Inferno or before the neotechnic Eutopia of the coming city, these extremes are what enable us to measure and to criticise the city of the present, and to make provision for its betterment, its essential renewal.

'Here or nowhere is our Utopia'; and our presentments of the city at its worst, in depressing shadow, or again at its best, at brightest dawn, are but the needful chiaroscuro. The hell and heaven of the theologian may have lost their traditional meaning, their old appeal to the multitude, yet may all the more for us here renew their significance. When they asked Dante, 'Where didst thou see Hell?' he answered, 'In the city around me,' as indeed the whole structure and story of the *Inferno* shows. And correspondingly, like plainer men, like simpler poets, he built his Paradise around his boyhood's love.

Absolutely, then, as zero and infinity are indispensable for the mathematician, so hell and heaven are 'the necessary stereoscopic device' of the social thinker, much as of his predecessor, the theologian. Even the material presentments of these – tremendous energies, dissipated and destructive in the one; orderly magnificence of environment and perfection of life in the other – are concretely applicable, are alike logically necessary for our economic and civic studies. Given the everyday life of our towns, at one time we see their brighter aspects, but at another we feel their extending glare and gloom. We say with Shelley, 'Hell is a city much like London', we see how slow must be our journey out of its Valley of the Shadow.

So, again, with the traditional psychologic presentments of hell and heaven – here of agony, of rage, of hatred, of despair and frost, or there of joys, of ideal fellowship, of individual ecstasy.

Hence are not pessimist and optimist each right, and each even in his extremest way? Yet nearer truth than either the image of the Inferno or of Paradise is that of Purgatory; for before us is the renewal of a great social hope, behind us the disappointment and the suffering of innumerable falls.

Yet less fiery presentment of the city's life-process is needed than any of these sternly mythopoetic ones. What better, then, that Blake's? – a veritable town-planner's hymn:

> I will not cease from mental strife,
> Nor shall my sword fall from my hand.
>
> Till I have built Jerusalem
> Within this green and pleasant land!

Now, as regards the Beauty of Cities. Those who are most in the habit of calling themselves 'practical', to maintain this character are also wont too easily to reckon as 'unpracticed' whatever advances of sciences or of art they have not yet considered, or which tend to disturb the paleotechnic set of working conventions. Hence they so easily say of us town planners and city revivers, 'All these prettifications may perhaps do very well for Continental cities, but after all they are mere luxuries, and won't pay us here,' and so on. Now, if anyone in that mind considers the argument of these pages, he will find that what they are primarily concerned with is very different from what he expects; and that our problem is – not prettification, not even architecture, mistress of the arts though she be – but what practical men – men of business, men of politics, men of war – consider to be the most practical of all, namely, their survival, at once local and regional, national and imperial, in the present intensifying struggle for existence, and this in competition with other countries; and with Germany for choice, since their thoughts at present turn so much that way. This fiercely practical reader will also find that all this is discussed without any more reference to aesthetic considerations than are given to them, say at the War Office, or at the nearest public Health office Bureau. The utmost difference is that at places in such grim earnest as these they do know the significance of cleanliness, good order, good looks. They know these as the best and most obvious of symptoms, as the outcome, the expression of health and well-being, alike for a child or for a regiment, for a home or for a city; while our manufacturing and our commercial world, and its traditional economists as yet do not, with exceptions still so rare as to be practically little more than individual ones.

Such individuals the practical man as yet fails to understand for what they really are – pioneers of the incipient neotechnic order. For does he not commonly say, 'All very well for them; they can afford it!' – thus missing the fact that their sense of order and efficiency, their desire of fitness and seemliness, and their diffusion of these throughout their whole concern, and not only in but by those who serve in it, are vital factors of their superiority, factors by which their already often conspicuous business success over those of more 'practical' competitors, may, as a matter of contemporary history, be often and very largely explained. Those few great industrialists – of the Continent, like Godin at Guise, Krupp in Germany, Van Marken in Holland, of America, like Patterson or Fels; of England, like Lever, Cadbury, and Rowntree – who have done best by their workers, have also been all the better served by them, as their eminence, alike to efficiency of output and in resultant fortunes, plainly enough shows.

It has long been known that to get the best work out of a horse, one must not put the worst in. The same has, in comparatively recent times, been discovered to hold good of the soldier, of the sailor, even in the long-depressed mercantile marine. So why should the great paleotechnic world be so slow in learning this lesson, and be so loyal, so sentimentally self-sacrificing to their economic superstitions as to leave the few neotechnic employers to make their fortunes, not a little through their application of it?

None will deny that the military world has always known the value of aesthetic appeals, and these of many and magnificent kinds, as a means of increasing alike its numbers and the efficiency of these. But it is a main disaster of our modern, i.e. paleotechnic, industry that our practical men are so largely blind to these considerations in their own dealings, and that they even pride themselves upon their limitations. The name 'practical' which they so habitually arrogate to themselves is but a sophism, self-deceptive thought it be, for where they really find their arguments and take their refuge is in the utilitarian philosophy. This it is which is the real inspiration, the sole justification of their practice. They think it strong because it still survives, despite the various and vivid protests of 19th century romance and sentiment, or rather of what to them but seemed so. What they as yet failed to realise is that, when weighed in the balances of the sciences, their philosophy is found but futilitarian, or worse. For the physicist their 'development of resources,' their 'progress of a district,' is too much the wasteful dissipation of the energies of Nature; to the biologist and physician the increasing numbers they boast as 'progress of population' are too obviously in deterioration rather than in progressive evolution. Nor are these criticisms of physics or of public health the sternest. The sociologist as historian has still fully to explain the practical man to himself. He has to analyse out the various factors which have gone to the making of him and his philosophy together – the uprooted rustic, the machine-driven labourer, and each as a half-starveling, too much even of the necessary food, and yet more of the good of life – the soured and blighted puritan degenerating into mammonised fanatic – the revolutionary and radical politician fossilising into doctrinaire. It cannot be too often repeated, too frequently presented in different ways, that the self-satisfied 'practical man' who looks down upon all our hopes of the redemption and ennoblement of his industrial and commercial would towards civic and social aims as 'mere sentiment', is himself the victim of sentiments gone wrong; nay, that his ledger-regulated mind is too often but an obsession of arithmetic, and his life of respectable acquisitiveness but its resulting Vitus' Dance, conducted by 'the least erected fiend that fell'.

Beauty, whether of Nature or art, has too long been without effective defence against the ever-advancing smoke-cloud and machine-blast and slum-progress of paleotechnic industry. Not but that her defenders have been of the very noblest, witness notably Carlyle, Ruskin, Morris, with their many disciples; yet they were too largely romantics – right in their treasuring of the world's heritage of the past, yet wrong in their reluctance, sometimes even passionate refusal, to admit the claims and needs of the present to live and labour in its turn, and according to its lights. So that they in too great measure but brought upon themselves that savage retort and war-cry of 'Yah! Sentiment!' with which the would-be utilitarian has so often increased his recklessness towards Nature, and coarsened his callousness to art. The romantics have too often been as blind in their righteous anger as were the mechanical utilitarians in their strenuous labour, their dull contentment with it. Both have failed to see, beyond the rude present, the better future now dawning – in which the applied physical sciences are advancing beyond their clumsy and noisy first apprenticeship, with its wasteful and dirty beginnings, towards a finer skill, a more subtle and more economic mastery of natural energies, and in which these, moreover, are increasingly supplemented by a corresponding advance of the organic sciences, with their new valuations of life, organic as well as human.

In their days, when education had withered down into mere memorisings for senile examining boards, for torpid bureaucracies, neither party could foresee the rebound which is now beginning towards the reassertion of the freedom and uniqueness of the individual mind, towards the guidance of its unfolding – witness, as a symptom of this, the world-wide interest in the teaching method of Dr. Montessori. In an age of extremis individualism, which had been necessitated by the escape from outworn trammels, neither foresaw that return of the sense of human fellowship and helpfulness which promises to rekindle the heart of religion; and still less that renascence of citizenship, that reconstruction of the City, on which we are now entering, and which inaugurates a new period of social and of political evolution. Too much lost by our predecessors of the industrial age, and as yet all too seldom realised by ourselves, the returning conception and ideal of Citizenship is offering us a new start-point of thought and labour. Here, in fact, is a new watchword, as definite, even more definite, than those of liberty, wealth, and power, of science and of mechanical skill, which have so fascinated our predecessors; one, moreover, transcending all these – one enabling us to retain them, to co-ordinate them with a new clearness, and towards the common weal.

From this standpoint the case for the conservation of Nature, and for the increase of our accesses to her, must be stated more seriously and strongly than is customary. Not merely begged for on all grounds of amenity, of recreation, and repose, sound though these are, but insisted upon. On what grounds? In terms of the maintenance and development of life; of the life of youth, of the health of all, which is surely the very foundation of any utilitarianism worth the name; and further, of that arousal of the mental life in youth, of its maintenance through age, which must be a main aim of higher utilitarianism, and is a main condition of its continued progress towards enlightenment.

At the very outset (Chapter II) we saw the need of protecting, were it but for the prime necessity of pure water supply, what remains of hills and moorlands between the rapidly growing cities and conurbations of modern industrial regions...

Plainly, the hygienist of water supply is the true utilitarian; and hence, even before our present awakening of citizenship, he has been set in authority above all minor utilitarians, each necessarily of narrower task and of more local vision – engineering, mechanical and chemical, manufacturing and monetary – and has so far been co-ordinating all these into the public service. But with this preservation of mountains and moorlands comes also the need of their access; a need for health, bodily and mental together. For health without the joys of life – of which one prime one is assuredly this nature-access – is but dullness; and this we begin to know as a main way of preparation for insidious disease. With this, again, comes forestry: no mere tree-cropping, but sylviculture, arboriculture too, and park-making at its greatest and best.

Such synoptic vision of Nature, such constructive conservation of its order and beauty towards the health of cities, and the simple yet vivid happiness of its holiday-makers (whom a wise citizenship will educate by admission, not exclusion) is more than engineering; it is a master-art; vaster than that of street planning, it is landscape making; and thus it meets and combines with city design.

But the children, the women, the workers of the town can come but rarely to the country. As hygienists, and utilitarians, we must therefore bring the country to them. While our friends the town planners and burgh engineers are adding street beyond street, and suburb beyond suburb, it is also for us to be up and doing, and 'make the field gain on the street, not merely the street gain on the field.' For all the main thoroughfares out from the city (henceforth, we hope, to be boulevards, and even more) and around every suburban railway station, the town planner is arranging his garden village, with its own individuality and charm, but we, with our converse perspective, coming in from country towards town, have to see to it that these growing suburbs no longer grow together, as past ones have too much done. Towns must now cease to spread like expanding inkstains and grease-spots; one in true development, they will repeat the star-like opening of the flower, with green leaves set in alternation with its golden rays.

The city parks, which are among the best monuments and legacies of our later nineteenth-century municipalities – and valuable, useful, often beautiful though they are, – have been far too much influenced by the standpoint natural to the prosperous city fathers who purchased them, and who took them over, like the mansion-house parks they often were, each with its ring-fence, jealously keeping it apart from a vulgar world. Their lay-out has as yet too much continued the tradition of the mansion-house drives, to which the people are admitted on holidays, and by courtesy; and where the little girls may sit on the grass. But the boys? They are at most granted a cricket-patch, or lent a space between football goals, but otherwise are jealously watched, as potential savages, who on the least symptom of their natural activities of wigwam-building, cave-digging, stream-damming, and so on – must instantly be chevied away, and are lucky if not handed over to the police.

Now, if the writer has learned anything from a life largely occupied with nature-study and with education, it is that these two need to be brought together, and this through nature-activities. But – though there is obviously nothing more important either for the future of industry or for the preservation of the State, than vigorous health and activity, guided by vivid intelligence – we have been stamping out the very germs of these by our policeman-like repression, both in school and out of it, of those natural boyish instincts of vital self-education, which are always constructive in impulse and in essence, however clumsy and awkward, or even mischievous and destructive when merely restrained, as they commonly have been, and still too much are.

It is primarily for lack of this touch of first-hand rustic experience that we have forced young energy into hooliganism; or, even worse, depressed it below that level. Whereas the boy-scout movement already triumphantly shows that even the young hooligan needs but some living touch of active responsibility to become much of a Hermes; and, with reconstructive opportunities and their vigorous labours, we shall next make of him a veritable Hercules.

With this dawning reclamation of our school-system, hitherto so bookish and enfeebling, there is coming naturally the building of better schools – open-air schools for the most part; and henceforth, as far as may be, situated upon the margins of these open spaces. With these, again, begin the allotments and the gardens which every city improver must increasingly provide – the whole connected up with tree-planted lanes and blossoming hedgerows, open to birds and lovers.

The upkeep of all this needs no costly increase of civic functionarism. It should be naturally undertaken by the regenerating schools and continuation classes, and by private associations too without number. What better training in citizenship, as well as opportunity of health, can be offered any of us than in sharing in the upkeep of our parks and gardens? Instead of paying increased park and school rates for these, we should be entering upon one of the methods of ancient and of coming citizenship, and with this of the keeping down of taxes, by paying at least this one of our social obligations increasingly in time and in service rather than in money. Thus too we shall be experimentally opening our eyes towards that substantial Resorption of Government, which is the natural and approaching reaction from the present multiplication of officialism, always so costly at best.

People volunteer for war; and it is a strange and a dark superstition that they will not volunteer for peace. On the contrary, every civic worker knows that, with a little judicious inquiry and management, any opportunity which can be found for public service is not very long of being accepted, if only the leadership for it can be given: that is still scarce, but grows with exercise and service. Thus before long our constructive activities would soon penetrate into the older existing town, and with energies Herculean indeed – cleansing its Augean stables in ways which municipal cleaning departments, responsible to the backward taxpayer, have not yet ventured upon – to a degree of washing and whitewashing on which the more bacteriologically informed rising generation will soon insist. In 'dirty Dublin', for instance, this civic volunteering is making conspicuous and effective beginnings.

But beyond these mere cleansings, we need both destructive and constructive energy. Nowhere better shall we find the smaller open spaces and people's gardens of the opening decade than in the very heart of the present slums. In the 'Historic Mile' of Old Edinburgh, that most overcrowded and difficult of slums, the 'Open Spaces Survey' of our Outlook Tower committee shows there are no less than seventy-six open spaces, with a total area of ten acres, lately awaiting reclamation, and of these already an appreciable proportion are now being gardened, year by year – all through voluntary agencies, of course, though now approved, and at various points assisted, by city departments and officials. This movement has lately been adopted by the Women's Health Association of Ireland, and such beginnings are in progress, with skilled leadership, in Dublin, London, and other cities.

Towards the reclamation of the slums, our industrialists and town planners have next their far larger opportunity. The innumerable and complicated muddle of workshops, large and small, which at present so largely and so ineffectively crowd up the working-class quarters of our towns, plainly suggest, and will richly reward, a large measure of thoughtful replanning. Many of our large industries – factories, breweries, and so on, as experience already shows, may with great advantage be moved to appropriate situations in the country, and in this way leave spacious buildings, which may often readily be adapted for the accommodation and grouping of smaller industries. Thus would be set free these minor workshops, largely for demolition, and their sites for open spacing, with a gain to health, to children's happiness, and therefore to civic economy and productivity, which would rapidly repay the city for the whole transaction. Hence of this the expense might, most fairly of all outlays, be charged for redemption during the generation now opening.

For a concrete illustration, let me take the cast of the West Princes Street Gardens of Edinburgh. These as yet retain the bounds of their former private ownership; but the map of the aforesaid open-spaces committee for Old Edinburgh shows how, as they already sweep round the castle, – they may next be made practically continuous with some of our slum gardens thus bringing public beauty into the very heart of what was lately, or still is, private squalor.

Mews, again, are rapidly becoming obsolete; and are often being utilised as private garages, stores, small workshops, etc. Now, however, is the very time for city improvers. Garages peculiarly lend themselves to concentration, not to dispersion; and private enterprise is already providing facilities for this here and there, though as yet on too small a scale…
… the throwing together of innumerable yards and drying greens, which at present disgrace the backs of even our best city-quarters, should be more and more comprehensively dealt with; and garden quadrangles should thus increasingly replace the present squalid labyrinth of wasted greens, cut up by innumerable walls. A single central drying-house for each garden-court might at the same time be provided, the whole thus setting free for vital uses over the city an aggregate of many acres, and these far more accessible, and therefore more useful, than are the parks, for the daily use of childhood and family life, and for happy garden-activities, both for youngsters and their elders.

Such minor (yet in aggregate considerable) changes need but beginnings; and not a few of these beginnings are in actual progress. Such modest initiatives, moreover, gently break down prejudices, and prepare the way for that large measure of municipal reorganisation which the public of our cities will soon desire. When this desire has been developed, there is no fear but that people will be willing to pay – that is, work – for its satisfaction. The present is the day of small things; our fellow-citizens have first to be persuaded hence this repeated emphasis on the need of private initiatives. But by all means let each possible step be taken within the municipality, and in its various departmental offices as well as without; and let public powers be obtained as far as possible, and as fast as they can, utilising precedents wherever these exist. Edinburgh, for instance, has taken more powers for the suppression of sky-signs, of winking abominations, and regulation of advertisements generally, than have as yet most other cities; while Glasgow has, of course, long been an example in larger matters…

Life and Its Science[40]

TO SOME READERS, as certainly to some of our brethren in science, it may seem a strange thing that we biologists should make much ado about the Seasons, and yet stranger that, forsaking our specialist societies with their Proceedings and Transactions, their Microscopical Journals and the rest, we should be seeking to range ourselves in pages like these along with the painter-exponents, the poet-observers, of the changing year. Nor can we wonder if these look at such self-invited allies somewhat askance.

In the poet and the artist, with their thirst for actual, their dream of possible beauty, such keen interest in the Seasons is familiar and intelligible enough; so, also, albeit in widely differing ways, in the farmer and the gardener, in the sportsman – and the mariner, in all who, outside the life of cities, have elected to do rather than to know or feel. As for Science, one remembers the astronomer and the geographer once explaining to us the Seasons in some dimly – remembered lecture, with their globes; but where should the biologist come in the reveller in cacophonous terminology, the man of lenses and scalpels, the reducer of things to their elements of deadness? What can he tell us of the seasons, what (beyond the time of getting this or that specimen) have they to say to him?

For is not the popular picture of the botanist, for instance, that of a mild yet somewhat mischievous creature, whose chief interest is in picking flowers to pieces, like the sparrow among the crocuses? His remaining occupation is supposed to be that of gentle exercise on holiday afternoons; when, as a kind of sober academic nursemaid, he has to march out with him upon his rounds the unwilling neophytes of medicine, each fitly equipped, in place of outgrown satchel (so prophetic is nature) with a small tin coffin upon his back.

His skill these measure by the frequency with which he stops like a truffle-hunter's pig, - say rather like a new, a vegetarian breed of pointer. See him loudly ejaculating in the most unmistakably canine Latin as he grubs up the unlucky specimen, as he coffins it with a snap, what the student (as his manner is) swiftly scribbles down and forgets, as the one thing needful to know, its technical 'name' really of course its index letter or reference mark in that great nature-catalogue, which so few consult at all.

Similarly, is not the zoologist a kind of mad huntsman who slays and grallocks[41] the meanest vermin for his game; or a child who pricks beetles and hoards shells and boxes butterflies into lines and battalions; or a pedant who 'pins faith on a basipterygoid process[42]'? And is not the physiologist the man

---

40. *The Evergeen*, Spring 1895 and *Edinburgh Review, Patrick Geddes Special Issue*, No. 88 Summer 1992, pp24-30.
41. Grallocks = disembowels (Chambers Twentieth Century Dictionary).
42. Basipterygoid process = joins the braincase to the palatal bones (Palaeos).

who gives electric shocks to frogs, and analyses their waste products? These appreciations are of course grotesque, but like all caricatures, they have one side of truth, and that the obvious one. The fact is that the Biologist has a familiar, a 'Doppelgänger,' his necessary and hence masterful, often tyrannous and usurping slave, whose name is Necrologist; and now-a-days most people know only him. The dead and the abnormal, being dissonant, are more striking than the living and the normal which are harmonious; and thus the doings of the necrological Mr Hyde attract more attention than those of the biological Dr Jekyll. Collection and dissection have their place, their necessary and ample place, but they are not all, they are not first. The study of life – the sum of living functions, and of their resultants in temperament, in sex, in variety, in species – is again beginning to claim, and will again recover, precedence in thought and in education over that post-mortem analysis of organs and tissues and cells which has for the present usurped its place. And as teachers of biology our serious desire and daily work is towards a distant revolution, which our pupils' pupils will accomplish, though we may never see. When this comes, those learned anatomical compendia, these text-books of 'Biology' falsely so called, which now dominate every School of Science in the world, shall be rewritten line by line, and from cover to cover. We shall have done with beginning with the analysis of dead structure; Physiology will precede Anatomy, and Bionomics will precede both. Physiology, too, despite popular and too authoritative manuals, Huxley's and the rest, sets out not by creaking a skeleton, by unpacking the digesting or the circulating organs, not even by observing the sensory or by experimenting upon the instinctive life. Not even with the marvel of the developing egg, nor with the mystery of seed-bearing in the flower, does the naturalist begin; but with the opening bud, with wandering deep into forest and high upon hill; in seeing, in feeling, with hunter and with savage, with husbandman and gypsy, with poet and with child, the verdant surge of Spring foaming from every branchlet, bursting from every sod, breaking here on naked rock-face, there on rugged tree-bole till even these are green with its clinging spray. Day after day he shall drift on the Sea of Life as it deepens in verdure over plain, as it eddies and ripples in blossom up the valleys; he shall keep unslaying watch upon the myriad creatures that teem upon its surface and crowd within its depths, till they show him the eager ways of their hunger, the fury and the terror of their struggle, the dim or joyous stirrings of their love. He shall listen to the Sounds of Life, the hum of insect and the coo of dove, the lilt of pairing mavises[43], the shivering child-cry of the lambs, till he too must lift up his voice with lover and with poet, with the greeting-song of the returned Prosperina, with the answering chant of Easter – Life is arisen! Life is arisen indeed! All this, quite seriously and definitely, is what we biologists want to teach him who would learn with us – say rather what we want him to see and hear, to

---

43. Mavises = song thrushes.

live and feel for himself. Only to him, we say, who has lived and felt with Life throughout the Seasons, till memories of Nature throng the labyrinths of brain and tingle the meshes of the blood, has there been any 'adequate preparation in Elementary Biology' at all. Only him would we admit into our winter-palace of museum, its crypt of laboratory; only him initiate into the perilous mystery, the alluring mastery, of analysis; only to him who can approach in contemplation no less reverent, in questioning no less vital than that of ancient sacrifice and augury, shall the corpse be opened, the skull laid bare, the magic glass be given, the secret of decay be told.

For among the initiates of Necrology, he and he only, and hardly even he, who has first gathered flowers with Prosperpine in her native valleys may ever return to a fuller Spring with her in the open world again. For the rest, their home is in the shades; for where the love and the wonder and the imagination of Life are dead, there remains only unceasing labour in the charnel-house and ossuary, here to disintegrate or there to embalm, with only, at best reward, the amassing of some mouldering treasure, the leaving for the bibliographer some fragment-record, the winning of some small mummy-garland upon a tomb.

But for him who has truly been in the greenwoods, who has met and kissed their faërie queen, the wealth of the museum palace still lies open; its very crypts are free. Yet with the spring her messengers come for him as for the Rhymer of old; her white hart and hind, unseen of other eyes, pace up the unlovely street; and he too must follow them back to their home, home to his love.

II

As the simplest greetings of 'good morning' and 'good day' remind us, some sympathy with Nature, some interest in our fellows, are instinctive and universal. No one but is so far a Nature-lover and a Season-observer; Spring with her buds and lambs and lovers, Autumn amid her fruits and sheaves, Summer in her green, and Winter with her holly, are all themes as unfailing as human life. Even the best-worn rhymes of dove and love, of youth and truth, will be fresh song-notes for adolescent sweethearts till rhyming and sweethearting end. And even the hardest day's labour closes sweetly which can pause at the home-coming and bathe its weariness in the evening sky.

That the child posy-gathering is a naturalist, the child drawing out of his own head an artist, the child singing and making believe a poet, are all obvious enough. Obvious, too, are becoming the general lines and conditions of these developments up to those children of larger growth whose impressions have been more richly gathered, more vitally assimilated, more fully organised, till they appear not as mere crude attempts in the child, mere fading memories in the adult, but in fresh life and new form which we call 'original' – discovery, picture, or poem. And were this the season, we might study the far strange (albeit more common) marvels of human failure. For what is that shortcoming of beauty, common in the human species above all others? How comes that blunting of sense and stunting of soul which befall us? How shall we unriddle the degeneration which the bio-pessimist has shown as well-nigh overspreading nature, the senescence which he has proved to begin at birth?

But from the strange abnormalities we group as ugliness, from that subtlest arrest of evolution which we once thought as well as called the Commonplace, let us return, as befits beginners, to the simple and the natural, the normal and the organic. That is, to the growth in activity and variety of sensory and psychic life, the growth of original and productive power, in discoverer, painter, and poet. Scant outline is indeed alone possible in these limits, yet every one has this latent in his own mind. The most inarticulate rustic knows and watches his fields from day to day; yet here is the stuff of biology. Simple satisfaction in fresh landscape, notice of at least some aspects of human face and form can hardly die wholly out of any mind; yet this is the stuff of painting. So in the prosaic description of place or person or event one detects the touch and tinge of literature, alike in thought and style.

As poetic intensity and poetic interpretation may be true at many deepening levels, so it is with the work of the painter; so too with the scientific study of Nature. And here, too, the extremes of thinker and child meet in the same mind. In twenty years of microscopic teaching, for instance, the writer has been rewarded by no such simple and joyous outburst of juvenile delight in any mortal as he once silently provoked by pushing his microscope, aswim with twirling Spirrilum and dancing Monads, under the eye of Darwin. 'Come here, come here; look! Look here! Look at this! They're all moving! They're all MOVING!' cried the veteran voyager, his deep eyes sparkling, his grey face bright with excitement; the aged leader of the century's science again a child who 'sees the wheels go round.'

The naturalist, as compared with his artist and poet comrades, is generally neither so much of a babe nor so much of a man as they; but primarily a boy or bird-nester, a hoarder of property in the old comprehensive schoolboy fashion, before the example of degenerate adults who specialise upon metal counters and paper securities had reduced his collecting to postage-stamps. Yet the naturalist, too, attains manhood upon the plane of intellect; and if his museum of accumulated wealth be not too much for him, he may gain new strength by systematising and organising it. Thus on the more abstract and philosophic side develops the systematist and thinker like Linnæus, on the more concrete and artistic the encyclopedist and stylist like Buffon. Each too in his way, in his world-museum and garden of life, is an Adam naming and describing the creatures.

From these great treasure-houses and libraries of the science the naturalist, too, may go out into the world not only to search and discover and collect, but to labour also. His level of action is primarily of a humbler and more fundamental sort than that of his artist comrades. Fishery and rustic labour are to his hand, he learns to dredge and to sow; forests, too, he may plant and tend. By-and-by, in ordered park and garden great, he even attains to artistic expression, and this upon a scale vaster than that of cities; he transforms Nature, shaping herself and not her mere image. Then strengthened and suppled in mind no less than in body he returns to his science with fresh questions and problems and perplexities, yet richer in resources, more fertile in devices for solving them. From the slight modification of certain forms of life by domestication and culture, from the breeding and selecting with farmer and fancier, he gains fresh light upon the problem of evolution; Darwin's, of course, being the familiar, the classic case, but not the only or the final one. But again riddles multiply and even those that seemed solved a few years ago appear anew from fresh sides and in slightly altered forms. Again he must observe and ponder, again also return to practice; and beyond the comparatively limited range of domesticated animals and plants he needs wider and more thorough observations. In course of these he must rear under known conditions in laboratory and garden, in field and farmyard, all manner of living things, low and high, wild and tame, useful and malignant – and pass, in fact, the life of his whole zoological and botanic garden under fresh and keener review. This is what we begin to speak of as Experimental Evolution. It is Comparative Agriculture, Hygiene, Medicine; and all these with widening range. Before long it will have its institutes as well as they.

The poet is but a simple poet who does not see that this is no dead science, but a very Alchemy, a higher Alchemy than that of metals – the Alchemy of Life – and that the search for the Elixir Vitae is indeed again begun.

Already at each stage of its progress the study of man has thrown light upon that of lower creatures; conversely their study upon our view of men. The interaction of these kindred lines of thought is even now entering a new and fuller phase, and a higher series of scientific institutes, those of the Experimental Evolution of Man, are thus logically necessary. These indeed are already to hand: asylum and hospital, prison, workhouse and school, orphanage and university (to name only the more obvious groups), are not far too seek. Each, too, has been changing its purpose and ideal within the past century, from the initial ones which were practically little more than of social rubbish-heaps into which society could more or less mercifully shoot its senile, diseased, or troublesome members, or of lumber-heaps for its immature and weak ones. First, common humanity showed us the festering of these social sores, opening the way for medicine, as this for hygiene; now psychology is entering upon school and asylum, even criminology forcing its way into court and prison; before long a fuller sociology and ethics will have entered all. The secrets of evolution and dissolution of body and mind, the corresponding interpretations, economic and ethical, of evolution and dissolution for each type of human society, are thus being laid bare. And here we may note in passing the scientific (necrological) justification of much of our contemporary decadent literature.

But the night of pessimism has passed its darkest. Its social explanation and standpoint remain clear enough. The physical sciences, their associated industrial evolution, have created a disorder they are powerless to reorganise – hence progressive ruin of all kinds, individual and social, material and moral, to which church, state, and the negations of these, are all alike powerless to find remedies. But such pessimists overlook an old saying of the prophets – of Descartes before Comte, doubtless of old Greeks before these, of older Egyptians before them – that 'if the regeneration of mankind is to be accomplished, it will be through the medical sciences.'

With this regeneration defined as Experimental Evolution, the prophecy is making a fresh start towards fulfilment. In the simpler institutes which we call school, college, or the like, the problem is to grow good fruit from good or average seed. In those of a pathological kind (asylum, prison, hospital) beyond the obvious aim of restoration to a low or average norm of health, is arising, however, the seemingly more difficult (perhaps easier problem, already hinted at – that of life-Alchemy, of Redemption. For again we are dreaming of a Secret of Transmutation, that of disease into higher health, of baseness into generosity, of treason into honour, of lust into love, of stupor into lucidity, phantasmagoria into drama, mania into vision.

Beyond this there is yet another step of practice; the physician is bringing experience and method from the hospital into the service of the home; so in their way are all his brother evolutionists. And thus they begin to discern and prepare for their immediate task to cleanse and change the face of cities, to reorganise the human hive.

For them as for their rustic fellows, the task begins with the humblest drudgery, the scavenging of dirt, the disposal of manure. Soon, however, they will grapple with the central and the supreme Art possible to mortals, the very Mystery of masonry itself, which has its beginnings in the anxieties of calculation and the perplexities of plan, in the chaotic heaps of quarry, in the deep and toilsome labour, the uncouth massiveness of the foundations: yet steadily rises to shelter and sacredness of hearth, to gloom of tower and glory of pinnacle, to leap of arch and float of dome. With this renewal of Environment, there arises a corresponding renewal of economic and moral Function which shall yet be Industry, the renewal and development of Life as well – what shall yet be Education. And thus even painter and poet find, through what seemed to them an irrelevant science, new space for beauty and new stimulus of song. Yet even here the Three comrades have no Continuing city.

For each, for all, the faërie messengers are waiting; and they must ever return to Her from whom they came.

The Sociology of Autumn[44]

ARGUMENT – I. How everyday experience differentiates into the Arts and Sciences; yet how their progress is not only towards diversity, but towards Unity. II. How this Unity may come into our experience, and that from childhood. III. How cities may be viewed in Nature and her Seasons. IV How their prevalent political economy is that of Autumn. V. Their literary and scientific culture likewise. VI. How decadent Art and Literature normally develop their colour, and produce their decay. VII. Decadence. VIII. How it passes into Renascence.

I

Behind our castle sable its field argent of white seething mist now lies later in the morning, gathers earlier towards the night, and the sea of swaying tree-tops from which its dark crags rise is crisping and yellowing towards the fall. Along the High Riggs on either hand, the distant specks hurry in denser crowd; and through the green lake-bed deep below, the engine drags under its lingering cloud a heavier train.

In some such phantasmagoria as may pass for each of us before the windows of his life, there lie latent our main possibilities both of Art and Science. Most of us, alas, are soon called back from our outlook to the workshop or the book-room, to the bed and table of our lives, and thence too seldom return. But now and then some chosen or forgotten child stays by his window all his life. Hence it is that at times we hear some strange voice of joy or sorrow and hail a new poet; or if his gaze be silent, but he make for us some colour-note of the phase of beauty he has seen and felt, we call him painter. One tells us of sky and trees, another sketches the passing faces, a third the incident; whence landscape, portrait, genre, and the rest.

While all these mainly observe and feel, others observe and wonder; and thus, your curious child wanders away from the world of Art to rediscover that of Science. This also must subdivide its field of observation, and this into narrower specialisms than those of the artist, and in a stranger way. One fixes his eyes upon the siege-scarred castle, and by and by we call him historian; another puzzles himself about the crags below, and becomes a geologist; another sees only trees and birds – the naturalist; a fourth sits peering into the mist and listening only to the wind – the meteorologist. So it is that science develops that strange mental habit for which plain folk at once and

---

44. 'The Sociology of Autumn', *The Evergreen* 1895, and *Edinburgh Review*, 88, 1992 pp. 31-39.

necessarily respect and ridicule the 'strange professor-bodie' – whose power of intensely seeing one class of phenomena, yet only one, leaves him 'absent-minded,' literally to all the rest.

In such ways, then, we need not wonder that there has arisen the marvellous heterogeneity of contemporary Art and Science; nor how each still goes on differentiating in its own way. Scientific Congresses and Art Exhibitions must needs multiply, as Science goes on isolating and analysing strange new fields of minute details, Art refracting subtler aspects of nature through more individual moods of mind. Who now speaks of Leonardo's, Dürer's dream of reuniting Art and Science, save as a mere echo of the days of alchemy? Little wonder, then, if our dreams of this should please few critics of either camp; yet, like themselves, we also speak that we do not know, and testify that we have seen.

For there is a larger view of nature and Life, a rebuilding of analyses into Synthesis, an integration of many solitary experiences into a large Experience, an exchange of the narrow window of the individual outlook for the open tower which overlooks college and city.

In such moments all the artificially isolated mind-pictures of mist and rock, of bird and tree, of man and his doings, reunite their special 'sciences' into Science. Nor does one lose this sense of unity when one descends again to one's own habitual outlook, but rather sees with new clearness all these diverse 'ologies' of which the half-informed think as of mazes beyond number, and within which even their special investigators are so often lost, as but orderly and parallel developments upon three planes – physical, organic, and social – which three are themselves not only parallel, but united by the world-process of Development, into a single Unit. The unnumbered descriptive specialisms of all three, like the mosaic facets of an insect's eye, are uniting into a single presentment of the world. In the science of life every one knows how of late years mind and body are again coming together, so that the psychologist is now also a physiologist; and even in the anatomist, so long an impenitent necrologist, the converse awakening has begun. So it is with the science of energy on the one hand, with that of society on the other; physics and æsthetics, economics and ethics are alike steadily recovering their long-forgotten unity. The age of mechanical dualism is ending; materialism and spiritualism have each had their day; that of an organic and idealist Monism is begun. The studies of sun and stars, of rock and flower, of beast and man, of race and destiny are becoming once more a single discipline; complex indeed, but no more a mere maze than a mere chaos, no more a mere fixed unity than a maze; but a growing Cosmos, a literal Uni-verse, of which the protean variety of Man and Nature are seen to be orderly developments; each phase of being, of becoming; each at once a Mode and Mood of the Universal Energy.

II

But this unity, the scientific man and the artist mostly agree in saying, may be all very well on the abstract and speculative level, but what can it do for us who are not content with philosophy, who live and labour in the concrete world? How can your fine talk of synthesis help us with that? Leave philosophy, the answer is, leave for a little your exhibitions and your congresses, and let us first begin with our children at school; for them all your descriptive sciences and much of your art will be absorbed into their 'Geography and History.' – Dull catalogues, you think? But forget your own woeful schooling, - and recall their real significance. Do they not cover Art and Science if they tell us, or rather teach us in some measure truly to imagine, the story of nature and Man through Space and Time?

Hence it is that the narrative of individual travel and experience, like that of Herodotus or Marco Polo, Robinson Crusoe or Humboldt and Darwin, has at all times and to all minds and ages so wide an appeal; for here is the very stuff of experience from which special science, art, and literature are made; while of their development into a higher and fuller unison there are already some great masterworks in which the style is worthy of the science. Such, for instance, are Buffon's 'Histoire Naturelle' in the last century, Elisée Reclus' 'Geographie Universelle' in this. In such an education as we are coming to, instead of books innumerable and pictures few or none, as at present, the books as in the ancient church will be few, but the pictures well-nigh infinite; and for this approaching demand of the school walls of the world let the foresighted painter be getting his imagination as well as his technique ready.

Again, then, as of old the child shall know how the earth and sun determine the seasons; these the plant and animal life; and thus also, indirectly as well as directly, our own essential life and labour. Into this simple chain, henceforward unbroken, all minor specialisms, their loose facts woven firmly into chains of causation, shall be securely linked. To develop this simple lesson, this House the Sun Built, all our specialists are needed, astronomer and meteorologist, zoologist and botanist, economist, writer, and critic. And (as in the educative initiations of the ancient mysteries) the lore of the seasons furnishes the central thread. Our glorious Autumn of harvest and woodland, her pathos of fall and decay have indeed been familiar from that very dawn of art and poetry, which her wealth and wine, her joy and sorrow, have done perhaps most of all the seasons to awaken. Yet our special sciences thrown together into the press yield new and rich elements to the old thought-vintage. They tell us where the harvest wind was warmed by the long-sunned sea, they signal from their observatories the Jôtuns, mustering white upon the hills, and warn us of their stormy breath; they follow the migrating bird across the sea, the fish into its depths, the seed into its appropriate soil. They follow, too, more deeply, the way in which our own lives are adapted to this Drama of nature.

They not only see as of old how the grapes or corn determine the autumn of the husbandman, or the descending cattle lead their herdman home; but ask if the herrings the fisherman has to follow are themselves borne landward upon a salter wave, see how the roots of the forest tree grow while the dryad seems in her winter sleep, or find how there lie amid the decay of autumn the witch-dreamed secrets of evil and good, sickness and wealth, disease and fertility.

Thus, too, our united physical and social geography will lead us straight into the very philosophy of History and amid the problems of Criticism. For it is the fundamental thesis of Human Evolution (there is also a supreme one) that the surroundings – the soil and climate, and hence the seasons – determine all the primary forms of labour; this labour again determines the nature of the family; this the structure of the society; and all these the individual man in life and thought. That literature may arise from the seasonal work of life, all see in the harvest dance or the shepherd's song, in Virgil or Burns, but few carry this far enough. Taine's great history of our literature has, of course, its errors (he was too much before the days of Le Play and 'La Science Sociale'), but his general idea was sound. 'Life the green leaf, say we, and Art the flower'. All the great flowers of literature and art rise straight from their great rootstocks, each deep within its soil. German commentators who teach, and critics who assume, that thought may be understood apart from its underlying life are, of course, not far to seek: yet such a view is untrue even for the most artificial flowers, false alike for the subtle devices of the decadent poet, and the sarcasms of his reviewer.

III

Yet the seasons – they may be all very well for trees and birds, for oxen and for them whose talk (or even song) is of such; but our rock-built cities – surely these are independent of your seasons – there is no place here for such rustic fancies! So indeed men were wont to think of the rocks themselves, but since Lyell determined certain 'Principles' we know how upon these the winter rains and frosts and snows all tell most swiftly and surely, albeit silently – 'they melt like mist, the solid lands'. And the city itself, does it really need anthropology and culture-history to remind us that its very existence is largely conditioned, its whole mode of life determined, by the approach of winter, for why else the crowding street, the heavier train? What are our stone houses but artificial caves, what we but the modern Troglodytes, who in our smoky labyrinths forget the outer world, and think no more of the seasons (save in society slang) because we have made ourselves a city life as near as may be to a perpetual winter?

We are indeed the New Troglodytes; hence our restless and ant-like crowding, our comfortable stupor of hibernation, our ugly and evil dreams.

Here is a main clue to the sociology and psychology of those wicked fairies who are such characteristic developments of the populations of the sunnier southern cities, of those sullen gnomes so common in the gloomier northern ones. So, too, we may understand much of the physical degradation of their inhabitants. We know the secrets of the metals, and forge new weapons and invent strange mechanisms and cunning fables like the dwarfs of old. And like them we are stunting ourselves anew.

IV

But our winter cave is a store of provision, and if some lack foresight, others have it overmuch. Hence arises the common 'mania of owning things' – a growing madness as of those, American squirrel-millionaires that spend their lives in feverishly heaping up great barns of plenty which they could not consume in years, and which they must leave to moulder and rot.

But in most cases it is not excess but lack of foresight that does the mischief. Population presses on subsistence, and so arises the strangest and most characteristic biological phenomenon of autumn, that keen competition at the margin of (degenerating not progressing) existence, which our modern cities have brought to that intensity of literally putrescent horror unknown before in history or life, at which we complacently sniff and pass by as 'merely and ordinary slum'.

The decaying leaf-heap of the garden, the manure-heap of the stable, are preyed upon, each by its appropriate mould. This swiftly digests all it can from the mass, scatters its multitudinous progeny abroad upon the wind, and dies of hunger. Yet not of hunger only, for meantime has been sprouting a lower form which has the same history, and is in its turn replaced; each generation thus expressing a lower stage of competition, a more complete decay, a more thorough burning of the ashes left by its predecessor.

In the same way it is to many minds of a quite clear and rational, though surely somewhat limited type, that the sole theory, nay, the whole practice also, of 'economic progress' lies in the steady development of a lower and lower life. Do we not tell the wretched millgirls of our Dundees and Oldhams how they must speedily give place to the cheaper drudges of Calcutta and Shanghai, or save themselves and slay these by diving into a yet lower circle of poverty? So where can we find a better opening for our capital than by removing it – to the East, or one in more obvious conformity with Nature? And what remedy is there? None that any one knows of – in autumn. For now is the golden age of Competition, as of Death.

V

In the same way it is in the intellectual world. Ideas once fresh from life wither and dry, but may still be utilised, infused anew, albeit in dilute form, by the help of commentaries. So commentary succeeds commentary, and criticism is piled upon criticism, copy upon copy; the lower industry must have its lower journalism, its lower art to match – so at length the slum newsagent's window, full of the strangest parodies of the art and science and literature of the educated classes. Are not the 'Police News' and its French congeners at the very fountainhead of Realism? the 'Family Herald' or 'Boys' Own Library' of Romance? Punch has surely not forgotten that he came from the Naples crowd? 'Tit-Bits' is to the commercial traveller exactly what 'Chambers's Encyclopedia' and the 'Britannica' are to the better-informed classes, nay, the British Association, the German University, with Cambridge and Johns Hopkins to boot, to the learned ones – a well-scissored chaos of interesting details, of 'Speciellen Arbeiten'. The culture of any city or period is really far more of a piece than we like to believe; yet the thought of the populace, like its labour, is full of the future as well as of the past, is literature of keynotes as well as echoes. And though the learned see their lore is vulgarised to the people, and often, of course, spoiled in the process, they seldom know the converse – truth. That is that the strength and weakness of their specialism are but a reflection and outcome of those of our modern industrial world, of the division and subdivision of labour, which have long kept so far in advance of the organisation of it.

Still harder is it to learn how the new synthesis we have seen as incipient in the world of thought must grow with advancing energy in the world of action. The wholesale social reformer, indeed, loudly proclaims this. He promises us much of both, but as yet lacks patience and skill to make much definite contribution to either. On the world's stage, as on the player's, labour and thought are indissoluble; and as the first is folly without the second, so the second is futile without the first. Would we be successful playwrights, either on the great stage, or on the small? We have to be more than wrights or authors merely; we must organise our labour to orchestrate our thought. Hence it is that each Renascence of Culture is the Story of a City.

VI

Amid the many problems of city life and degeneration some consideration of those of Sex is especially in these days forced upon us. The naturalist student must here again, as always look below literature into the life from which it springs, and so he sees, in all the strange phenomena of passion and horror which the latter-day novelist so unsparingly reveals, the extreme cases of Variation under Domestication.

For with food and shelter for winter, man becomes the first of his own domesticated animals, and the consequences of domestication inexorably follow. First comes the extension of the breeding season more and more fully throughout the year (so distinguishing, indeed, domestication from mere captivity), witness in varying measure all truly domesticated races, notably cat and mouse, dove and rabbit. That individuality blossoms not with the self-regarding, but the sex-regarding life, the development of child into Woman or Man is, of course, the main example; and here is a prime condition of intenser and fuller development, of organic and psychical individuation. Watch for a little your common doves at play, and see how passion and desire inspire gesture, these pouting their bosoms and those spreading their tails. But in some, gesture has become habit, and habit been established as variety; and so fantails and pouters are the result – for most purposes distinct and higher species. Domestication also involves precocity, and other consequences, and with all these degeneration seems more easy and frequent than advance. But we need not here trace the ignoble side of the evolution of sex (say rather Evolution through Sex). We are but naturalists and rustics; let the fashionable novelist go on till the mad doctor is ready.

Domestication involves disease of all sorts, or at any rate, increased liability to disease – again a matter in which breeder and physician are at one; and we see how increasingly medical treatment and hygiene agree in prescribing more and more of that Return to Nature, which, even as it is, is our yearly source of health and sanity.

VII

It is time to come to another great doctrine of the Decadence. We have heard abundantly of Art for Art's sake, and we all know how superior Art is to any restraints of morality – how indifferent to any call to action. Well, so far true. The thesis is not only defensible, but, on a fresh side, that of Science, of which we have already noted the kindred limitations. 'Here is the germ of the disease,' says the microscopist, 'but do not ask me for the remedy'. 'Je n'impose rien, je ne propose même rien, j'expose', calmly explains the student of social science, despite the cry for bread. Artist and man of science alike can be mirror to the world without. Hence it is that for the æsthetic appreciation of the world-phantasmagoria, the questioning intellect must be calmed, the call to action ignored; the rich variety and contrast of modern life must be impartially observed, dispassionately absorbed; and hence sheltered amid the wealth and comfort of our city life our æsthete develops as never before, his impressionist mirror growing more and more perfect in its polished calm. So develop new subtleties of sense; and given this wealth of impressions, this perfection of sensibility, new combinations must weave themselves in the fantasias of reverie. Our new Merlins thus brighten our winter with their gardens of dream.

Here then is the standpoint from which to appreciate that keenly observant yet deeply subjective 'Realism' which has been so characteristic of literature and art, as indeed also its complementary movement, that strange and wayward subjective Romanticism which has run parallel with it. So far both movements amply vindicate themselves against the Philistine criticism they have been wont to meet; yet, alas, they too easily make that step further which justifies it. For this attitude of life becomes fixed by habit, the lotus land is not easily left. For the gentler natures a deepening melancholy suffuses life, though in the stronger types passion may distil new subtleties of art or song. In time, inaction rouses the morbid strain latent in every life, and so the degeneration of the artist may set in from the physical side; and if strength remains, it must find outlet, or be lulled asleep. So arise and increase the temptations of the urban æsthete; who not only like any other man is no saint to resist them, but whose training we have seen has steadily relaxed both the intellectual and the moral fibre of resistance: and hence it is at the end of every epoch of decadence has been the same – an orgy of strange narcotics and of the strangest sins.

> I did but taste the honey of romance;
> And must I lose a soul's inheritance?

VIII

Is all æstheticism then evil, and only activity good? Has art only been an *ignis fatuus*[45], and is the jeer of the coarse utilitarian, the triumph of the joyless ascetic, to be the last word? Not so: the road of life ever lies forward, through the present phase of evolution, not back from it, be its dangers what they may. This so-called Decadence of literature and art which, as we have seen, science fully shares, is no hopeless decline, but only an autumn sickness, and one of rapid growth and adolescence. For man is increasingly master of the world and of his fate; he does not merely rest in his environment and take its mould, but rises superior to environment and remoulds it. So art and science, which we have seen unite in imagination, find unity in Action also, in that detailed reorganisation of urban and rustic life into health and beauty, which is the ideal of the Incipient Civilisation, and which distinguishes it from the confusion of the Contemporary yet Disappearing one. Here in fact lies the task of our urban autumn as harvest is that of the field; and to this men return with health and hopefulness gained from contact with nature. Autumn is indeed in many ways the urban spring, and spring, when we are weary with city life, is the urban autumn. Thanks then, and even honour, to the art and

---

45. *Ignis fatuus* = phosphorescent light over marshy ground; a delusion.

science of the Decadence, since from it we have learned to see the thing as it is; it has even helped us likewise to imagine it as it might be; it remains only to ask if in some measure we can make it as it should be, and here lies intact such originality as is left open to us – that of Renascence. To everything there is a season, and a time to every purpose under the heaven; so in this rhythm of passive with active life, of contemplation with constructive energy, lies the health and the future of the Individual and of the Race.

Artist and æsthete, writer and critic in this social Autumn, this ending of an age, all shrink from its active life, and indeed rightly. What profit these men of industry who can be mechanically construct, these men of science who but analyse, these emperors and revolutionists who dream but to destroy – Philistine decadents all! Little wonder that with the world-weary theologian or pessimist they proclaim, their passive doctrine as final, their standpoint as permanent – and even as they speak their flowers fade, their garlands fall; then comes despair and silence.

> Some little talk awhile of ME and THEE
> There was – and then no more of THEE and ME.

The first word of the Sociology of Autumn is of the beauty of Nature, the glory of Life, both culminating (as our urban culture only more fully teaches us) in their Decadence. Hence there inevitably comes the second word, the pessimist antithesis: yet a third – the vital one – remains. Amid decay lies the best soil of Renascence: in Autumn its secret: that of survival yet initiative, of inheritance yet fresh variation – the seed; who wills may find, may sow, and in another Autumn also reap. This last word, then, leaves Omar's death-son and returns to the prose of homely life. 'Il faut cultiver son jardin'.

Letters

The *Halakarshana* (Plough Festival) at Santiniketan

Geneva
May Afferid 5. 1921

Dear Geddes

I am sorry for your not being able to come and for the cause of it. I hope that your friend is out of danger and your mind is at ease.

I send you herewith a draft copy of an invitation letter from which you will know that I am arranging a conference of some representative men of the West and of Japan and China if possible. I wish to have your advice both with regards to names as well as the details of the programme. I need not say that it would help me greatly if you could personally take part in organising it. My scheme of the University has been well received in this country and I feel certain that I shall have volunteers who will join me from all parts of Europe. I have already received some very valuable offers of service. However, tell me how I am to proceed about this conference. Incidentally let me mention that I am willing to bear the travelling expenses of those for whom it is likely to be a burden. If you suggest any alterations in the wordings of the invitation letter I shall gratefully accept them. My intention is to hold in connection with the conference an exhibition representing different aspects of Indian life and culture.

yours
Rabindranath Tagore

My next address will be:
C/o Dr Hans Bodmer
Lesezirkel Hottingen
Zurich

SANTINIKETAN
BEERBHUM (BENGAL)
Dec. 28, 1922

Dear Geddes,
    Andrews has told me all the trouble you are taking over us and of your hope for the institution. Elmhirst tells us that you were quite keen on Arthur coming here. It would be delightful to have him here to advise us on the carrying out of your schemes which we will gladly follow within the limits of our resources. I see no reason at all why he should not keep his health at Surul. Miss Green has promised to try and act as a mother to him. She has made a different man of Elmhirst and I think you could trust her to guard him from malaria. Besides this the malaria season does not get into full swing until July. With his help Surul could be malaria-proof within three months. We can offer him Rs 150/ per month for his expenses. Lodging is free, board will come to about Rs 30-40, and servant Rs 30-40.

Your idea of the graphic representation of the growth of human life and mind, the cycle of their activities and varied manifestations has strongly captured my mind. I wish we could make a place for it in our institution. It is not in our power to collect at once all the materials necessary for it, but we can make a start if we have an efficient guidance. Will Arthur be able to help us if it becomes possible for him to come? I hope some day some of your students may take up this work here. While I was in Bombay I was so fatigued and my mind distracted with work for which I have no aptitude that I could not see you as often as I wished. I am waiting for Andrews to come when I shall know something about the interviews he had with you.

Yours
Rabindranath Tagore

President
Dr. RABINDRANATH TAGORE
Vice-Presidents
Sir JAGADIS BOSE
Sir MICHAEL SADLER
Sir BRAJENDRANATH SEAL
Chairman of Executive
The MAYOR OF MONTPELLIER
Directors
Prof. PATRICK GEDDES
Mr. E. B. HAVELL
Secretary
Dr. G. G. ADVANI

INDIAN COLLEGE
PLAN DES QUATRE SEIGNEURS
MONTPELLIER

Montpellier, le 20/II/29.

Dear Poet and Honoured Friend,

(Yours of Oct. 3I) I quite understand: you will let us know if and when you can come.

Yes, pray write something - in Visvabhareta or where you think fit - of your ideals and aims in Santineketan School and University ! For that will be at once (I) an impulse to education over the wide world - and (2) a document of testamen--tary value to your successors, towards continuing and developing your initiatives there, instead of "tying them up in the napkin", as successors so often do. That happened not only in Jesus' parable, but in the resultant Christian Church, beginning even from St-Paul, and continued too much to this day. It is the tragedy of initiatives that the disciples close and enshrine the teaching of their master. That has happened in every religion, has it not ? Thus, had not the last Sikh Guru done this himself, where might not the Sikhs be now - with still growing Scriptures !

In science too, despite its "progress", the same thing too often happens; and in philosophy no less. Thus from Descartes came the modern mechanistic obsessions; and from Newton an absolutism which has had to wait for Einstein to relativise it. From Linnaeus (whose "System of Nature" gave the "Principia" of the world of Nature,) the evolutionists, from Buffon to Darwin and ouwards, have found it hard to escape ! And so too for Darwin, since most Darwinians hardened into mechanists and "struggle-for-lifers" (as the French call them) idealising wars, and master-castes, and all other devilments of competition. So too Comte's elements too much remained for Positivists, and so on.

I dont often trouble you with my own papers; but if you have time ro tun through the accompanying three, you will see, I hope that with Branford, Arthur Thomson and others, we are getting towards clearness and even policy. The general idea of these papers (marked I. II. III is that:

I - We have constantly to be re-surveying our world and interpreting it, at once in science and in philosophy, both of nature and of man ("Voir" and "Savoir" - even "prévoir" (Pro-Synthesis).

II - To discern this as definitely from Urban to Rustic, mechanical to vital, hence renewal of social feeling and thought towards action "Penser pour Agir!"

III - to coordinate our action, as Social Transition, active and thoughtful, together by turns.

We have thus to get beyond our Outlook Towers, telescope, botanic gardens and geologic, historic chateaus &c, and towards fuller utilisation of vital and spiritual outlook, and constructive and creative expression, such as are yours.

As example: Bose (I mean your Prof. of Philosophy) is welcome here - and the more since striving to correlate Indian and European philosophy. Here is the ideal link; between our Scots College, with its garden literally "peripatetic" - since its walks and terraces are being adjusted to illustrate the viewpoints of the west from Greeks onwards to today; and we are puzzling now over how to do the like for Indian Philosophy, on the adjacent terraces, and garden, of the Indian College, now rising fast. Thus towards a higher and fuller outlook than either alone. (Interesting that my Edinburgh architectural partner, without suggestion from me, has sketched Asoka's pillar on its corner Tower!)

So, pray, send Bose a message of encouragement towards this unification of philosophies; it is sure to help him.

Yours always
P. Geddes

Town Planning Office
Chiman Bagh Indore [illegible]
11 June 1918

Dear Sir Rabindranath,

Admirable! The parrot is being avenged! – and what is yet better, future parrots will be protected! rescued, [illegible][46] It would have pleased you – the delight with which my friend C.E. Dobson here, Rector of the big High School (1500 boys – far too many) carried off this and gloated over it; & showed it to the very people it is meant to kill! – (or cure?)

I am sure it will help the cause everywhere.

Even the weakness of our hesitating yet would-be friends is due to the feeling that Indians want the poorest treatment, because people like Sadhu do. A converse opinion has now to be stirred to expression. So pray continue to fight – now – before the Commission furnishes its report this month at Darjeeling, & then takes it to Simla (to be watered down by reactionaries, I fear, there!)

Yours always cordially

P. Geddes

    With such caricaturists to help you there is a great field of action – Go on! There is a time for War; and this is it! I am writing to Thacker to ask him terms for 250-500 copies to send through Universities and Colleges etc. through Europe and USA!
    I have only delayed replying promptly, to send you extract reprint of my report here on 'proposed University'. I have got 500 copies, and shall send to any you suggest. Pray do let you see me a list. *(sic)* My feeling and hope are that these simultaneous appearances, yet totally different and independent attacks may help each other in various minds.
    Thus Dr. Sadhu etc. of University Committee for CU are far more with us that you perhaps realise. Do send them copies! (Address c/o Govt. House Darjeeling) I am of course sending him all I write, and he was delighted with my Evidence of which I read you part at Bolpur – So all this will give them more courage.

[All the letters are taken from Bashabi Fraser, Ed. A Meeting of Two Minds: The Geddes-Tagore Letters, 3rd Rev Edn, 2005; 4th Rev Edn. 2017. P. 57.

---

46. There are two words that are not legible.

Santiniketan
15 June 1918

Dear Professor,

I have sent a copy of 'Parrot's Training' to Dr. Sadhu. He had already read it when it appeared in the Modern Review and expressed his enthusiastic appreciation of it in a letter to the Editor. Sometime ago he spent a night here in our school when I had an opportunity of long conversations with him. I was delighted to find that in all vital things about education we agreed. But I am afraid the commission is composed of members more of whom differ in their views from Dr. Sadhu – and the people are already explaining their doubt about the result. What we need now is an ideal university in some of our Native States. A few months ago I received a letter from the Nizam State asking my opinion about the advisability of introducing Urdu to be the medium of instruction in a new university they intend to start. Do you know anything about it? I do hope you will be able to purchase some of our ruling chiefs to give Education a freer scope.

Please send me twenty copies of your Report which I will distribute among men who are interested.

Yours very sincerely

Rabindranath Tagore

[Fraser, p. 58.]

GEDDES AND COLLEAGUES
Town Planners, Park and Garden
Designers, Museum Planners, etc.

OUTLOOK TOWER, EDINBURGH.
MORE'S GARDEN, CHELSEA. S.W.
TOWN PLANNING OFFICE, CALCUTTA

CITY SURVEYS AND REPORTS
CITY PLANS AND IMPROVEMENTS

GARDEN SUBURBS AND VILLAGES
PARKS AND GARDENS

UNIVERSITY AND COLLEGE BUILDINGS, HOSTELS, etc.
TYPE MUSEUMS

EXHIBITIONS:-
    THE CIVIC EXHIBITION
    of Cities and Town Planning
    DIRECTOR:- PROF. GEDDES

TOWN PLANNING OFFICE[47]

Calcutta,
1 April 1919
Dear Sir Rabindranath,

Congratulations on your lectures on "Education", & on "<u>Forest</u>" here, each so fine in its way. I hope you'll <u>erupt</u> again over the Calcutta University Commission question and other things. (Don't you even sing better after a hard battle, like the warrior of old?) (And pray make your publisher sends a good packet of Parrot's Training to England, where as needed).

    I have been writing a "Life of Bose", in which his service and some of his battles too are set forth. He will send it you when published (I trust with Autumn season by Longmans).

    Young B. Ganguly has made me a good sketch of Bose for a frontispiece, - better than any photo, of course. He would like to sketch you too some

---

47. This is the letterhead.

day – will you allow him? – I give him this to send on to you, as I shall be gone – till autumn at least – sailing on Tuesday.

Always very cordially – and appreciatively –

Yours
P. Geddes

[Fraser, p. 60]

4 August 1920
PS I have just written this about Dr. Patrick Geddes

What so strongly attracted me in Dr. Patrick Geddes when I came to know him in India was not his scientific achievements, but, on the contrary, the rare fact of the fulness of his personality rising far above his science. Whatever he has studied and mastered has become vitally one with his humanity. He has the precision of the scientist and the vision of the prophet, at the same time, the power of an artist to make his ideas visible through the language of symbols. His love of Man has given him the insight to see the truth of Man, and his imagination to realise in the world the infinite mystery of life and not merely its mechanical aspect.

Rabindranath Tagore

August. 4. 1920

[Fraser, p. 60]

H.M. the Maharaja's Guest House
Patiala, Punjab.
15 April 1922

Dear Tagore,
    It was a pleasure to meet at Paris last summer, and a great regret that my engagements with my two home collaborators (Branford also being seriously ill, & Arthur Thomson not too well) prevented me from accepting your call to Geneva, which I would otherwise be delighted to do. But I have been getting on with my University planning, for Jerusalem etc.; first helped by stimulating contact with Paul Otlet etc. at the University International at Brussels, then with kindred beginnings at London and at my Outlook Tower in Edinburgh, but also especially last winter at Bombay. For there I have been fortunate in getting long galleries in the Institute of Science, and have thus not only installed my growing <u>Library and Dept of Sociology & Civics</u>, but my <u>Cities and Town Planning Exhibition</u> – a long picture book of cities (and their regions too in small measure) covering ¼ mile and more of screens, crowded as close and high as may be, and outlining their past and present, and sometimes, their possible improvement too, as from Edinburgh to Jerusalem, and with something of Indian Cities also. (In fact very much of what I proposed to Mr. Tata 20 years ago when he was planning his big benefaction, and though then Sir William Ramsay managed to turn it all towards Chemistry and Physical Science, and at Bangalore, it is something to be able to express in Bombay, as <u>Gate to the West for India, and of India to the West</u>, how their respective cities may be studied and better understood in their qualities and defects, and with development of the one and domination of the other.)
    But while I should like to show you this 'picture-book', I think you would be more interested in the scheme of the associated Department, since not simply for its special theories and technical applications, but as also presenting in miniature, the mobilisation of resources of the University. For what are all our arts and sciences, and how have they arisen, how too certain of the social lives of past and present. And how can we apply them better than towards mending the old lives, or starting the new as you are specially doing?
    Consider the plan of this Department as miniature outline of the University's resources, applied towards clearer social thought, and better civic practice. For social science needs all that the preliminary sciences can teach it, and civics needs all the corresponding and independent arts. We need to be logical in our reasoning, and mathematical in our statistics and graphics, physical in our construction, biological in our agriculture, horticulture and hygiene, economic in our general undertakings: yet of all these sciences

and arts, as you peculiarly and clearly see, (just as Ruskin saw before us or younger leaders now) are ineffective, when not calamitous, while expressing only the sciences and arts of the material and mechanical order, still so predominant, and so characteristic of the West. Poet and Artist, psychologist and educationist, moralist and mystic (and indeed even the traditionally religious) all necessarily sees the crudeness, weakness and failure of such 'science' and such 'progress' – (*sic*) Yet they hardly do justice to the finer science, the truer progress for which some of us – Bose, Otlet, Paul Desjardins, and other mutual friends for example – are working. Consider then this diagram-plan of my department, with the various academic specialisms arranged, but now with the subjective arts and sciences co-ordinated with these, and dominant accordingly. Beginning first in the conventional academic way, which University men are ready for accordingly, (we shall come to your way, or at least nearer it, presently) – we have the essentials of

Logic   (as Science)
  '   (' Art)   evolving together as 'thematic metrics'
  ────────────────

Mathematics as Science
  '   (' Art, metrics, graphics, etc.)
Physics (energics)
Technics   ' ' ' Eutechnics
──────────

Esthetics
Fine Arts

Biology
Biotechnics (Agriculture Horticulture Medicine and Hygiene etc.)
──

Psychology   ' ' ' Psychorganics
Education

Economics
Politics
────────

Ethics as Science   ' ' ' Etho-polity/ics
 ' in practice (with Religions)

But while the traditional University began with logic, (and thus too often stuck there, or now at various stages on the Mathematical, Physical, etc) we now have to read upwards: - and in truer order, right first:- for the preceding technical terms but disguise for the moment, in our academic jargon, the world-old simplicity, since, unity of Life.

Life as 'Conduct' ('Dharma' righteousness' Duty' etc)	(Social) = Etho-polity . economics now at one, 'duty' and 'efficiency' together the concave-convex of the same curve and thus inseparable.
Life as 'Behaviour' (Individual)	= Psychorganics: *i.e.* withpsychology and biology – mind and body 'sanity' and 'health' together
Life as 'Activity' (Practical & applied in social service)	= Eutechnics: i.e. with esthetics and physics, art and industries at one, 'gesture' and 'grasp' together.

If the preceding e clear, (uncongenial though may be the diagrammatic method and presentment, since this suspends any attempt at literary expression, - as mere foundation-plans lack architecture, yet I trust prepare for it) you will, I hope agree that this is not the conventional and 'hard shell' presentment of science, but at least contains a germ of the life we are all seeking, in however different ways.

(In my actual Department, the tables laid out all for the outlines of the arts face towards the City (in Exhibition), and those with outlines of the sciences face towards the library; yet on the opposite wall are brought together, and into the right order as above; *i.e.* from the 'spiritual' to 'temporal', from 'transcendental' to 'material and mechanical', or whatever other terms are preferred).

So far then the present attempt towards a step in University planning, which I am putting to Otlet, to Branford, and to my friends of the Jerusalem University. I should indeed be grateful if it turns out to be in harmony with your own vision; and so far as it falls short of this, I hope you will tell me.

Let me hear from you then, at leisure. I am here for another month or so, planning such improvements as may be for this old city, and for its College also, as also for one or two other towns of the state. After that my plans are uncertain. – I am tempted to return to Darjeeling, and sit down quietly to some writing there, (and learning too what I can from the unending wizardry of our friend Bose!) But I do not return to Bombay till the end of October.

Pardon this long letter (which has grown as I wrote!); and believe me, with all good wishes for your educational as well as other creative work, always very cordially yours, (and gratefully also,)

Pat. Geddes[48]

[Fraser, pp. 64-67]

Santiniketan
9 May 1922
Dear Geddes,

You ask me for my opinion about the scheme of your Department. I find it rather difficult to answer your question because my own work in Santiniketan has been from first to last a growth, which has had to meet all the obstacles and obstructions due to shortage of funds, paucity of workers, obtuseness in those who were called upon to carry out my ideal. But just because it was *a* living growth it has surmounted these difficulties and taken its own shape. In writing my stories, I hardly ever have a distinct plot in my mind. I start with some general emotional motive which goes on creating its story form, very often forgetting in the process its own original boundaries. If I had, in the commencement, a definite outline which I was merely to fill in, it would certainly bore me, - for I need the consistent stimulation of surprises, which comes only to a semi-passive medium through some living truth's gradual self-unfoldment.

The same thing happened with my Santiniketan Institution. I merely started with this one simple idea, that education should never be dissociated from life. I had no experience of teaching, no special gift for organisation; and therefore I had no plan which I could put before the public in order to win their confidence. I had not their power to anticipate what line my work was going to take. I began anyhow. All that I could do was to offer to the five little boys who were my first students my company. I talked and sang to them, played with them, recited to them our epics, improvised stories specially given to them by evening, took them on excursions into neighbouring villages.

It was an incessant lesson to me, and the institution grew with the growth of my own mind and life. With the increase of its population and the widening of its range, elements have constantly been intruding which go against its

---
48. There is a slight difference in this letter to the version at the National Library of Scotland, which ends with the paragraph 'So far then… University planning'.

spirit of freedom and spontaneity. The consequent struggle has been helpful in strengthening and making us realise the fundamental truth which is in the heart of our ashram.

But that which keeps up my enthusiasm is the fact, that we have not yet come to a conclusion. And therefore our task is not a perpetual repetition of a plan perfected one for all.

My first idea was to emancipate children's minds from the dead grip of a mechanical method and a narrow purpose. This idea has gone on developing itself, comprehending all different branches of life's activities from Arts to Agriculture. Now it has come to a period, when we are fully aware of the absolute necessity of widening, across all barriers, the human sympathies of our students, – thus leading them to the fulfilment of their Education. This stage we have reached, as I have said, not through planning out my system, but by an inner life-growth, in which the subconscious has ever been bursting up with the conscious plans.

Lately it has come to us, almost like a sudden discovery, that our Institution is to represent that creative force which is acting in the bosom of the present age; passing through repeated conflicts and reconciliations, failures and readjustments, while making for the realisation of the spiritual unity of human races.

I have often wished, for my own mission, the help of men like yourself, who not only have a vast comprehensive sympathy and imagination, but also a wide range of knowledge and critical acumen. It has been with a bewilderment of admiration, that I have so often followed the architectural immensity of your own vision. But at the same moment, I have had to acknowledge that it was beyond my power to make a practical use of the background of perspective which your vision provides us with. The temperamental characteristics of my own nature require the greatest part of my work to remain in the sub-soil obscurity of mind. All my activities have the character of 'play' in them, – they are more or less like writing poems, only in different media of expression. Your own schemes also, in a great measure, have the same element which strongly attracts me, but they have a different idiom, which I have not the power to use. You will understand from this, my dear friend, that though I have always enjoyed listening to you, when you formulate your ideas, and my mind [illegible] is the vastness of their unity, I cannot criticise them. I suppose they are being stored in my conscious memory waiting for living assimilation with my own thoughts.

Cordially yours

Rabindranath Tagore

[Fraser, pp. 68-69]

H.M'S Guest House
Patiala, Punjab
17 May 1922

Dear Tagore,

Yes, I feared that my technical plan of my Dept. of Sociology and Civic would be too dry for you! All plans must be so: that is their mathematical nature and limitation. But they express concrete foundations also, and for City and University alike – the latter too in its spiritual and ideal completeness, – not for knowledge only, but *for* Good, True and Beautiful together; as the best mind have always seen, but as each age and civilization has to express anew, and as you are trying! (And with unusual share of success!)

So think of us technical workers and students as planning out the foundations for your and other ideal Universities – and locating more clearly – and more spaciously too, the gardens of the Muses upon this sacred Hill.

It was thus an agreeable result to find, for instance, as I said at Jerusalem, that the *Great* Hall I had to plan for the University there worked out into the hexagon and interesting triangles[49] which are the symbol of Israel[50] (as the crescent for Islam, or the cross for Christianity). This gave a new style of done – for all others are on square or octagon – and thus a new style in architecture.

But this came not to me not at all as seeking to realise the Jewish symbol for them, as my Zionist friends at first naturally thought. It was really worked out sixteen years or more before, before I had ever heard of Zionism – and as an ideal Temple for the Unity of Life; (usually the Jewish Ideal!) yet thus strictly derived from synthetising, in graphic forms, my general knowledge of Biology – (Environment functioning on Organism, yet Organism mastering Environment) and of Sociology and Civics –
Place conditioning People, yet People re-conditioning Place

    (- working)   [re-illegible]
                                              [re-illegible]
                More (briefly) still =
                     (simply)
             Life-dynamic (E f o : O f e   (= Bergson etc. where developed)

                                      and
                          - Social {Pl w pe : Pe w Pl}

---

49. There is a hand sketch of a star here with intersecting triangles.
50. There is a sketch of a swastika-like symbol just after and above 'Israel'.

Mathematics and Logic – Technics and Physics, Arts and Esthetics, (Biotechnics = Agriculture, Medicine, etc.) and Biology, Education and Psychology, Politics and Economics, Religion and Ethics, are thus all in tune, so many strings for the philosophic harp, as well as of the poet's lyre! (Hence they helped in planning these University Buildings).

But you may say I am off again into my world of theories; so stop bothering you with these!

But just read the accompanying short Bombay University circular, as the first published product of this technical looking Department Plan of mine! You will, I am convinced, feel it has some human interest, and I trust more or less agree that it is on the lines of progress you can approve. (The preface is by Harold Mann especially – but all now adopted by University Committee and circulated accordingly.)

The difference between us is that while I work out (the equivalents of) musical <u>notations</u>, the <u>prosody</u> of thought, you can make songs as well as poems! (Yet you know your musical notation, your verse-notation too.) (Why not then notation for <u>thought</u>? Not impossible, though ideas occur without them!)[51]

Ever yours

P Geddes

[Fraser, pp. 70-71]

---

51. This paragraph is added to the left-hand margin.

University of Bombay
Deptt of Sociology and Civics letterhead
(emblem)

Department of Sociology and Civics,
Bombay,
10 November 1922

Dear Tagore,

(My son &) I have spent two active days at Santiniketan and Sherul, following on one with Mahalanobis beforehand, in which he explained to me as much of the situation as might be.

They are sending me survey plans on which I can work, and I shall hope to send you what suggestions, report and developed plans as I can – say, by new year vacation, or sooner, - work here may allow. *(sic)*

In the meantime pray write me anything you can as to the future developments which you have in mind, even though not realizable soon, or with present means, so that I may at any rate leave room for them. Above all, give me your ideas as to the <u>numbers</u> you expect to provide for, in Boys School, in Girls and Women Students Departments, in College of Art, College of Music (and Drama?), College of Agriculture, etc. For these are each and all real and promising beginnings, invaluably supplementing (and I trust in time stimulating) the existing University Departments and Faculties elsewhere, as of Law, Medicine, Engineering etc. What, too, are your expectations of numbers of students and of teachers in Modern Literature (Indian & European) in Classics Sanskrit, Pali etc. and Philosophy? Do you intend making these varied – *i.e.* including French and German (if not Italian) as well as English, and also Hindi etc. with Bengali?

Again, are you to teach Latin and Greek as well as Sanskrit, Pali etc.? What scale and scope do you intend to give to mathematics, physics and chemistry? And what to Geological Sciences? Do you admit Sociology and Civics within your scheme? (Tacitly of course they are evident; but what of a specific teacher?).

I am sending a copy of this letter to Mahalanobis as secretary and as you will be seeing him, you need not spend precious time in writing me; he will do this. But pray be considering these questions and others, and give me your ideas as clearly as you can – <u>boldly</u> for the future – (and trusting to my keeping confidence, as to anything you may not wish announced or promised). For as the essence of all planning is foresight, it is your vision and ideal which must guide the whole scheme. Have you written of this anywhere? If so, can I have it (in Translation if need be)?

The term 'International University' suggests comparison with that of my old friends Otlet and Lafontaine in Brussels, who have also the warmest sympathy with you. Are you in possession of their publications of which I have here only imperfect samples? If so, it will save time if you can spare it me for a brief perusal afresh, for though I have been over their scheme, buildings etc. I have not yet seen it in operation. (It is essentially a greatly developed 'Summer School', such as I ran for many years at Edinburgh, and found stimulating all round to teachers & students alike.)

You, however, aim more distinctly at all the year round work.

But you cannot compete with Universities on the great world scale – at least for many years to come (such as I have been planning at Jerusalem – on a scale surpassing Oxford & Cambridge, Harvard & Chicago).

Your Colleges as aforesaid, of Agriculture, Fine Arts and Music, Modern and Ancient Literature, etc. I take to be your main concern, leaving boys who wish to enter law, medicine, engineering etc. to go elsewhere; yet as for preparing these also, as school may do. Am I right in this?

This seems to me also an opportunity for drawing out the ideas and dreams of development of the various responsible collaborations you have gathered round you, (and of whose character and spirit, as well as technical qualifications I have a very high and deep impression, and so cannot but congratulate you accordingly). Thus what do your artists groups, scholar groups, agricultural group, scientific groups, feel that they could (1) best immediately utilise? – and (2) will gradually and ultimately require? Similarly as to provision for girls and women, so far as these requirements differ from those of men?

All these are large demands: but if I am to plan (of course as economically as may be, and) in such a way as to meet growing and future requirements, I cannot be too fully 'briefed', or too speedily.

- With congratulations and good wishes, *great* hopes also, believe me always

Yours faithfully and cordially

P Geddes

[Fraser, pp. 72-74]

Santiniketan
17 January 1923

Dear Professor Geddes,

The poet has handed to me your letter of Jan 10th and I feel guilty for not having written in answer to your previous one. I am trying to save my brain from bursting before March! And I'm almost on the verge of disaster but think I can hold out till then. These lectures in Calcutta take it all out of me mentally, though physically I'm fit enough.

Quite a number of villages round us have their old *Jatra*[52] parties which act folk plays etc. and we are doing our best to stimulate and encourage them. Our theatre will be of great service there, but at the moment we haven't funds to finish digging the tank.

So the poet says by all means let them come and survey the field. As to the rest, the wretched Kanungo, (Government surveyor) who drew our plan, which rightly disgusted you, is back – but I see no prospect yet of our getting another. Rathi Tagore is trying to get what pictures he can from the school and I believe has a surveyor at work.

Between[53] ourselves I am afraid delay is inevitable, though I hate to say it, and I am simply trying to prepare the ground so that Arthur can give the necessary guidance when he comes. I do hope he can come here before the end of February, and I'm sure you need have little fear for him so long as he is cooked for and mothered by Mrs. Green. I'd have been in a lunatic asylum long ago if it had not been for her.

Andrews is hopeless, off to the flood areas and likely to be engrossed in Relief for some time to come. My only hope here now is in Suren Tagore[54] who though unsuccessful in business has a head on him and real understanding of the practical means for carrying out the poet's schemes. Andrews means

---

52. *Jatras* belong to the folk theatre tradition of Bengal, performed on an open stage with the audience sitting all round it. The plays are usually based on the stories from the Indian epics, the *Ramayana* and the *Mahabharata* and Hindu mythology. Sometimes popular stories are used and even historical and topical themes. Villages have their own Jatra group with its equipment and the actors are amateurs from amongst the village population. There are also some itinerant professional groups. The plays are performed on makeshift stages in temporary tents and whole villages turn out to witness performances which can last through the night.
53. This reads like an abbreviation of 'Between', though the fountain pen strokes do make it more of a guess than a certainty.
54. The pen strokes read like 'Suren Tagore' and not 'Kar'. We know that Suren Kar, the architect, did help in the designing and implementation of many of the buildings at Shantiniketan and that Suren Tagore, Tagore's nephew, was a literary figure in his own right.

well and is a man of good heart, but I cannot see that he comprehends much of what the poet is really aiming at and politics, strike and reliefs occupy the balls of his energy, necessary no doubt, but in the end the energy invested hardly bears any true interest?

I've just got my camera working and am getting all the pictures I can.

I'm worried too over funds for my own place here, and I'm investing rather heavily in a cinema film to carry with me via China to America, giving this end of the poet's work.

I expect to be in Ithaca NY about the end of June, so if you are in USA write me c/o The Telluride (*sic*) Association Ithaca New York (to await arrival)

The poet says he has written regarding Arthur – did he make condition of pay, board etc. plain or what is to be the arrangement, – let's have it clear, – for they are awfully casual in these matters here.

As to the Surul tank – lease is impossible, but all the leaders in the village have promised to carry out a full programme which I have sketched, and through Miss G's[55] work the big division has been healed and we hope for united action.

I feel guilty *somehow* that I haven't properly backed up your end of the work, but I know you'll realise how almost impossible it is to get things to move here, delay, delay – delay, we'll see, – tomorrow, and so forth and even the best labour is inefficient.

However, dairy, weaving and tannery schemes are coming along.

Lord Lytton lunched with the poet and myself here two days ago and was apparently delighted. He promised every support.

Yours very sincerely

L.K. Elmhirst
I sail *in* March![56]

[Fraser, p. 85-87]

---

55. Probably 'Green's'?
56. And in March we do find Arthur writing to his father from Shantiniketan

Plays and Poetry

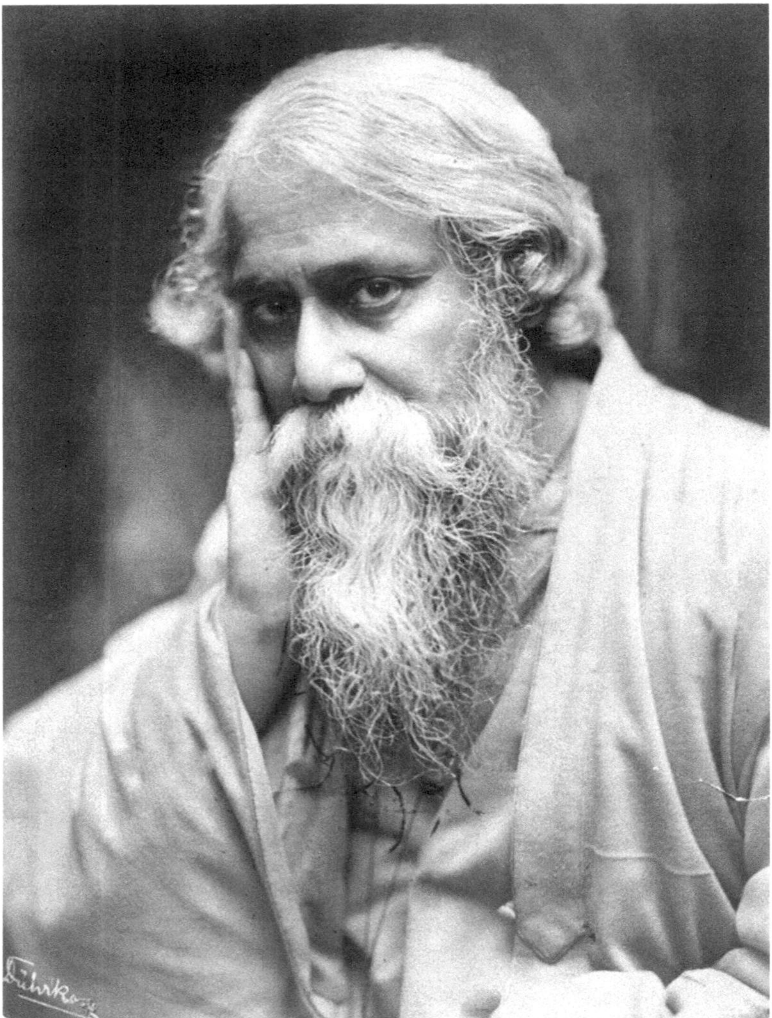

The Waterfall[57]

Scene. A mountainous country, with a road leading to the temple of Bhairava.[58] The scene remains the same through the play.

In the background is represented the upper framework of a big iron machine; opposite to this is the spire of the Bhairava temple, with its trident.

Ranajit, the king of Uttarakut, has his royal tent in the mango grove by the side of the road. He is resting there on the way to celebrate the evening festival, on the dark night of the moon. After twenty-five years of strenuous effort, his royal engineer, Bibhuti, has succeeded in building up an embankment across the waterfall called Muktadhâra.[59]

The inhabitants of Uttarakut are seen visiting the temple with their offerings and preparing to hold in the temple court-yard the festival, which is to celebrate the achievement of the royal engineer, Bibhuti.

The temple *devotees* of Bhairava are in the foreground. They are seen making a long circuit in religious procession round the temple. As they sing the praises of the god Bhairava, some are swinging their censers, some are beating the gongs, some are blowing the conch shells.

> [*The* DEVOTEES *sing, in procession,* –]
> Victory to Him, the Terrible,
> The Lord of Destruction,
> The uttermost Peace,
> The Dissolver of doubts,
> The Breaker of fetters,
> Who carries us beyond all conflicts,
> The Terrible, the Terrible!

[*They go in.*]
[*A* STRANGER *comes with his offerings of worship and meets a* CITIZEN *of Uttarakut.*]
STRANGER. What's that there put up against the sky? It is frightful!
CITIZEN. Don't you know? You're a strange, I see, – It's the Machine.
STRANGER. Machine! What Machine?

---
57 Sisir K. Das, The English Writings of Rabindranath Tagore, vol 2, pp. 163-208.
1 One of the names of the God Shiva, meaning 'Terrible'.
2 'Free Current'.

CITIZEN. The Royal Engineer, Bibhuti, has been working at it for the last twenty-five years. It's just been finished. A festival is now being held in honour of the occasion.
STRANGER. What's the object of the Machine?
CITIZEN. It has bound up the waterfall of Muktadhârâ.
STRANGER. What a monster! It looks like a dragon's skull with its fleshless jaws hanging down! The constant sight of it would make the life within you withered and dead.
CITIZEN. The life within *us* has got a thick hide to protect it! You needn't have any fear for *us!*
STRANGER. All the same, this isn't a thing to put up nakedly before the sun and stars. Can't you see how it seems to irritate the whole sky by its obtrusion?
CITIZEN. But aren't you going to attend the evening worship of Bhairava?
STRANGER. Yes, I've come out for that object. Every year I bring my offering at this time. But I've never seen such a monstrous obstruction in the sky before. Don't you think it's a sacrilege to allow it to overtop the spire of the Temple? *[He goes.]*[60]

* * * * * *

---

60. Das, p. 65

[The MESSENGER from Abhijit, the Crown Prince of Uttarakut, meets BIBHUTI, while he is on his way to the Temple.]

MESSENGER. Bibhuti! The Crown Prince has sent me to you.
BIBHUTI. What is his wish?
MESSENGER. You have been for a long time building up an embankment across the waterfall of Muktadhârâ. Over and over again it gave way, and men perished smothered with sand and earth; and others got washed away by the flood at last, to-day –
BIBHUTI. My object is accomplished and the sacrifice of their lives has met with its fulfilment.
MESSENGER. The inhabitants of Shiu-tarai are still ignorant of this fact. They cannot believe, that any man can deprive them of the water, which has been to them the gift of God.
BIBHUTI. God has given them the water; but He has given me the power to bind that water.
MESSENGER. They don't know that, within a week, their fields –
BIBHUTI. Why talk about their fields? What have I to do with their fields?
MESSENGER. Wasn't it your object to devastate their fields with drought?
BIBHUTI. My object was to make Man triumphant over the sands and water and stones, which conspired against him. I had not the time to trouble my mind about what would happen to some wretched maize fields of some wretched cultivator in some place or other.
MESSENGER. The Crown Prince asks you, if the time has not come at last for you to trouble your mind about it.
BIBHUTI. No! My mind is occupied with the contemplation of the majesty of the Machine.
MESSENGER. Cannot the cry of hunger interrupt that contemplation?
BIBHUTI. No! The pressure of water cannot break my embankment; the cry of hunger cannot sway my Machine.
MESSENGER. Aren't you afraid of curses?
BIBHUTI. Curses? – When labourers became scarce in Uttarakut, I had all the young men of over eighteen years of age from every house of Pattana village brought out by the King's command, and a great number of them never returned to their homes. My Machine has triumphed against the storm of mothers' curses. He who fights God's own power, is not afraid of man's malediction.
MESSENGER. The Crown Prince says that you have already attained the glory of a creation; and now it is time for you to attain a greater glory by demolishing that creation.
BIBHUTI. So long as my work remained unfinished, it was mine. But now that it is finished, it belongs to all Uttarakut. I have no longer the right to demolish it.

MESSENGER. The Crown Prince declares, that he will take this right into his own hands.
BIBHUTI. Are these words from our own Crown Prince himself? Does he not belong to us?
MESSENGER. He says, that it has yet to be proved, whether God's Will has found its entrance into the Government of Uttarakut; the Machine must not stand between.
BIBHUTI. It is my mission to prove, by the force of the Machine, that God's throne is ours. Tell the Crown Prince, that no road is left open to make the Machine slacken its grip.
MESSENGER. The God, who breaks, does not need the broad road for his passage. The smallest holes, which escape our notice, are enough for him.
BIBHUTI. Holes! What do you know about them?
MESSENGER. Nothing. But He knows, who makes use of them.
[MESSENGER *goes*.]

[CITIZENS *of Uttarakut, on their way to the Temple, meet* BIBHUTI.]

FIRST CITIZEN. Engineer, you're a wonderful fellow! We never noticed when you got ahead of us!
SECOND CITIZEN. That's ever been his habit. Nobody knows how he wins in the race. That shaven-headed Bibhuti of our Chabua village got his ears pulled along with ourselves at the village school. And yet he's done such wonders, surpassing us all!
THIRD CITIZEN. Hallo, Gobru! why'd you stand there, basket in hand, with your mouth wide open? Is this the first time you've seen Bibhuti? Bring out the garlands. Let's garland him.
BIBHUTI. No, no! What's the use of doing that?
THIRD CITIZEN. Why do you say 'no'? If the length of your neck could keep pace with your greatness, it'd grow like a camel's and we'd load it up to the tip of your nose with garlands.
SECOND CITIZEN. Harish, our drummer, hasn't yet arrived.
FIRST CITIZEN. That man's the very prince of the sluggards! He needs a good beating on the drum of his back.
THIRD CITIZEN. Nonsense, he can beat the drum far better than we can.
FOURTH CITIZEN. The idea came to me, that we might borrow the chariot from Samanta, to drive Bibhuti on it to the Temple. But we hear that the king himself'll go walking to the temple. Let's carry him on our shoulders.
FIFTH CITIZEN. Not at all! You were born in the lap of Uttarakut, and now you've got to be raised on its shoulders.

[*They all take him up and sing.*]
The Song of the Machine.

We salute the Machine, the Machine!
   Loud with its rumbling of wheels,
  Quick with its thunder flame,
        Fastening its fangs
    into the breast of the world.
 Hurling against obstructions
     its fiery defiance
That melts iron, crushes rocks,
       And drives the inert from its rest.
We salute the Machine, the Machine!
    Now stolidly stable, with timber and stones.
 Now light and free, like a storm cloud.
Sailing across earth, water and sky.
   The Machine, whose claws wrench bare.
      The entrails of the earth.
Whose magic net captures in its meshes.
  The elements elusive and subtle.
We salute the Machine, the Machine!

[*They all go out.*][61]

---

61. Das, pp. 167-169

[A SCHOOLMASTER *enters, with a group of* BOYS.]

SCHOOLMASTER. These wretched boys are in for a good caning, I can see. Shout, with your loudest voices boys: 'Salve Imperator.'
BOYS. 'Salve Im-'
SCHOOLMASTER. '- perātor!'
BOYS. '- perātor!'
SCHOOLMASTER. 'Salve Imperātor Imperātorum!'
BOYS. 'Salve Imperātorum! –'
SCHOOLMASTER. – 'Imperātorum!'
BOYS. 'Imperātorum!'
RANAJIT. Where are you going?
SCHOOLMASTER. Your Majesty is about to confer special honour on the Royal Engineer, Bibhuti; and I am taking my boys to the festival, in order to share in the rejoicing. I do not want my boys to miss any opportunity of participating in the glory of Uttarakut.
RANAJIT. Do these boys know what Bibhuti has done?
THE BOYS [*clapping their hands and jumping*]. Yes! Yes! We know. He has shut up the drinking water of the Shiu-tarai people!
RANAJIT. Why has he shut it up?
BOYS. To give them a good lesson.
RANAJIT. What for?
BOYS. To make them smart!
RANAJIT. Why?
BOYS. Because they are bad!
RANAJIT. Why bad?
BOYS. Oh they are terribly bad. Everybody knows it!
RANAJIT. Then, *you* do not know why they are bad?
SCHOOLMASTER. Certainly, they know it, Your Majesty. – [*To the* BOYS] What's happened to you, you blockheads? Haven't you Haven't you, – in your books? – Haven't you in your books? – [*In a low voice, whispering*] Their religion is rotten!
BOYS. Yes! Yes! Their religion is rotten!
SCHOOLMASTER. And they are not like us, – come, answer, boys, – don't you remember [*pointing to his nose*].
BOYS. Yes, they haven't got high-bridged noses.
SCHOOLMASTER. Good! Of course you know what has been proved by our Professor. What does a high-bridged nose denote?
BOYS. The greatness of the race!
SCHOOLMASTER. Good! Good! And what is the mission of the greater races? – Speak out! They conquer – peak out! – They conquer, – the world, – for themselves. Is not that so?

BOYS. Yes! They conquer the world for themselves.
SCHOOLMASTER. Is there a single case in which Uttarakut has been defeated in a war?
BOYS. No, never!
SCHOOLMASTER. You all know how the grandfather of our king, with only 293 soldiers, put to flight 31,700 barbarians from the South. Isn't that true, boys?
BOYS. Yes!
SCHOOLMASTER. Your Majesty may rest assured that these very boys will one day be a terror to all those who have the misfortune to be born outside our boundaries. I shall be false to my vocation as a schoolmaster if this does not happen. I never allow myself to forget for one moment the great responsibility – which we teachers have. We build up *men*! Your statesmen merely use them. And yet Your Majesty should take the trouble to compare the pay which *they* draw, with what *we* get.
MINISTER. But those very students are your best reward.
SCHOOLMASTER. Wonderfully uttered! Indeed, they are our best reward! Beautiful! But, Sir, food is becoming so dear now-a-days. For instance, the butter from cow's milk was once –
MINISTER. You needn't go on. I shall ponder over this question of the butter from cow's milk. Now you may take your leave.
[*The* SCHOOLMASTER, *with his* BOYS, *departs.*]
RANAJIT. Inside the skull of this schoolmaster of yours, there is nothing but the butter made of cow's milk.
MINISTER. Nevertheless, Sire, such people are useful. He loyally repeats the lesson, day after day, according to the instruction that he has received. If he had more brains, such a thing as this would not be possible.[62]

* * * * * *

[*Enter* RANAJIT *and* MINISTER.]
MINISTER. Sire, the camp is deserted and a great part of it is burnt away. The few guards, who were there –
RANAJIT. Never mind about them. Where is Abhijit? I *must* know!
KANKAR. King! We claim punishment for the Crown Prince.
RANAJIT. Do I ever wait for your claim, in order to punish the one who deserves it?
KANKAR. The people harbour suspicions in their minds, when they cannot find him.

---

62. Das, pp. 174-175

RANAJIT. Suspicions? Against whom?
KANKAR. Pardon me, Sire! You must understand the state of mind of your subjects. Owing to the delay in finding the Crown Prince, their impatience has grown to such a degree, that they will never wait for your judgement, when he is discovered.
BIBHUTI. Of our own accord we have taken in hand the duty of building up again the Fort of Nandi Pass.
RANAJIT. Why could you not leave it in my hands?
BIBHUTI. We have the right to suspect your secret sanction to this outrage done by the Crown Prince.
MINISTER. Sire, the mind of the public is excited by their self-glorification on the one hand and by their anger on the other. Do not add to *their* impatience, and make it still more turbulent by *your* impatience.
RANAJIT. Who is there? Is it Dhananjay?
DHANANJAY. I am happy to find that you have not forgotten me!
RANAJIT. You certainly know where Abhijit is.
DHANANJAY. I can never keep secret what I know for certain.
RANAJIT. Then what are you doing here?

DHANANJAY. I am waiting for the appearance of the Crown Prince.

[*From outside, the voice is heard of* AMBA.]
AMBA. Suman! Suman, my darling! It's dark. It's so dark!
RANAJIT. Who is that calling?
MINISTER. It is that mad woman, Amba.
[*Enters* AMBA.]
AMBA. He has not yet come back.
RANAJIT. Why do you see him? The time came, and Bhairava called him away.
AMBA. Does Bhairava only call away and never restore, - secretly? In the depth of the night? – My Suman!
   [AMBA *goes out.*]

[*Enters a* MESSENGER.]
MESSENGER. A multitude of men from Shiu-tarai is marching up.
BIBHUTI. How is that? We had planned to disarm them, by falling on them suddenly. There must be some traitor among us! Kankar! Very few people knew, except your party. Then how was it, –?
KANKAR. Bibhuti! You suspect even us!
BIBHUTI. Suspicion knows no limits.
KANKAR. Then we also suspect you.
BIBHUTI. You have the right! But when the time comes, there will be a reckoning.

RANAJIT [*to the* MESSENGER]. Do you know, why they are coming?
MESSENGER. They have heard that the Crown Prince is in prison, and they have come to seek him out and rescue him.
BIBHUTI. We are also seeking him, as well as they. Let us see who can find him!
DHANANJAY. Both of you will find him. He has no favourites.
MESSENGER. There comes Ganesh, the leader of Shiu-tarai.
[*Enters* GANESH.]
GHANESH [*to* DHANANJAY]. Father, shall we find him?
DHANANJAY. Yes.
GANESH. Promise us!
DHANANJAY. Yes, you shall find him.
RANAJIT. Whom are you seeking?
GANESH. King! You must release him.
RANAJIT. Whom?
GANESH. Our Crown Prince! You do not want him, but we do! Would you shut up everything that we need for our life, – even him?
DHANANJAY. Fool! Who has the power to shut *him* up?
GANESH. We shall make him our King.
DHANANJAY. Yes, you shall! He is coming with his King's crown.

[*Enter the* DEVOTEES, *singing.*]

Victory to the fearful Flame,
That tears the heart of Darkness,
That burns to ashes things which are dead.
Victory to Him whose voice thunders forth Truth.
Whose right arm smites the unrighteous.
Whose guidance leads mortals across Death.

[*From outside is heard the cry of* AMBA.]

AMBA. Mother calls, Suman! Mother calls! Come back, Suman! come back!
[*A sound is heard in the distance.*]
BIBHUTI. Hark! What is that? What is that sound?
DHANANJAY. It is laughter, bubbling up from the heart of darkness.
BIBHUTI. Hush! Let me find out from what direction the sound comes.
[*In the distance, the cry is faintly heard,* 'Victory to Bhairava!'
BIBHUTI [*listening with his head bent towards the ground*]. It is the sound of water.
DHANANJAY. The first beat of the drum before the dance
BIBHUTI. The sound grows in strength!
KANKAR. It seems –

NARSINGH. Yes! It certainly seems –
BIBHUTI. My God! There is no doubt of it. The water of Muktadhârâ is freed! – Who has done it? – Who has broken the embankment? He shall pay the price! There is no escape for him!
[*He rushes out.*]
[KANKAR *and* NARSINGH *rush out, following him.*]
RANAJIT. Minister! What is this!
DHANJAY. It is the call to the Feast of the Breaking of Bondage –
[*Sings.*]
The drum beats;
It beats into the beatings of my heart.

MINISTER. Sire, it is –
RANAJIT. Yes, it must be his!
MINISTER. It can be no other man than –
RANAJIT. Who is so b rave as he?
DHANJAY [*sings*].
His feet dance,
 They dance in the depth of my life.

RANJIT. I shall punish him, if punished he must be. But these people, maddened with rage, – Only Abhijit! He is favoured of the Gods! May the Gods save him!
GANESH. I do not understand what has happened, Master!
DHANANJAY [*sings*].
The night watches,
And watches also the Watchman.
    The silent stars throb with dread.

RANAJIT. I hear some steps! – Abhijit! Abhijit!
MINISTER. It must be he, who comes.
DHANANJAY [sings].
My heart aches and aches,
  While the fetters fall to pieces.

[*Enters* SANJAY.]

RANAJIT. Here comes Sanjay! – Where is Abhijit?
SANJAY. The waterfall of Muktadhārā has borne him away, and we have lost him.
RANAJIT. What say you, Prince?

SANJAY. He has broken the embankment.
RANAJIT. I understand! And with this he has found his freedom! Sanjay! Did he take you with him?
SANJAY. No! But I was certain he would go there. And so I preceded him, and waited in the dark. – But there it ends. He kept me back. He would not let me go.
RANAJIT. Tell me more!
SANJAY. Somehow he had come to know about a weakness in the structure, and at that point he gave his blow to the monster Machine. The monster returned that blow against him. Then Muktadhârâ, like a mother, took up his stricken body into her arms and carried him away.
GANESH. We came to seek our Prince! Shall we never find him again!

DHANANJAY. You have found him for ever!

[*Enter the* DEVOTEEES *of Bhairava, singing.*]
Victory to Him, the Terrible,
    The Lord of Destruction,
  The uttermost Peace,
     The Dissolver of doubts,
  The Breaker of fetters,
Who carries us beyond all conflicts,
  The Terrible, the Terrible!
Victory to the fearful Flame,
        That tears the heart of Darkness,
    That Turns to ashes things which are dead.
Victory to Him whose voice thunders forth Truth.
      Whose right arm smites the unrighteous.
    Whose guidance leads mortals across death!
The Terrible! the Terrible![63]

THE END

---

63. Das, pp. 203-207

HOMAGE TO THE TREE

Deep down under the earth you heard the call of the sun in your dark chamber and felt the first stir of consciousness.
O Tree, O primal spring of life, you raised your head above the passive rock and uttered the first prayer in praise of light.
The harsh and sapless desert got from you its first sensation.

On that day, in varied tones and hues, you declared the glory of this earth to the firmament with its assemblage of stars and planets.
Facing the great unknown you held aloft the victorious banner of life – of life that crosses the mighty gate of death age after age and in ever-new chariots hurries on to make its pilgrimage on ever-new paths.

At your silent call the earth woke up. Her dream was broken. She quivered and recalled her own chronicle.
A reckless daughter of the gods, dressed in lowly rags and smeared with ash, she sought the bliss of heaven, wandering through fragments of space and time.
She longed to shatter that bliss with blows of strife and pain for the pleasure of making it whole again.

Valiant offspring of the dust, you waged a continuous war to liberate the earth from the fortress-prison of aridity.
Mounted on the ocean's soaring wave you reached distant islands, and on their barren shores established the royal power of verdure with supreme confidence.
You scaled forbidding mountainsides and upon their stony pages wrote an epic of victory in leafy alphabet.
You charmed the dust, and fashioned for yourself in trackless regions a web of verdant paths.
There was a day when all were dumb – the earth, the oceans
   and the empty vault of heaven – while the seasons knew no music.
You came, and your tuneful branches brought comfort to the

world. In your melody the restless wind first discovered itself,
painted its own invisible body with varied hues of sound, and
etched the rainbow of song upon the sky.

On the eart's canvas you were the first to sketch the living
image of beauty. From the sun you extracted its formative
power, fused it with your own breath, and scattered the treasure
of light in countless colours.
One day the nymphs of Indra's heavenly court struck the clouds
with their jingling bracelets, broke those jars of vapour, and
in playful dance poured out the wine of youth.
You saved that nectar in your leaves and flowers, and with them
you beautified the earth, making her eternally young.

O Tree, O silent solemn tree, it was you who first joined patience
    to valour and showed how power can incarnate itself in peace.
I take refuge in you. Initiate me into the fellowship of
    tranquility, that I may hear the profound message of silence.
I bend my head, burdened with anxious thoughts, and touch the
dust in your soothing shade.
There I seek the varied forms of Life: the generous form, the
form of ever-new joys, the heroic form, splendid, world-conquering,
and the eloquent form which the earth displays.

I have meditated, entered into your spirit, have understood how
the sun – the holy flame that burns for the sacrificial ritual of
creation – through your being silently assumes a glossy, tender
form.
O Tree, O sunbeam-quickened, for centuries you milked the
days – as though they were white cows – and the vigour acquired
from this nourishment you gave away to mankind as a gift.
With your own strength you made man invincible, raised him
to the pitch of honour until he dared to rival the gods.
And now his flaming power breaks all barriers while the universe
stares in deep amazement.

From the realm of man I come to you, O Tree, as a messenger.
I speak for him – for man who is animated by your breath, who rests in your cool loving shade, who wears your flowery garland.
O friend of man, I am a poet charmed by your music, and I bring to you with humble greetings this verse-offering.

March, 1927

Bibliography

Alam, F and Radha C, eds., *The Essential Tagore* (Harvard and Visva-Bharati, 2011).

Bhattacharya, S., *Rabindranath Tagore: An Interpretation* (New Delhi: Penguin Books, 2011).

Das, S K, ed., *The English Writings of Rabindranath Tagore* (New Delhi: SahityaAkademi, 1996), Vol 2.

Das, S K, ed., *The English Writings of Rabindranath Tagore* (New Delhi: SahityaAkademi, 1996) Vol 3.

Elmhirst, L., *The Poet and the Plowman*, (Calcutta: Visva-Bharati, 1975).

Defries, A., *The Interpreter: Geddes*, Routledge, 1927.

Fraser, B, ed., *The Tagore Geddes Correspondence* (Shantiniketan: Visva-Bharati, India, 2004, 2nd Rev Edn).

Fraser, B, ed., *A Meeting of Two Minds: the Geddes-Tagore Letters* (Edinburgh: Wordpower Books, 2005 3rd Rev Ed.)

Geddes, P., *'Scottish University Needs and Aims'* University College, Dundee, Closing Address for 1889–90 and Scots Magazine Aug 1890.

Geddes, P., 'Life and its Science' *The Evergeen*, Spring 1895 and *Edinburgh Review, Patrick Geddes Special Issue,* No. 88, Summer 1992.

Geddes, P., 'The Sociology of Autumn', *The Evergreen* 1895, and *Edinburgh Review*, 88, 1992.

Geddes, P., *The World Without and the World Within: Sunday Talks with my Children* (Bournville: St. George Press and London: George Allen, 1905) Part 1.

Geddes, P., *Cities in Evolution* (London: Williams and Norgate, 1915).

Geddes, P., 'Talks from my Outlook Tower', *Survey Graphic,* 53-55, Feb–Sept 1925.

Geddes, P., 'The Notation of Life', in *Edinburgh Review, Patrick Geddes Special Issue,* No. 88, Summer 1992.

Ghosh, N., ed., *The English Writings of Rabindranath Tagore* (New Delhi: SahityaAkademi, 2007, 2011), Vol 4.

Kabir, H., ed., *Towards Universal Man: Rabindranath Tagore*, (Bombay:Asia Publishing House, 1961).

Reilly, J.P., *The Early Social Thought of Patrick Geddes*, PhD thesis (New York: University of Columbia, 1972).

Sen, Amartya., *The Argumentative Indian: Writings on Indian Culture, History and Identity* (Harmondsworth: Penguin Books, 2005).

Stalley, M., *Patrick Geddes: Spokesman for Man & Environment*, Rutgers University Press, 1972

Tagore, R., *Sadhana/The Realization of Life*, (London: Macmillan, October 1913).

Tagore, R., *Creative Unity* (New York: Macmillan, 1922).

Acknowledgments

This *book* would not have been possible without the generous permission of the Rabindra-Bhavana Archives, Visva-Bharati and Dr. Jan Merchant, Senior Curator and her staff at the Dundee University Archives who have granted us the permission to publish the essays/talks/articles/chapters by Patrick Geddes.

We have found the library staff as the National Library of Scotland, the Stathclyde University Archives, the Devon Record Office and the University of Edinburgh both helpful and enlightening.

This book owes much to the generous encouragement of Marion and Clare Geddes, the daughters of Arthur Geddes and granddaughters of Patrick Geddes who have been forthcoming with information regarding the papers of Patrick Geddes.

Our deep gratitude to Saptarshi Mallik whose dedicated research, material gathering and analysis has strengthened this project.

Many thanks to Dr Tom Kane who 'discovered' one crucial letter at the RabindraBhavana from Patrick Geddes to Rabindranath Tagore, which has not been published before, which Saptarshi then typed up for this volume.

A big thank you to Anna Shepherd of Peacock Solutions of Edinburgh for her meticulously typing up all the documents in what is a flawless reproduction of the original sources.

We thank Sri Nilanjan Banerjee for his cover design for the book. Our sincere gratitude to Sri Utpal Mitra who made many of the resources at the RabindraBhavana Archives available to us, to Madhumita Roy for her meticulous research and to Priyabrata Roy for patiently typing out parts of the manuscript.

Thank you to Visva-Bharati and Luath Press (Edinburgh) for agreeing to publish this seminal *Reader* in India and the UK, respectively, which will bring the ideas, thought and work of two great men on education and the environment for a global audience.

Bashabi Fraser
Tapati Mukherjee
Amrit Sen

Luath Press Limited

committed to publishing well written books worth reading

LUATH PRESS takes its name from Robert Burns, whose little collie Luath (*Gael.*, swift or nimble) tripped up Jean Armour at a wedding and gave him the chance to speak to the woman who was to be his wife and the abiding love of his life. Burns called one of the 'Twa Dogs' Luath after Cuchullin's hunting dog in Ossian's *Fingal*. Luath Press was established in 1981 in the heart of Burns country, and is now based a few steps up the road from Burns' first lodgings on Edinburgh's Royal Mile. Luath offers you distinctive writing with a hint of unexpected pleasures.

Most bookshops in the UK, the US, Canada, Australia, New Zealand and parts of Europe, either carry our books in stock or can order them for you. To order direct from us, please send a £sterling cheque, postal order, international money order or your credit card details (number, address of cardholder and expiry date) to us at the address below. Please add post and packing as follows: UK – £1.00 per delivery address; overseas surface mail – £2.50 per delivery address; overseas airmail – £3.50 for the first book to each delivery address, plus £1.00 for each additional book by airmail to the same address. If your order is a gift, we will happily enclose your card or message at no extra charge.

Luath Press Limited
543/2 Castlehill
The Royal Mile
Edinburgh EH1 2ND
Scotland
Telephone: +44 (0)131 225 4326 (24 hours)
email: sales@luath.co.uk
Website: www.luath.co.uk